Successful Corporate Turnarounds

Successful Corporate Turnarounds

A GUIDE FOR BOARD MEMBERS, FINANCIAL MANAGERS, FINANCIAL INSTITUTIONS, AND OTHER CREDITORS

Eugene F. Finkin

Quorum Books

NEW YORK • WESTPORT, CONNECTICUT • LONDON

Library of Congress Cataloging-in-Publication Data

Finkin, Eugene F.
  Successful corporate turnarounds.

  Includes index.
  1. Organizational change.   2. Organizational
effectiveness.   I. Title.
HD58.8.F52   1987   658.4'063   86-25280
ISBN 0-89930-232-7 (lib. bdg. : alk. paper)

Library of Congress Catalog Card Number: 86-25280
ISBN: 0-89930-232-7

First published in 1987 by Quorum Books

Greenwood Press, Inc.
88 Post Road West, Westport, Connecticut 06881

Printed in the United States of America

The paper used in this book complies with the
Permanent Paper Standard issued by the National
Information Standards Organization (Z39.48-1984).

10 9 8 7 6 5 4 3 2 1

Copyright Acknowledgment

The author and the publisher gratefully acknowledge permission to use a portion of the following
copyright material:

  R. J. Schonberger, ''Just in Time Production,'' *Quality Progress* (October 1984): 22–24.

To Dennis Unkovic, whose
inspiration and persuasion led to the creation of this book

CONTENTS

EXHIBITS

PREFACE

The business pages of our newspapers and magazines are filled with accounts of the troubled condition or failure of well-known industrial companies. A new management is brought in to save a company, or the old management announces sweeping changes, claiming that these are what were needed. Are they? Can the troubled company be successfully turned around? Are the approaches being taken to achieve the turnaround the right ones?

This book answers these and other questions. It gives insight into the turnaround process and gets into specifics. It details the approaches and actions needed to achieve a successful turnaround for all important functional areas—finance, purchasing, marketing, personnel, engineering, manufacturing, inventory control, foreign operations, and others.

Reading this book will give an observer the understanding needed to judge the ability of the players and the appropriateness of their tactics while watching the game in progress. It will guide the management of a troubled company to improve their chances of success.

This book removes the veil of mystery surrounding successful turnaround management. It provides important insight to board members, lenders, stockholders, suppliers, customers, employees, securities dealers, the press corps, and the interested general public.

ACKNOWLEDGMENTS

Having been long involved in the turnaround of troubled industrial companies, it bothered me to see the high degree of ignorance and lack of understanding of how turnarounds are achieved on the part of many executives who have the responsibility of accomplishing a turnaround. Therefore, with a sense of civic responsibility, I set out to write a lengthy article to provide some of the missing guidance. Robert Paul (president, Ampco-Pittsburgh Corporation) became interested in my project and was kind enough to devote much time to reading and assessing the original article draft. He suggested useful deletions and a reorganization of the presentation. The finished article was published with much interest and further led to a well-received speech before the North American Society for Corporate Planning.

Dennis Unkovic (partner, Meyer, Unkovic, and Scott) then convinced me that the article was not enough. To really do justice to this subject, a book had to be written and, because of my comprehensive and wide-ranging turnaround experience, I was the one to write it. Dennis Unkovic's confidence and enthusiasm convinced me to start what became an increasingly larger endeavor. He also spent much time reading sections of the manuscript and suggesting improvements.

As the book evolved, significant editorial suggestions and comments were received from the following experienced and knowledgeable executives: Richard Beutel (vice-president, Continental Illinois National Bank and Trust Company of Chicago); James Bortle (Danly Machine Corporation); Clare Brown (Danly

Machine Corporation); Richard Cawley (president, Rain Hill Group, Inc.); Edmond Corry (president, Corry, Howe Associates, Inc.); Kim Gordon Davis (general partner, Weiss, Peck & Greer); Walter Dollard (Westinghouse Electric Corporation); Daniel Dye (vice-president, Security Pacific Capital Corp.); Melvyn Goetz (Westinghouse Electric Corporation); Sherman Goldberg (senior vice-president, The First National Bank of Chicago); Herbert Graves (vice-president, Allegheny International, Inc.); Steven Jones (vice-president, Danly Machine Corporation); Warren Kearns (former president, L. B. Foster Co.); Robert Lear (Columbia University); Eugene Malinowski (Coopers & Lybrand); Joseph Mandia (vice-president, Avondale Industries, Inc.); Richard Missar (president, DeSoto, Inc.); Robert Morrison (vice-president, Continental Illinois National Bank and Trust Company of Chicago); Laurence Mullen (consultant); Thurman Naylor (retired chairman, Standard-Thompson Corp.); Francis O'Neil (consultant); John Pridgeon (former president, Special Metals Corp.); Steven Reichman (Wyman-Gordon Company); Edward Robert (president, P.V.F., Inc.); Frederick Ross (former president, Raymark Corp.); William Scharffenberger (former president, Saxon Industries, Inc.); Joseph Scuillo (Allegheny Ludlum Steel Corp.), Herbert Shields (Alberto Culver Co.); and Joseph Steinman (Ethyl Corp.).

Ideas were also received from: Michel Besson (president, CertainTeed Corp.); William Billington (president, Billington, Fox & Ellis, Inc.); John Fogarty (former president, Kentucky Electric Steel Company); John Gallagher (former chairman, Chemetron Corp.); Gerald Hale (president, Hale Minerals, Inc.); Gordon Lohman (vice-president, AMSTED Industries, Inc.); R. James Lotz (president, International Management Advisors, Inc.); Morton Mandel (chairman, Premier Industrial Corp.); William Manly (former executive vice-president, Cabot Corp.); Donald Melville (president, Norton Company); and Theodore Stern (executive vice-president, Westinghouse Electric Corp.).

Successful Corporate Turnarounds

1

COMING TO GRIPS WITH THE PROBLEM

The American economy is in a permanent state of turmoil. Prominent firms are in serious trouble in such industries as steel, machine tools, fasteners, meat packing, textiles, steam turbines, cranes, copper, shipbuilding, farm machinery, and railroad products.

Almost daily, newspapers and magazines report well-known companies suffering deep financial problems. Some articles read like preliminary obituaries—and often they are. Desperation moves are commonplace. New managements are brought in. Will the fine old-name company survive? Be sure to read tomorrow's installment.

Troubled companies usually are not inherently destined to fail. Their successful turnaround is frequently possible. But possible doesn't necessarily imply probable. The successful turnaround doesn't just spontaneously happen. It must be made to happen. Management is the key.

Obviously, some people are more than just bystanders. The drama for them involves personal risk. As employees, will they lose their jobs? Are the life savings of stockholders or bondholders at risk? What happens to the small business that is a supplier? Will the members of the turnaround management be harmed in their careers?

To accomplish a successful turnaround, you must understand what needs to be done. The successful turnaround is not the result of luck, but a little luck never hurts. Then you have to do what needs to be done. If you are not responsible for leading the turnaround, but are personally at risk, you need to understand the fundamentals of what is at hand in order to gauge the likelihood of the turnaround's success.

The task of this book is to explain, to the turnaround management and the others at risk (e.g., stockholders, bankers, and employees), the perspectives and actions needed for achieving a successful industrial turnaround. It will help interested observers to judge whether or not a turnaround attempt is being properly managed and is likely to succeed.

This book focuses attention on the most crucial elements of a successful turnaround and the methods used to identify and solve problems. Because it is impossible to cover all conceivable situations, I have concentrated on those areas of greatest importance, based on my personal experience and observations in more than twenty-five companies—many subsidiaries or divisions of well-known conglomerates. Additional ideas and comments have been received from three dozen knowledgeable executives from a wide spectrum of companies.

Many business managers are faced with the challenge of turning around a failing industrial corporation, or a subsidiary or division. The company's potentially terminal condition may result from excessive operating and overhead costs, lagging sales, depressed prices, severe competition, or other factors. Unfortunately, managers who are accustomed to more "normal" business conditions usually lack an appreciation of the perspectives, skills, and special actions that are necessary to accomplish a turnaround. As a consequence, many turnaround efforts fail.

Many companies that fail do so needlessly. After the fact, people claim that achieving a turnaround was an inherently impossible task, but they gave it their best. They may have given it their best, but is was not necessarily an impossible task.

The inability of upper management, not experienced in turnaround management, to handle the situation is the first problem to be faced in a turnaround. Managements incorrectly assume that business as usual can continue. Because the normal business practices have placed the firm in mortal jeopardy, they cannot continue. Wrenching psychological changes, and cultural changes, are invariably required. Long-standing employees will need to be fired. Product lines long associated with the company name will have to be eliminated. Plants that are the keystones of local economies will have to be closed. Policies and procedures will need to be replaced. The people responsible for the past cannot usually bring themselves to make these types of changes.

Leadership of a turnaround, therefore, is usually put in the hands of someone new, someone without a past (from the employees' perspective). This person must have the needed freedom and ability to act. If he or she cannot act decisively and quickly, the turnaround is probably doomed.

Where the turnaround is entrusted to the old management, the psychology of the situation is far different. Employees, customers, and suppliers are dubious and suspicious of management's actions and motives. Sometimes this can be overcome, in time, if the management pursues what are the right steps, providing it has sufficient cash resources to do so. However, achieving a turnaround becomes a far more difficult task.

Some of the existing company management, say, the heads of some departments and functions, will be found by the management leader to be competent and able to react to the changed circumstances. These managers must be retained, as they provide continuity and knowledge as well as competent management. Those managers who the turnaround leader finds cannot provide effective leadership during a time of change will have to be replaced. But there must be no attitude of change for change's sake. It is foolish and needlessly expensive to replace an entire management. There must also be a link between the new turnaround management and the existing middle management and professional staff. This link should be the retained members of the previous management who are found to be competent.

People are at the heart of a successful turnaround. The employees of a company must want the turnaround to occur and feel personally involved in achieving it. A sense of urgency, care, and participation must permeate the environment. Deliberate team-building measures must be instituted to convert dispirited employees into believers, confident that the turnaround will succeed, that the company will survive, and that they will continue to have a future as employees. What the company achieves it will achieve through the actions of its employees, all its employees, not just the few in upper management. Top management cannot lose sight of this fact.

Besides motivating, training, and properly directing the activities of its current employees, the turnaround management must take whatever steps are needed to ensure that the organization has the proper mix of critical skills. This will necessitate hiring people with those key skills that are missing. Invariably some important skills will be found to be missing.

A successful turnaround is not accomplished through achieving a consensus on what needs to be changed and what painful actions need to be taken. Major change can only occur through decree. One person needs the authority to give orders. These orders may contradict decades-long practices and ways of doing business. They may turn the company culture inside out. This is necessary; therefore it is futile to entrust the turnaround to someone without the authority to impose radical change. Needed changes will occur by directive rather than by conversion of belief.

A turnaround needs a leader, not a caretaker. But a strong leader is not a dictator. Subordinate managers must be expected to act of their own accord, and not just carry out the leader's orders. Too many decisions must be made for one person to make them all.

Sometimes turnaround is sought by hiring a consultant to assist the chief executive officer or, in the case of a subsidiary, having an executive from the parent company spend much time assisting its president. Such approaches are futile. They indicate that the person who must act decisively lacks the knowledge and perspectives needed to properly do so.

Establish new values and priorities. This means a new corporate culture, which must quickly permeate the operating environment. Use positive reinforcement and negative feedback to show your employees what is now wanted and expected. People will adapt quickly to the changes as they sense that this is what is needed to make the company survive.

You must immediately set up an employee communications program, which makes the employees part of the effort to solve the company's problems. People need information if they are to respond appropriately and be properly motivated.

All people fear losing their jobs and the unknown. They have a need to know what is going on: how bad sales and losses are; what management will be doing to save the company; what they are expected to do. A sense of personal involvement and urgency in doing their jobs will exist only if people feel that they are part of the team. This requires specific action. A turnaround situation is a highly stressful environment for all concerned. Communications will also help reduce the level of personal stress.

The turnaround management faces a number of powerful constituencies who will have much to say on key elements in the turnaround program. Sometimes there are three or more constituencies. This can complicate the situation. The first group is the board of directors or the parent company (where a subsidiary is experiencing problems). The board has to be convinced that the proper actions, programs, reorganizations, and the like are being implemented. They must be made confident that the turnaround management is competent and will succeed in saving the firm. The lenders are the next constituency. They have much to say about the financial resources available to the turnaround and such aspects as asset disposition and use of the proceeds. Unfortunately, lenders often demand management time that is critically needed elsewhere. Government may be the third constituency. If the business is primarily selling defense products, this will be a key and very time-consuming constituency. However, do not overlook other governmental bodies that are important as well. For example, you may need to work with your local Environmental Protection Agency office. You may need to convince it to hold back on citing the company for poisoning the soil with lead wastes; you may argue that a citation too easily issued would put the firm out of business. Another constituency is a powerful labor union. Just consider how important the United Auto Workers was in the Chrysler turnaround. Then there are major customers. If customers cannot be convinced to stick with the firm through its turnaround, all may be lost. Last, there are major suppliers. They also may have the ability to put the firm out of business. Remember, successfully dealing with all these important constituencies is a critical element of a turnaround.

The usual turnaround management has far less freedom of action than it would like. It has to deal successfully with at least some powerful constituencies in order to obtain the financial resources it needs and remain in business. As a general rule, the approach the company is taking in achieving a turnaround must be made known and seem sensible to these external groups. They must believe that their best interests are served by supporting the turnaround effort and that, within a reasonable period of time, the company will once again be viable.

To come to grips with the viability of the business, the turnaround leader will need to rapidly develop a strategic concept of the business. That is, he or she will need to define the corporate objective—not some glittering generality, but a specific statement of business purpose. For example: the Jones Company will design and manufacture custom-engineered automatic assembly equipment for the automotive industry.

In order to win in the competitive marketplace, you have to start with an evaluation of your strengths and weaknesses in relation to the competition. Only then can you devise a program that might enable you to differentiate your company's offerings in terms of cost, product design, quality, and distribution. Decide which of your business segments or product areas are protentially viable. Determine which ones are intrinsically unprofitable. Those must be eliminated. For the potentially viable product segments, decide what strategic changes are needed to make them viable. Understanding must lead to action and include the market and what makes it work. In some cases everything else becomes secondary.

Up to now we have assumed that the company should be turned around, but should it? Is the company worth the turnaround effort? This is a fundamental question. Suprisingly, this question is seldom asked. What is left after so much effort and additional financial resources have been expended? The bottom line is the net present value of achieving the turnaround. The troubled company may be the victim of an industry technological or structural change, or it may be faced with a huge worldwide permanent overcapacity in its industry. It may have many far larger and more capable competitors. Logically, it may be one of the participants that does not deserve to survive the shakeout. Then again, a company may need to so restructure its products and orientation that starting over may be far more desirable than a transformation. A good example of this reasoning is the manufacture of railroad car wheels. For many years quite a few companies supplied the railroad wheel market, using specialized forging plants. Then cast railroad car wheels came along. Cast wheels cost much less to make. A huge cast wheel-manufacturing overcapacity developed. The makers of forged wheels were faced with the prospects of either being driven out of the wheel business or making large research and development (R & D) and capital investments in order to be able to make cast railroad car wheels. If they made these investments, their projected returns were unreasonably low, owing to the glut of cast wheel-manufacturing capacity. As a consequence, most forged railroad wheel manufacturers chose to exit the business.

At the outset, however, of developing a strategic concept of the business, top management must answer the question of whether or not a turnaround is worth the effort.

Amazingly, companies in trouble often cannot define their strategic business units, product market segments, and the tactics and strategies that apply to each.

A company in more than one business will have a number of business units. The characteristics of each unit are different. They can range from low growth to high growth, from cash use to cash generation. These units need to be identified, their characteristics enumerated, and a strategic concept and assessment made for each one. The company may have transfer price policies and cost allocation methods that make good businesses look bad and bad businesses look good.

You must have a *stated* plan for all the various types of turnaround activities. The sum of the individual departmental or functional turnaround plans may be considered a form of master plan. A hit-or-miss approach will fail because too many types of changes must be defined and implemented at the same time. For example, purchasing should prepare a purchasing plan showing how its mode of operation will be changed to be more effective, how it will obtain lower prices, how price increases will be contained, and what types of procedural and organizational changes will be made to accomplish this. Product Engineering, as another example, should detail the approaches it will be taking to substantially decrease product cost through product design and engineering analysis efforts. This should include a timetable and plan for adopting or increasing its use of computer-aided design, finite element engineering analysis, and value engineering. Avoid the use of task forces to solve most of a troubled firm's problems. Begin to institutionalize the processes of reducing product and operating costs. This is done by following plans and improving operating procedures, which include appropriate changes in organizational and reporting relationships.

It is not enough to have carefully prepared written plans for the various turnaround activities and cost reduction steps. A comprehensive business plan is needed as well. You need a prior prospective view of what is likely to occur, month by month, for the foreseeable future, in such things as sales, costs, profits, and cash flow. Financial sources will demand it, but the turnaround management group will need it as well, to know just where it stands. You have to know how bad things really are and will probably get financially, and how much financial latitude actually exists in taking cash-using turnaround actions.

Improving operations alone is usually not enough to achieve a successful turnaround. You must pay particular attention to cash flow. If debts or bills cannot be paid when they are due, some form of bankruptcy proceeding is inevitable. This can prematurely terminate the turnaround effort, so it should not be allowed to happen. Cash generation is needed to overcome the rough spots, while cash demands have to be reduced.

Often the long-in-place management of a troubled company, as well as outside constituencies, will have views about what is the critical problem and what needs to be done to fix it.

Time after time the perceived problem and the real problem will be quite different. The turnaround management must quickly come to grips with this possibility. One example is the True Temper Corporation hand tools operation, which thought its problem was obsolete production equipment. In actuality, problems were numerous and included an improper manufacturing strategy, which placed labor-intensive operations in high-labor-cost plants. Another example is a machinery company that thought foreign competitors were under-pricing it through unfair competition. In actuality, the firm's prices were excessive, owing to obsolescent product designs, poor manufacturing productivity, and excessive purchased-item costs arising from an unskilled Purchasing Department.

The methods and procedures used for operational control are invariably a problem in a turnaround situation. A troubled business is usually one out of control. Operational controls, if absent or ineffective, must be created or improved, and this must be done for all areas of the business. A troubled company doesn't know its costs. It doesn't know its inventory. It doesn't meet production schedules. Frequently, not fully implemented and overly complex electronic data-processing systems are a contributor to the lack of control. Simple procedures, reports, and mandatory internal communications will provide the coordination and knowledge needed for all functions and executives to do their jobs properly. Encourage people to talk to one another, each telling the other the information needed to do the job properly. Regularly scheduled meetings help bring this about. Specific approval authority for various actions at various levels has to be thought out and instituted; this is important to both gaining control and properly disseminating information. This may range from the authority to create a personnel requisition, that is, job opening, to authorization to place a purchase order.

In a troubled company a new management team may find fault with almost everything. Remember, all problems are not equally important. In a turnaround everything cannot receive the same degree of attention. Initially, the one or two factors that are most important for the business to be successful must be identified. These factors will differ from industry to industry. Therefore, you must learn what they are for a particular company. These factors dictate what needs to be fixed first. The factor could be manufacturing costs, purchasing effectiveness, product design, quality of personnel, pricing, or market share.

In evaluating the existing policies, procedures, methods, and products of the troubled company, understand that there is no such thing as a stupid question. The conventionalism of the wisdom and length of duration of a business practice are no substitute for common sense. Everything is open to question. Many of the answers to those questions are surprising.

In short, a turnaround must focus on those people-inspiration aspects, cost areas, cash needs, operational improvements, and personnel problems that are of the greatest significance and immediacy. Because most costs are controlled at the profit center level (division, strategic business unit, subsidiary, or company as a whole), the methodology for averting disaster must be implemented at that level.

In a turnaround there is seldom time for new technology, new products, and long-range considerations. Realistically, the time horizon is usually one year or less—frequently much less. Approaches that will take three years or more are simply out of the question. You must concentrate on the short term.

The question often arises, "How does one get started in accomplishing a turnaround?" Successful turnarounds frequently take the following course.

PHASE 1: THE BEGINNING

Approach the turnaround with a positive, can-do attitude. Expect to breathe life into a dispirited organization. Be dynamic, or the staff will sit back and fearfully wait for the company to fail. Immediately initiate a system of timely reports (e.g., daily and weekly) covering those areas where control and reemphasis are needed. These may focus on accounts receivable, new orders, factory labor usage, productivity, inventories, and purchases. Do not rush to prematurely terminate management and professional employees. Wait until you have developed an understanding of the key strategic and operating problems and have identified unmet needs. Accomplish this quickly.

PHASE 2: THE AWAKENING

Move forward, based on the new strategic concept of the enterprise. Identify the 20 percent of elements that contribute to 80 percent of costs. Purchased-material costs, inventories, pricing, product design, plant work force, and manufacturing productivity are usually the areas that demand priority attention. Wade in and make bold, decisive, and significant improvements. Encouraged by your progress, staff members will begin to become enthusiastic and start contributing their own ideas and suggestions. The turnaround chain reaction has begun!

PHASE 3: STREAMLINING

Some individuals will still sit back at this point. They are unable to respond to the new corporate culture. It is likely that they are the ones who are largely responsible for the company's problems. Now is the time to rebuild, and form a lean and capable team that believes in its ability to make things happen. The time is now right to replace managers and professionals who lack the required skills. Upgrade your staff with new and needed skills that will lead to better controls in all phases of the business. Further efficiencies and cost reductions should follow.

Remember, turnarounds are usually all about:

- cutting direct costs,
- reducing overhead,
- fixing quality and customer service problems,

- stopping the making of unprofitable products, and
- pricing and marketing strategically.

If these things are done correctly, you can turn around anything that is *turnable*.

In the final analysis, common sense is the key to a successful turnaround. You must, through hard work and unrelenting attention to details, ascertain what is truly important. Then focus on those areas, leaving minor deficiencies for subsequent "mopping up operations." In the learning process, you must solicit information from all, while maintaining a skeptical attitude toward everything and everyone.

2

DANLY MACHINE CORPORATION: A TURNAROUND EXAMPLE

The 1983–84 turnaround of Danly Machine Corporation embodies the drama and human elements found in all industrial turnarounds. Danly Machine Corporation is a $170 million in sales capital goods and fabricated metal products manufacturer. Historically it has been an important machinery innovator. Danly's products have a reputation for quality and have been copied in Europe and Japan.

Danly Machine has approximately 1,500 employees. Its headquarters and major plant are in Cicero, Illinois, a suburb of Chicago. This plant, which is unionized, manufactures the company's three types of products: large custom-engineered mechanical stamping presses, automation systems, and die set products. Customers use these products in stamping plants. The company also has five small nonunion regional U.S. die set manufacturing plants and five small foreign die set plants.

Danly Machine became the leading U.S. builder of large mechanical stamping presses in the 1950s, driving many competitors from the field. Stamping presses are the basis of the company's reputation. When sales are good, they account for about 60 percent of Danly Machine's business. In the past three years the company has become a leading supplier of computer-controlled stamping press automation equipment. These systems are bought by auto companies as part of their efforts to reduce automobile manufacturing costs.

Danly Machine is the largest U.S. die set and die set component manufacturer. A die set is a fixture that permits a parts manufacturer to make a rapid stamping press die change.

Danly Machine was suffering from unproductive union agreement work rules and high product costs. The arrival of Japanese and German competitors with low-priced products, who succeeded in taking major market shares, spelled trouble for Danly, which began to lose big money. Pre-tax losses in 1983 exceeded $8 million.

Attitudes within the firm varied. A few in senior management were of the opinion that the problems would blow over. The more common view, from middle management to hourly worker, was, "When will we close down?"

Could Danly Machine be saved? In 1983 no one looking at the company from the outside could say for sure. Everything pointed downward. Losses mounted. Market share fell. The work force was discouraged.

Under new leadership, brought in to achieve a turnaround, Danly Machine was successfully turned around within approximately a year. Danly reduced its product costs by more than 25 percent. It regained customer confidence, winning back enough business to strain its manufacturing capacity! Danly also withstood a strike by a major industrial union, which attracted national attention, and successfully continued to operate while on strike.

Danly Machine went from being a dinosaur headed for extinction to being a survivor. Few inside and outside Danly had thought it possible. What happened represents good turnaround management. The turnaround of Danly Machine Corporation is a casebook example of the many perspectives and varying approaches needed in all industrial turnarounds.

In 1981 Danly Machine, which had been a family-controlled company, was sold to a large conglomerate. Shortly thereafter the recession of 1981–82 hit and the market for stamping presses collapsed. Along with the recession, an even more damaging event, of lasting importance, occurred—the arrival of foreign competition. Three Japanese stamping press manufacturers (Hitachi, Komatsu, and Ishikawajima-Harima Heavy Ind. [I.H.I.]) and two German stamping press manufacturers (Shuler and Weingarten), all well-established in their home markets, decided at about the same time to seriously compete in the U.S. custom-engineered stamping press market. Their equipment is technologically equivalent to U.S. products, being largely derived from them. This foreign equipment is also acceptable to U.S. customers, particularly to automobile companies, who buy the majority of this type of equipment.

Danly Machine had made a strategic error years before by licensing its technology to I.H.I., thereby creating a future competitor. It did not realize back then that the day might come when I.H.I. would refuse to renew its license agreement and become a full-fledged competitor.

The foreign stamping press builders established a new U.S. price level that was 25 percent below the previous price level. The new entrants rapidly gained market share: about 5 percent of the large mechanical stamping press market in 1981; 27 percent in 1982; 50 percent in 1983; and 65 percent in 1984. All U.S. stamping press builders felt the impact—a shakeout began. In bidding against foreign competitors to equip the new Toyota–General Motors California automotive stamping plant in May 1983, Danly's prices were so much higher as to indicate that the company was no longer a viable competitor.

In August 1983 I was brought in to turn Danly Machine around. My mandate was to revive Danly Machine Corporation as a viable company and win back market share from the Japanese and German competitors. After taking a month to assess the situation and get my hands around the operation, I devised the following strategic concept: reduce the cost of making a stamping press by more than 25 percent and quote new press orders at the foreign-determined price level. Although this price was far below current costs, it would be above the actual product cost at the time of delivery. I assumed that customers, given equally low prices, good quality, a greater ease of communication, and a better availability of spare parts, would prefer to buy from Danly and, consequently, market share would return. The strategy worked.

To announce that costs will be reduced by 25 percent is easy. Doing it is another matter. Accomplishing a significant cost reduction at Danly required devising and implementing improvements in many facets of the business. Like most turnarounds, Danly Machine, in 1983, needed to fix nearly everything. At the start, few things were satisfactory. Priorities had to be established and the most important things improved first; you can't expect to fix everything at once.

To begin with, I formulated a plan for achieving major product-cost reductions. This was the keystone of the turnaround. The plan targeted where reductions in product cost, for mechanical stamping presses, would occur. Table 2–1 shows the 1984 plan that was instituted late in 1983. In aggregate, these cost reductions arising from product-engineering efforts, better purchasing, and improved manufacturing management have been achieved. The table shows *average* values for the year. Actually, there is an ascending curve of cost reductions, which should keep rising over the years. According to the plan, after one year, cost reductions would have been well beyond the yearly average and would exceed 25 percent. Let us look at Danly Machine's specific product-cost reduction steps because they can apply to many troubled companies.

PRODUCT ENGINEERING COST SAVINGS

Danly manufactures products of its own design. Therefore, it has the ability to change its designs in order to reduce their manufacturing costs. In this situation, Product Engineering is the area in which, over time, the greatest product-cost reductions had to originate. The product had to be redesigned to be intrinsically less expensive to manufacture, and this had to be done again and again and again. Let's look at the specific approaches taken, which are applicable to many types of manufacturing companies.

1. *Preliminary design.* Danly, like many companies, responded to customer needs by copying or modifying its previous designs. This locks a firm into yesterday's designs, yesterday's technology. This approach was replaced by creating and critically ex-

Table 2–1.
1984 Product Cost Reduction Plan

SOURCE	AVERAGE TOTAL SAVINGS
ENGINEERING:	
Preliminary Design	1.0%
Critical Component Analysis	1.0%
Value Engineering	1.0%
Use of High-Strength Alloys	-
User-Friendly Drawings	0.3%
Switch to Catalog Items	0.5%
	3.8%
PURCHASING:	
Steel Plate	5.1%
Other Purchases	2.7%
	7.8%
MANUFACTURING MANAGEMENT:	
Welding Procedure	0.3%
Preparation of Work	0.3%
Central Work Scheduling	0.5%
Work Productivity	3.6%
Improved Assembly Planning	2.8%
	8.3%
TOTAL	19.9%

amining a new preliminary design for each stamping press order, rather than directly copying previous designs. Design improvements can be found by this method that reduce overall product cost by, say, 2 percent per year.

2. *Critical component analysis*. Modern engineering analysis tools are widely available—finite element analysis in particular—that allow the function of every cubic inch of material in a design to be scrutinized for need. Often inadvertent weak points are found, say, a lifting hole put in a location of high stress concentration. Changing the placement of this hole, and other such corrections, may permit significant reductions in size or thickness. Thinner, smaller parts mean less expensive parts. Overall product costs can be reduced this way by, say, 2 percent per year.

3. *Value engineering*. A specific responsibility has to be assigned to ask questions about

cost-generating elements of a design. For example, must the part have these tight tolerances, or does it need to be made in this shape to do its function effectively? Value engineering can reduce cost by, say, 2 percent per year.

4. *Use of high-strength alloys*. Companies get into a rut of using only a few convenient materials, such as low-carbon steel. This ignores readily available cost reductions from changing materials. For example, a switch from medium-carbon steel to 4340 alloy steel allowed a tie rod design to be reduced from a 12-inch diameter to an 8-inch diameter. The actual cost of tie rod metal was lowered, and significant economies resulted from the size reduction on mating parts. This type of change can bring overall savings of, say, 1 percent per year.

5. *User-friendly drawings*. Expansion of a CADAM computer-aided design system from two to ten work stations and two plotters, used on two shifts, meant that it became possible to generate as many variants of a design stored in the computer's memory as one wished. It would no longer be necessary to use the same drawing for different purposes. For a machined weldment, specialized drawing versions could be prepared for both the weld and the machine shops, showing notes and dimensions most appropriate for each purpose. This would save significant employee comprehension time and prevent manufacturing errors. This can reduce overall cost by, say, 0.6 percent per year.

6. *Switch to catalog items*. Many small components, such as valves and switches, were designed and manufactured that could have been selected from the catalogs of outside vendors at lower cost and higher reliability. Switching to outside vendor catalog items reduces overall costs by, say, 1 percent per year.

These engineering-based cost reductions have a common thread. They are all substitution of brains for brawn. Higher intellectual costs serve as a multiplier to achieve greatly reduced manufacturing costs. It works.

PURCHASING COST SAVINGS

Purchasing was made a major player in the Danly Machine turnaround. The steps it took, which are applicable to most manufacturing companies, were these:

1. *Steel plate*. Sixteen percent of the total cost of a stamping press is the steel plate used in making it. By demanding large discounts from steel companies and convincing them that significant supplier competition exists for Danly's purchases, domestic mills met foreign prices, and discounts of as much as $180 per ton were realized.

2. *Lower purchase price levels*. Major savings were realized by making buys of all items more competitive and obtaining significant quantity discounts for electric motors, electronic controls, and other expensive components.

3. *Make/buy*. Creating an effective make/buy function, by adopting appropriate procedures, adding necessary support staff, and coordinating needed information, permits the identification and the subcontracting of the manufacture of those items that can be bought for less than their internal manufacturing cost. This resulted in significant economies.

MANUFACTURING MANAGEMENT COST SAVINGS

Manufacturing management was the third leg to the Danly Machine product-cost reduction plan. Let us review the steps taken.

1. *Worker productivity improvement.* A comprehensive labor use and productivity tracking system was instituted. It provided manufacturing supervision with a basis for taking corrective action. For a one-year period it results in a product-cost reduction at the rate of 7.2 percent.

2. *Welding procedure.* A company that does as much welding as Danly Machine needs professional welding expertise. A welding engineer was hired to implement advanced welding procedures, more cost-effective welding design practices, the purchase of improved welding equipment, and the use of more cost-effective welding materials. These activities should reduce product cost by, say, 0.6 percent per year.

3. *Preparation of work.* Preparation of work in machining, by having the work, tools, and drawing pulled together by a laborer before giving the work to a machinist, reduces the overall time required. The queueing of such setups allows the easier switching of a worker from one job to another, with a resultant recapture of time that would have been lost if a problem developed with the first job. This procedure should reduce total cost by, say, 0.6 percent per year.

4. *Central work center scheduling.* Work center scheduling had been done by the foreman of each activity, who acted to optimize his own area. By transferring this function to a centralized authority, optimization of the plant's activities as a whole could be realized. This will result in reduced lead times, reduced work-in-process levels, and reduced manpower. The overall product savings will be about 1 percent per year.

5. *Improved assembly planning.* It is difficult to control the productivity of an event taking thousands of hours, such as the assembly of a large machine. By breaking this event into a number of smaller, manageable events, taking typically four or eight hours, control of productivity is reestablished. Application of short-interval scheduling approaches to the tasks of assembling large machinery substantially reduces the total assembly time. The total cost improvement from this is about 5.6 percent per year.

6. *CNC (Computer Numerical Control) torch cutting, nesting, and plasma cutting.* Improving this activity, by analyzing how to get more parts from a given steel plate, achieves, through material savings, a cost reduction of, say, 1.6 percent per year.

Although the Danly Machine cost reduction plan was focused on the major product line, which is the manufacture of large custom-engineered mechanical stamping presses, the cost reduction efforts carried over to the automation and die set products as well. One should not lose sight of the fact that if Purchasing buys steel at a lower price, all other products made of steel will similarly benefit. Therefore, the die set and automation businesses both experienced improved profit margins.

Manufacturing companies are—or should be—always evaluating new machine tools that have a fast payback and cut costs. The Danly cost reduction plan did not include the savings that would result from new capital equipment. At Danly Machine it was felt that whatever these savings were, they would be considered a bonus and not planned for. Much of the Danly equipment is old but well maintained; the average machine tool in Danly's plants is twenty-two years old. Yet this machinery is being used to produce state-of-the-art equipment. Having old equipment, then, did not provide an important impediment to the turnaround. New machine tools are being bought, to the extent capital is available, but the average age of the equipment will remain old.

Important but less urgent cost reductions arose from pruning two product lines. Danly Machine had once been an active supplier of milling machines to the aircraft industry—aircraft spar mills and woodworking equipment—although neither constituted a major percentage of sales. Foreign companies had developed more cost-effective designs, so little more than a repair parts business remained. However, sales quotations continued to be made, engineers were in place to develop customer proposals and improved models, and manufacturing capacity was kept in place in the event an order materialized. Most of this was eliminated, as waste, but the profitable replacement parts business was retained.

The second business to be pruned was the manufacture of small stamping presses—25 tons to 150 tons. The market for high-quality models of such machines disappeared as a technological change occurred in the auto industry. A market remained for machines of lesser quality, and in attempting to sell equipment to this market, Danly Machine was experiencing product costs averaging 180 percent of sales price. The material costs alone were running 95 percent of sales price. Danly Machine's manufacturing was geared to making large custom machines, not to making batches of standard design machines. The product line didn't fit. Quotations on new orders were stopped but, again, the profitable replacement parts business was retained. Every turnaround must face the elimination from the product line of no longer viable products. Danly Machine did this successfully.

THE HUMAN ELEMENT

People are the most important element in all turnarounds. Danly Machine was no exception. Top management could only succeed by working through them. People want to do the right things to save the company and their own jobs. Unfortunately, they often lack the understanding of what must be done. The employees had to become part of the turnaround process.

A major employee communications effort was the first step. The purpose was to convince employees that a turnaround was possible and that the new management was determined to achieve it. This restored employee self-confidence and motivation, which are both essential to making a turnaround effort succeed.

Specifically, Danly hired a public relations firm to draft a constant flow of letters sent to the employees' homes. The letters were sent there so spouses could read them too. They described the state of the industry and the state of the company. These letters were to raise employee consciousness and build team spirit. They countered fear of the unknown and of the future. Fear had to be countered because it seriously debilitates employee effectiveness. People were made to understand that costs had to be reduced if their jobs were to be saved. The point was made that featherbedding doesn't protect jobs, it destroys them. Employees were encouraged to ask questions by mail and in person and were given straight answers when they did.

As part of the communication effort, a speech was given to 850 assembled employees, near the spot in the Cicero plant where another impassioned speech had been given soon after December 7, 1941. The 1983 speech told them that, like the last time, we were here to stay and we would turn back the Japanese threat. Danly Machine would not close and, with their participation, we intended to survive.

One consciousness-raising approach was to prepare a fifty-foot-long banner, hung across a public street between Danly plant buildings, saying "WE WANT MORE JOBS IN CICERO NOT TOKYO." Soon thereafter a Japanese machine tool company delegation arrived to discuss ways for the two companies to collaborate. Both groups chose not to discuss the banner. The Japanese company's idea of collaboration turned out to be somewhat peculiar. It had Danly Machine giving them American dollars, and their giving Danly Machine Japanese machine tools in return. To some people it was pointed out that there was another way to interpret the banner that was not hostile to the Japanese. That is to say that Danly Machine was determined to survive and have jobs in Cicero, and to accomplish this it would do whatever it took. This included buying Japanese machine tools if they were a better buy and superior to American-made tools.

An example of the impact of the communications program on people was a $1,200 savings achieved by a machine assembler. When the worker heard that "no one knows your job better than you do" and was urged to help, he abandoned decades of the company culture. Given the task of assembling a hydraulic manifold, the worker realized, because he had made such items for years, that the design was needlessly elaborate. The worker took the initiative by sketching a simple arrangement and sought out the chief engineer, who agreed with the idea. The new design was immediately adopted, and the savings from eliminating unnecessary parts exceeded $1,200 in parts alone.

As in all turnarounds, leadership was needed. It had to come from the top. Changes occurred through decree, not consensus. Explanations had to be given because people need to know why radical changes are being made. Nonetheless, someone had to set the course.

Proper leadership had to be exercised at all levels. It was needed from the heads of all Danly's departments and functions. In working with these senior executives, it was clear to me that many of them did not and could not do their jobs well. An exception was the head of Engineering, who was a capable, longtime employee. About a year before the turnaround began, Danly had enhanced an early retirement window, so many of the best Danly people had retired.

This meant that many of the present senior executives had been in their current positions for less than a year. New executives were obviously needed and recruited for Employee Relations, Manufacturing, Purchasing, and Finance.

An important step within the first month of the turnaround was getting the various members of management talking to one another and working together. Weekly staff meetings were set up for the first time in the company's history. At the initial operations staff meeting, people seemed afraid to voice an opinion. Recognizing the fear and getting little give and take, I abruptly stopped the meeting, asking, "What are you afraid of? Why are you afraid to talk?" Eventually someone replied, "We are normally called together only to hear bad news or to be shouted at." Expressing this cleared the air and allowed interaction, although on a small scale to begin.

Regularly scheduled coordination meetings became commonplace. These included a general staff meeting for all those concerned with sales, operations, and finance aspects, and staff meetings within each of the departments, say Engineering and Manufacturing. These meetings provided coordination that was previously nonexistent. Minor problems were kept from developing into full-blown crises.

To come to grips with manufacturing productivity, a simple manual labor reporting and productivity measurement report was instituted. This helped to establish what productivity level actually prevailed and identified where improvement was most glaringly needed. It showed where time was being buried and where the number of employees was excessive for the current level of business. The report was based on data contained in a vast, but generally useless, electronic data processing-generated report.

The productivity report became a powerful tool in the hands of manufacturing management and shop floor supervision. They now had a weekly report card. A greater analysis of these aspects and techniques appears in a later chapter.

Long evening meetings (at which cold cuts were served), held weekly for several months, were used to train shop supervision how to do their jobs better. They learned how to properly discipline employees and how to achieve higher productivity. The productivity report card compelled them to act and the training taught them how to act. The result was a week-to-week improvement in shopwide productivity, measured in terms of output per hour, using a standard cost system. After seven months, productivity had increased by 37 percent. This was achieved rapidly, without significant expense, with no capital investment.

The shop supervision training changed the culture within Manufacturing. In the new culture, productivity is important, whereas previously simply producing the goods had been the objective. The role of shop supervision became recognized, and these men's self-esteem and authority rose. Questions once asked of union stewards now were asked of foremen. The changes pleased almost everyone. Foremen now felt like part of management and received more respect. Hourly workers became confident that Danly knew what it was doing.

The training of shop supervisors and their increasing authority allowed Danly to face the issue of its poor manufacturing work rules. A detailed look at this follows in the chapter on Manufacturing. Although the labor union contract protected many poor work practices, even worse practices actually occurred. Union stewards claimed that certain undesirable practices were protected by the agreement, and the foremen hadn't known they weren't. Workers who were fired usually won reinstatement for two reasons: poor procedures accompanying their firing and management weakness. This weakened foremen's authority. After training provided during the turnaround, the foremen learned what was in the labor contract and so couldn't be misled about nonprotected poor practices. Techniques were taught on how to properly discipline a worker so the charge would be upheld. It only took the firings of two workers for the news to spread that a new day was at hand. Training and improved shop floor discipline were important elements in obtaining the large increase in productivity.

Cultural changes had to be achieved everywhere in the organization, not just among hourly manufacturing employees. For this, top management had to drive the cultural conversion process. Whenever something was spotted that wasn't consistent with the new themes, it had to be corrected at once. The person involved was helped to understand why we at Danly no longer did it the old way. Take, for example, a request from a customer for a duplicate of a machine the customer had bought from Danly before. The Engineering staff was forced to realize that the "duplicate" could *not* be a true duplicate because Danly Machine would lose money making a true duplicate. The machine that would be designed would meet the same specifications, look similar, and be of the same quality. But in many detailed aspects it would have value improvements. If this customer ordered another duplicate machine in a few years, it wouldn't be just like the one the company was currently designing. The idea was implanted that the company must be continually improving its products—technologically frozen designs must be banished from our minds. In product design there must be no such thing as good enough.

THE STRIKE

There are always some who resist change. At Danly, the labor union was one. In order to accomplish a turnaround, the old, unproductive work rules were no longer tolerable. Danly management had to face the problem squarely. The union local president was sent, at company expense, to Japan to see the work environment in Japanese plants and the nature of what the company faced. It had been hoped that he would realize that protecting his members' future employment depended on allowing the company to successfully face the productivity and cost challenges presented by Japanese competitors. Apparently the trip had no positive effect.

Danly drew up a list of those work rule changes essential to having the flexibility needed to be productive and, thus, competitive. Management tried to negotiate, in the fall of 1983, an early labor contract based on work rule improvements. It seemed to management that the union was determined to have a strike to prove to the new management just who was in charge. Detailed planning went into Danly Machine's strike preparations. The company went to great lengths to let politicians, police, and employees know that it would not permit itself to be shut down by a strike. No violence or other illegal acts would be tolerated. Police were expected to enforce the law. Transportation of people and goods in and out of the Cicero facility would continue. T.V. cameras and tape recorders were visibly installed in advance, to ensure availability of hard evidence if illegal acts were committed. Plywood was placed over all windows. A Danly strike six years before had caused $10,000 worth of window damage. The 1984 management would not let this happen. Security was beefed up; more guards were added and patrols in off-hours were made more frequent.

The union called a meeting of its members and took a strike vote. It was careful to not take any chances on this vote; no secret ballot here. Each member was asked to individually proceed to the front of the meeting, where, assisted by union leaders, he was asked to openly vote, by writing in pencil on a pad, whether he was for or against a strike. If he made a mistake, those standing around him were available to help him erase his error and vote correctly. By this process the vote came out about 600 to 19. Under the circumstances it was remarkable that nineteen persons insisted on voting against a strike. Federal law does not require that strike votes be taken by secret ballot.

May 1, 1984, the strike came. The union, it was felt, expected the company to buckle within a few weeks—it did not.

Hundreds of salaried employees were drafted to work in the manufacturing areas of the Cicero plant under the guidance of experienced foremen. A twelve-hour day was instituted. Danly provided free lunches and dinners. The experience was valuable for all. It taught the office staff what the company made and how it was made. Engineers finally understood the complaints they had heard over the years from Manufacturing about how hard it was to make or assemble the products they designed. The result was the swift simplification of a number of product designs and resulting cost reductions.

Circumstances forced foremen to do production work themselves, helping them to learn how long it took to do certain operations. They learned just where the company had been getting less than a day's work for a day's pay. Feath-erbedding beyond original estimates was uncovered. These were valuable lessons. They meant that Danly would be made more productive in the future. This information would never have been learned without the strike.

During the six months before the strike, the communications program had won the hearts and minds of the salaried employees. They donned jeans and willingly worked production machines. It surprised many a secretary to learn that she could make something in the shop. Several of them, visibly proud, brought me parts to show what they had made.

After the first month of the strike, hours were reduced to a more tolerable ten hours per day. Striking workers began to trickle across the picket line to come back to work. They, too, had been influenced by the communications program, which continued during the first months of the strike. They felt that the company was being fair and reasonable and wanted to protect their jobs.

The union had told its members that the company couldn't run without them. Two weeks into the strike a large stamping press was completed. It was shipped at night by rail because it was cheaper to ship this way. The rumor was spread among the strikers by those hostile to Danly that this shipment never occurred. Two weeks later another press was readied and shipped by rail. This time it was shipped in daylight, decked out with American flags and with the locomotive whistle tooting. There could be no mistake about what had happened this time. The company was operating.

The initial minor violence in the strike was met with immediate arrests—two the first day. In this incident, strikers dropped nails on the roadway in front of Danly Machine's driveway, one reaching over a policeman to do it. The striker was amazed to be immediately handcuffed. This set the tone. Pickets who went to workers' homes to harass them were met by police, who arrested them. In one case, Danly Machine's security was so effective that it got to the intended victim's house before the criminals did. One dark night a group of strikers crept up to a Danly gate and, after looking around for guards or police, tore down a small section of fence. They did not realize that the scene was being captured on new night-vision video equipment. An arrest quickly ensued. One early picket line crossover received telephone calls threatening his life and the lives of his wife and children. After the second call the equipment was ready for a telephone trace. When a third call occurred, it was simultaneously traced to a telephone in the union's headquarters and the arrest was made. One night a former employee, a union activist fired before the strike for insubordination, threw a flammable substance against a wooden door of the plant, lit it, and ran. A guard noticed the flames almost immediately. The fire was quickly extinguished. The guard recognized the fleeing arsonist. The arsonist was arrested and faces a criminal felony trial. Because people were in the building, under Illinois law, the act of arson is akin to attempted murder. The situation never got out of hand because Danly Machine was vigilant.

After ten weeks on strike the company began hiring economic replacements. With the writing on the wall, increasing numbers of strikers gave up the strike and crossed the picket line to regain their jobs. After fourteen weeks large newspaper advertisements for new employees were published. Thousands applied. Danly could afford to be selective in interviewing job candidates. New employees were assured that Danly would give them job protection; they would not be fired to make room for returning strikers.

By the fall of 1984 the strike ceased to be an important operating issue. The Cicero plant was fully manned and meeting production schedules. The plant was operating under the work rule changes the company felt were essential to its survival. After six months the hourly work force consisted of half new hires and half former union members. I say former union members because they resigned from their union to prevent the union from fining them. It is important to understand that in many states, unions have the right to fine members who violate a strike. The communications effort served to convince many workers that striking was in no one's best interest. They chose to vote against the continuation of the strike with their feet; they crossed the picket line and returned to work.

Although a strike was in progress, placing severe demands on the staff organizations, the company continued to achieve product-cost reductions, almost to the plan that had anticipated no strike. The finance organization found that, after six months on strike, Danly Machine was still on the planned cost reduction curve, with only a two-month delay.

THE MARKET

A manufacturing company needs to sell its products in order to remain in business, and Danly Machine was no exception. At the start of the turnaround, almost no one was ordering Danly stamping presses. Buyers were letting Danly Machine quote but with little expectation that they would place an order—Danly Machine's prices were just uncompetitive. With the cost reduction program, shown before, the company understood that its costs would become competitive in time and started quoting prices below its then current costs. The expectation was that, in the year or so it takes between receiving an order and shipping a custom-engineered stamping press, costs would have sufficiently declined to permit a break-even. In time, the cost reduction effort would lead to profitability.

Customers were genuinely surprised at Danly Machine's new price competitiveness. In addition, the company began offering features no one else had thought of, such as a five-year guarantee and a twenty-four-hour, seven-day-a-week hot line for service questions.

As 1984 progressed, the Danly share of large contracts awarded to press builders rose. It was helped, in large part, by orders from different organizations within General Motors Corporation, which is the largest customer for Danly Machine's types of stamping press equipment.

Senator Charles Percy stopped by Danly Machine on a campaign swing. He shook hands with about 200 office employees, many of whom stopped him to show him their campaign buttons, remind him of past campaigns in which they worked for him, and tell him of contributions they had made. I then maneuvered Senator Percy into my office and told him that General Motors was making one of the largest buys in the history of the press industry, and if they went entirely foreign, it would destroy the American press industry. I went on to say that Danly would make the best machine at the lowest price but wanted and needed fair consideration. The people at Danly Machine needed his help. Chuck Percy made notes, analyzed the situation, and then picked up the telephone and called the White House. He told them to get him the chairman of General Motors. In five minutes General Motors' chairman Roger Smith was on the line. Senator Percy gave Roger Smith a well-thought-out, cogent exposition that lasted for more than twenty minutes. Senator Percy discussed the role of the American machine tool industry and the importance to that industry of G.M.'s press-buying program. He outlined the business reasons why General Motors should deal with Danly. He concluded with the request that, if all thing were equal—and only if all things were equal—care should be taken to give Danly fair consideration in this competition (against six, mostly foreign, competitors). By the next morning the results of the Percy telephone call were being felt.

General Motors ultimately placed orders with six press builders. Danly Machine came out with a much larger share, vis-à-vis the foreign builders, than many people expected. These were the largest orders the company had ever received. Since this event many other customers have come back to Danly Machine.

SUMMARY

The turnaround of Danly Machine Corporation was a hard fought but successful effort, with many broadly applicable lessons. Its high points included the following:

- Changing the corporate culture to include a willingness to accept change, and a sensitivity to cost
- Replacing key executives in Manufacturing, Purchasing, Employee Relations, and Finance, in order to obtain competent functional leadership
- Obtaining major price reductions for important purchased items through more effective purchasing management
- Retraining the entire corps of first-line manufacturing supervision to become effective managers
- Replacing rigid work rules in manufacturing with flexible, productive ones
- Improving hourly labor productivity by 37 percent
- Adopting high-technology approaches to product engineering, a substitution in product designs of intellectual content for metal, ''brains for brawn''
- Successfully decreasing product cost by more than 25 percent
- Pruning unprofitable product lines
- Reducing inventories
- Restoring customer confidence
- Winning back significant market share from the Japanese and Germans in a smokestack industry—not many have done that
- Increasing the order backlog from $8 million to $200 million; the highest level in the company's history
- Successfully operating during a strike by the United Steelworkers of America, and continuing to reduce product costs during the strike
- Ending the threat of extinction as a company

Not all of these points apply to every turnaround situation. But a good many of them do. The key is to have a specifically designed turnaround program for each situation that is lead by a strong, experienced individual at the top.

3

COMMUNICATIONS

The purpose of a communications program is to influence people—how they think and how they act. Communications is a means to motivate individuals to change their behavior: employees to work with greater diligence; unions to give up featherbedding work rules; lenders to give more time and concessions in debt repayment; customers to forgive past poor service and continue buying. A communications program is analogous to the function of a wartime Allies Propaganda Ministry. The analogy is fitting because the company really is in a war—a war of survival. Everything said by the company must be completely truthful. Establishing the credibility of company statements is a major and necessary objective.

People are at the heart of the majority of the company's problems. They are also at the heart of the solution to these problems. The way you influence people is through good communications.

A troubled company seldom has the internal resources needed for an effective communications program. If it does, it signifies the existence of excessive corporate overhead. This type of capability should be obtained on an as-needed basis from a large public relations firm. Only a large firm has the variety of resources and depth of contacts needed to do the job comprehensively and effectively. For example, this means being able to learn, in advance, that a potentially damaging story will appear on television or in the press and being able to influence the presentation of the story so as to include the company's side, or even to slant the story the company's way.

A communications program cannot be given entirely over to a public relations firm. Only the turnaround management can decide the program's theme, which must reflect the firm's strategic concept. Company executives must become the company spokesmen. Frequently the turnaround leader becomes the leading spokesman, except for labor relations matters, which are left to the head of Employee Relations. A public relations firm can train these executives to become more effective spokesmen.

People give greater credence to what they learn from third parties they either respect or consider to be neutral. The public relations firm must, therefore, develop newspaper and magazine reports of things that will increase confidence in the company—things such as, "Jones Company receiving support from its suppliers." Similarly, third-party pronouncements that can influence employee attitudes need to be developed and widely disseminated. For example, "Senator Jones says that widget manufacturers that don't reduce costs will be driven out of business by foreign widget makers."

An effective communications program costs money. A troubled company must watch this expense, like all others, and spend no more than it really needs. Public relations firms, being paid consultants, will always want a company to do more, to spend more.

EMPLOYEE COMMUNICATIONS

A company in a turnaround is a company in upheaval. Vast changes will be required and people's support needed in implementing these changes, rather than in opposing them. Long-accepted norms and procedures will disappear. People will disappear. A cultural revolution will occur. Effective employee communications will be needed to accomplish this as smoothly and painlessly as possible. But it will never be truly smooth or painless.

The employees have to know why change is needed. They may see for themselves, by the lack of activity in the manufacturing plant, that business is terrible and be fearful of losing their jobs. But they may still not understand why major changes are needed to save the company. The facts should be presented to them. Even if employees don't fully understand the facts, they will appreciate the company's taking the time and trouble to inform them. By treating the employees as adults and sharing its problems with them, the company will bring its employees back into the mainstream. The employees, as a result, will also feel a closer psychological bond to the company and be more understanding of its needs.

For employees to be motivated and end their demoralization, you must keep them informed about the status of the business, competition, and matters affecting the firm. Demoralized employees show disinterest and boredom in the way they do their jobs and antipathy toward the changes that need to be made. Troubled companies often keep their employees in the dark, trying to keep the bad news away from them. This is futile; employees know when there are problems and usually what many of the problems are.

The confidence of the employees must be reestablished: confidence that the company will survive; that the plant will not close down; that the turnaround management knows what it is doing; that the turnaround program will succeed; and confidence in themselves.

Restoring the confidence of the employees that they can succeed in turning the company around is a key turnaround step. Fearful, demoralized employees are ineffective employees. Confident employees, urged to try harder, to measure up to the challenge, to get the job done, will try harder and be more innovative.

Employees and their attitudes are behind most of a troubled company's problems. Poorly made products reflect the attitudes of the people who make them. Featherbedding plant work rules and bloated salaried staff organizations also reflect people's attitudes. Making a cultural revolution, using effective employee communications, will not solve all of a troubled company's problems, but it will solve a good many of them.

All of a company's employees, hourly, salaried, and management, have personally much at stake in the success or failure of the business. Their interest, vigor, and initiative in doing their jobs are important elements that you can motivate in the solution to the company's problems. A one-shot employee communications effort will not do the job. You must continue to keep employees informed of things they should know, the good things as well as the bad. Positive news must be spread, as it helps to build confidence.

Keeping employees informed takes continuing and regular effort. Frequent notices, bulletins, letters, and some meetings are normally required. The company cannot count solely on an employee newspaper. This may require the help of a public relations firm to establish a program. The employees must, psychologically, become part of the team with management. They have to feel that the management knows what it is doing and is committed to making the company succeed. Every employee must be made to feel that what he or she does matters and that his or her contributions to the turnaround are not only welcome, but also essential, as indeed they are.

It is a mistake for a company to communicate solely with its employees through a union, whose messages are often one-sided, parochial, and adversarial. The development of trust and perception of mutual interests requires direct communication. In addition, major problems are usually not solely those of union versus management, but often more global in scope. Direct communication, ignoring the union and thereby undermining its officials, is essential to create the feeling of ''we,'' consisting of all employees (including management), and ''they,'' the enemy—the competition.

Communications must be upward as well as downward. All employees, whether salaried professional staff or hourly production worker, must feel free to ask you questions, to offer suggestions, and to express complaints. When they do it shows that people feel involved, that the communications effort is working. People feel better when they can complain to the boss, even if he does nothing but hear them out. Sometimes it is easy to solve their problem, and when you do news travels fast.

The employee communications program used at Danly Machine Corporation shows the comprehensiveness of the needed effort. It was aimed at all employees, not just those in management, and contained the following elements:

- At least one letter a month from top management sent to every employee, relating things he or she might possibly want to know, such as the state of the business and the competitive situation. A public relations firm helped to prepare the letters
- A telephone hot line for important information, such as a major order won or lost
- Bulletins to the foremen so they can get vital information to the workers quickly
- No holds barred—ask any questions you want—sessions between top management and groups of employees
- Solicitation of ideas from the employees on cost reduction
- Prepaid envelopes and cards, marked confidential, to allow any employee to communicate directly with top management
- A banner across a major artery stating, ''WE WANT MORE JOBS IN CICERO NOT TOKYO''
- Visits from important political figures, such as Senator Charles Percy, showing the employees that they and their company are important
- Speeches by top management to the assembled work force

In addition, weekly meetings of all manufacturing supervision and weekly staff meetings held by all the various professional functional staffs also promote communications.

This comprehensive communications program had the desired effect. Productivity improved, costs were brought down, and many, many salaried employees were inspired to put in long hours of unpaid overtime without being asked. In retrospect, the value of the unpaid overtime may have exceeded the cost of the employee communications program.

The Danly Machine Corporation employee communications program maintained a central source of information. It kept control of what was said, to whom, and where. This control is quite necessary.

An interesting comparison is to look at the very different communications program used in the turnaround of Kentucky Electric Steel Corporation, which also saw a need for improved employee communications. The elements of their communications program were as follows:

- Daily department head luncheons
- Formal out-of-plant monthly meetings between department heads and supervisors
- Formation of a supervisor's club
- Bimonthly Manufacturing Policy Committee meetings

- Bimonthly Commercial Policy Committee meetings
- Monthly President's Staff meetings
- Quarterly department head letters to employee's homes
- Periodic letters to employees' homes from the president
- Monthly labor/management Productivity Committee meetings
- Frequent meetings between the Executive Committee of the union and labor relations executives
- Formation of a First Ladies' Club for spouses of supervisors

As you can see, the Danly Machine Corporation communications program focused on *all* employees (i.e., hourly workers, salaried employees, and all levels of management). In contrast, Kentucky Electric Steel's program focused primarily on improving communication among the management. A possible consequence of this difference in emphasis was an attempt to unionize Kentucky Electric Steel's clerical staff sometime after their communications program began. This may have been a symptom of a polarization, which had been at the core of the original problem. The communications program may have exacerbated the situation. Ultimately, Kentucky Electric Steel failed to survive a ruinous strike, and the closed-down company was sold off.

The turnaround of a company requires many changes to be made in the way a business is run. These changes can best be accomplished by the people the company already has. In short, you must accept that demoralization has begun; that it can only be modified by gross attitudinal changes; that these can be effected only by strong leadership exhibited through positive communications efforts. To succeed, you must motivate the company's current employees to accept and advance change. An employee communications program is essential in this task.

EXTERNAL COMMUNICATIONS AND RELATIONS

People are distrustful when they are not fully informed. Hiding or minimizing negative information corrodes credibility and adversely affects the motivation of the very people whose support is most essential. Troubled companies tend to generate cynicism in their workers, suppliers, customers, shareholders, and lenders. Despite the aphorism "no news is good news," most of the interested parties want to know many of the same things:

- What is the strategic problem and what will be the company's response to this problem.
- What plans, programs, and specific corrective actions will be undertaken, with what timetable.
- What are the expected benefits from these actions and how long before the company can expect to regain profitability.
- How is the company progressing in achieving its stated financial and other objectives (a report card).

• How long will the cash generated by various asset dispositions be used in health-restoring ways (so as to reassure the people that it will not be merely dissipated on continuing operating losses).

Employee communications and external communications have to be consistent. You need to tell the external groups much of the same things that the employees will want to know. Their confidence in the turnaround management's ability to succeed will have to be built. Providing them timely information will help to create confidence in the management, and thereby a willingness to go along with you. Confidence in the ability of the company to survive and in the ability of the management to achieve a successful turnaround must be consciously developed.

In situations where community support is required, one excellent form of external communications is the "spreading of the word" by informed employees. More often than not this forms the basis of the community's opinion of the company.

The following sections examine some of the special aspects presented by the more important external parties.

Dealing with the Board and the Parent Company

The board of directors must have absolute confidence in the turnaround leadership and support it completely, giving it full authority to make the required changes. The board must have a realistic view of the company and its expectations. If not, this could be the source of an important problem.

The board members may have considerable personal expertise, which can and should be brought to bear. The various problems and alternative solutions should be discussed with those individual members who might be able to provide additional insight, as well as with the board as a whole. The action of reviewing and presenting the problem and the solutions being considered will help to clarify matters and, by itself, improve your ability to make the right choice. The board member, by looking at the problem afresh, may be able to suggest alternatives that hadn't been considered, or pitfalls that were unknown. Involving the board and keeping it well informed are necessary to keeping its support during the innumerable crises that are bound to occur.

Sometimes communicating with the board involves the greatest political sensitivity. This must be handled with great care.

In some instances it may be advisable to have counsel present at board meetings when particularly sensitive subjects are to be discussed. This provides a basis to assert that the discussions were privileged and not discoverable in litigation.

Most boards prefer written action plans and written measurements against plan. This is another reason the company needs a complete and well-conceived business plan. The business plan is explored in the chapter on finance.

For the turnaround of subsidiaries or divisions, the upper management of the parent company functions much like the board of a freestanding company. Again, communication builds confidence, and confidence creates support.

Dealing with Major Lenders

Lenders need to feel, with some confidence, that their loans will be repaid, that their asset is sound and not seriously at risk. If they aren't made to feel this way, they will have a greater proclivity to calling in the loans and most certainly truncating the credit line. This they will be able to do at various times, when the firm is technically in default, by unintentionally violating restrictive covenants in the loan agreements, such as requirements on minimum net worth or on a minimum current ratio. The company will also need the lender's support in easing the loan restrictions in the event this becomes necessary.

Lenders like to know that the company's financial and business plan is realistic. They should be brought into the turnaround's planning at an early stage, and the sensitive lenders must be kept continually advised. You must keep them convinced that whether the early results are good or bad, the firm is on top of the situation, with adequate controls. Surprises at month's end are not welcome, particularly on a regular basis.

The turnaround may not be able to generate sufficient cash in its early period to keep the firm liquid. The lenders may have to be persuaded to put in more money in order to tide the firm over this period. The lenders have to be made to feel that they are going to be much better off by being patient and supportive. Otherwise, the turnaround will fail and, in all probability, they will recover far less. It may also be necessary to convince them to reschedule and restructure the debt; say, to convert a significant portion of the debt into preferred stock.

The turnaround of Memorex in the 1970s hinged on this very aspect. The company owed the Bank of America $150 million and other lenders millions more. A restructuring was worked out that converted $30 million of the debt to the Bank of America and $10 million of the debt to thirteen other lenders into preferred stock. The lenders also accepted 4 percent interest and a new stretched out schedule for repayment of the remaining debt. On top of this the Bank of America provided Memorex a new $35 million line of credit.

Lenders have a tendency, once the turnaround has begun to succeed, to want to withdraw too much cash from the business too soon. If this happens, it will jeopardize the firm's being able to ever really become completely healthy. The lenders must be convinced therefore, that substantial progress is not the same as achieving success. Their long-range interests would be better served by staying with what is turning into a healthy borrower until the company becomes that.

Every lender wants to keep nonperforming loans to a low level. Attention must, therefore, be given to being able to pay down the loans to a reasonable level.

Loan officers like to visit regularly to see for themselves the actions purported to be under way to accomplish the turnaround. These visits should be encouraged, within the limits of time availability of top management. Time spent with lenders may seem to consume too much valuable management time—it comes with the uncertainty of a turnaround. This time needs to be managed if it is not to become excessive. Both the chief financial officer and the chief executive officer need to be involved and, with skill, both need not be present at all meetings. Good business and financial plans, discussed in a later chapter, will help reduce the time needed to be spent in this activity.

In multibank situations it may be best to concentrate senior management's time on visits to the lead or agent bank, but no bank can be slighted.

Outside members of the board of directors can sometimes help in dealing with lenders. This help should be solicited.

Dealing with Suppliers and Other Creditors

A troubled company is usually late in paying its bills. The creditors will be concerned about getting paid at all and on what basis. The firm should not dodge its creditors. It can turn these encounters to its advantage. One way is to ask for significant price reductions and better terms. Chrysler, for example, aggressively pushed its suppliers to lower their prices and extend dating. Many did.

The company can ask for extended payment arrangements, particularly when it can give some assurance that these payments will be made. A slow pay will often be acceptable, once the condition of the firm is understood, if this is what is needed for the vendor to retain the business. The company can also ask the supplier for an improvement in quality and delivery.

Negotiations with suppliers should reinforce the importance of the company's business to them. It should review dollar purchase amounts, the length of the business relationship, and the like—it all helps. If the supplier is also a customer, this aspect may be intertwined.

If at all possible, a firm must try to avoid being put on a C.O.D. basis or, worse, partial payment in advance. It should try to guarantee credit and remove any existing C.O.D. arrangement. Extending payment for thirty, sixty, or ninety additional days can be equated to the value of money, using the prime rate, with significant resultant savings.

Dealing with Press and Broadcasters

You would be surprised how many sharks a potential corpse attracts. A company must expect, and be prepared for, media scrutiny. Remember, normally *good* news is *no* news where the media are concerned. They are going to be looking for bad things to happen and will exercise a large amount of journalistic license in attempts to gain rating points or subscribers.

Troubled companies breed rumors. One must expect the worst—it's probably what many people believe—and develop plans to counteract these damaging falsehoods. The firm has to decide what is its message. The message is better communicated if it is simple and clear. For example:

- We do not intend to close the plant.
- We have to reduce costs to meet foreign competition; lower labor costs and higher productivity are needed for company survival.
- We are regaining market share through lower costs and, therefore, lower prices.
- Our customers and lenders are cooperating.
- No union is helping the turnaround by making economic concessions.

A single spokesman has to be selected. All press and broadcasting inquiries should be directed to this person. The spokesman will need a day's media training by a public relations firm to do the job properly. He should reiterate the message, whatever it is, on all occasions. It is important to encourage press and broadcasting coverage in order to restore confidence in the company, its products, its management, its turnaround program, and its likelihood of survival.

Depending on the situation, it may be wise to avoid the term turnaround in communications to the media; a more positive image of a company fighting for survival and determined to succeed should be projected.

Issuing press releases for every positive step, particularly trivial ones, may make some people skeptical of the presented versus the real situation. In the manner of Shakespeare, "Me thinks thou dost protest too loudly."

The communications effort will influence and possibly motivate employees and external constituencies. People believe what they read in newspapers and see on television.

Dealing with Customers

Customers must receive the same message given to press and broadcasters. Their confidence has to be built if sales are to be retained, further sales erosion halted, and market share recaptured. People don't like to buy from vendors they think are going out of business. The goal must be to stop further erosion. The company may not be able, in the short run, to obtain a sales gain, but as a result of a good communications effort, it is unlikely to lose more market participation.

Public statements, and private reassurances given to customers other than the general public, that is, to distributors and industrial customers, are extremely important issues in a turnaround. Every industry has its rumor mill; there are few true secrets. Customers must be properly informed or they will draw their own, possibly unfavorable conclusions from rumors started and spread by competitors. Urgency should be given to counteracting the falsehoods disseminated by competitors.

If customers develop confidence in the turnaround program, they will tend to return. An example is Chrysler Corporation, which didn't hide the fact that it was in trouble. Chrysler almost seemed to exalt in going through a turnaround, and the customers responded favorably.

There is an aphorism "people love a loser," but they tend not to buy from him. The firm must change its image from loser to fighter. Chrysler is the best example of this. Customers are also reassured when the company's chief executive officer projects a strong, confident image. Successful examples are Sanford Sigoloff of Wickes and Lee Iacocca of Chrysler.

Dealing with Consultants

Troubled companies with a new turnaround management do not need consultants to do long, expensive studies to find out what is fundamentally wrong. Figuring out what is wrong and what should be done is the role of the new turnaround management. Companies don't have the money and, most important, the available time of key staff members that would be taken up by consultants. Major consulting firms have a propensity for devising expensive, unworkable solutions and should be avoided if possible.

Troubled companies can and should use consultants to advantage when they know there is a problem of a specific type in a specific function. Consulting firms are a necessity, in these times of governmental regulation. Dealing with the complexities of such governmental agencies as EPA, OSHA, IRS, FTC, SEC, NLRB, DOC, DOD, etc., alone justifies their existence. Specialists can do a short consulting effort to identify improvements or solutions and chart a path through the government's mine fields. Troubled companies tend to throw up their hands and give the problem over to all types of consultants, rather than using these firms as teachers and keeping close to the problem and proposed solutions. Consultants don't necessarily have good business sense, which is why the company must be able to choose among solutions, rather than meekly accept what a consultant thinks is best.

Lenders may insist that a consultant of their recommendation be allowed to study the situation. If a company has no choice but to allow it, to maintain a key lender's support, then, pragmatically, it has to allow it. But the company shouldn't expect to benefit from this effort, unless it takes control of the project. The turnaround leader should try to either get his money's worth from this consulting effort, or try to help the lender find a consultant with the right point of view.

Dealing with Outside Attorneys and Accountants

Attorneys and accountants, representing other parties, may make demands for information or verification. If a firm is, in general, forthright and informative in its communications, which this book suggests, then these demands may be lessened.

However, if the demands go beyond the general, they should be measured against certain tests. Is the information readily available? Does the requester have a real need or right to know? Would a significant additional effort be required to satisfy the request? Is this information too proprietary to disclose? In view of these tests, if it would take only a little effort to satisfy the request and doing so represents no risk, then consider doing so. If it would be imprudent to satisfy the request, then don't.

However, there must be control within the company of the source of information. The company must keep control of what is said to whom, and when, and advise employees of the risk of deviating from these procedures. People must also be aware of regulatory guidelines concerning dissemination of significant data. A "party line" must be established to unify the information that people give out. People must be cautioned to exercise close care and not give speculative information.

You should also consider requiring a confidentiality agreement if inside or proprietary information is to be provided.

Dealing with Shareholders and Investment Analysts

Shareholders and investment analysts often receive bland, obfuscating communications that destroy confidence in management. These create doubts about the wisdom of the investment in a company's shares. For example, read the chairman's letter in the typical annual report of a company experiencing a major drop in profits.

What shareholders and investment analysts need is the same type of direct, informative communications, which thereby inspire confidence, given to others. Gilding the lily doesn't work and shouldn't even be considered. In addition to the opportunity for communicating with shareholders presented by the annual report and quarterly statements, top management should consider interim statements or shareholder letters. These communications should state plans in brief, indicate potentials in new efforts, and admit past inadequacies. They should not make rash promises involving earnings or market expansion. Rather, they should communicate a feeling of the dynamic that the turnaround management is instilling in the company.

COMPANY NAME

Companies take on personalities, much as people do. Over the years an image develops among employees and customers, an image triggered by the company's name. A turnaround grapples with making fundamental changes in a business— its methods of operating, its products, its marketing. These changes, frequently cultural changes, are needed if the business is to survive. Once these changes are completed, or even started, it becomes important to influence people to react to the company in a new way.

Employees, possibly used to a slothful, authoritarian environment, must begin to feel that their actions count and become self-motivated. Quality and excellence in products and services must be made the norm. Customers long accustomed to, say, late delivery, poor technical service, and the like must look on the company in a new light—as a capable, responsive supplier. All this is impeded by existing psychological connotations attached to the company name.

Solution: Alter the name, or change it entirely. This announces to the world that it's a new game and a new company. People are willing to give the newly named firm a fresh start, or at least some benefit of the doubt, whereas they had come to utterly reject the company under its old name.

The change in name will have an important effect on the company's employees. It will rally them to the challenge and reinforce the cultural changes under way (discussed in another chapter). It will tell them we are going up from here.

Stockholders may take on some of the same feeling. They may have quite a bit of hostility to the old name.

The name change reinforces your position as the leader of the turnaround. It allows you to drive the company away from its historical baggage of negative perceptions and problems. Name is an image.

Your visits to major customers, or potential major customers, to solicit their advice on how to serve them better will now be taken seriously. Much valuable advice can be given at these meetings, as well as possibly obtaining some new business. Under the old name such a meeting, if possible, would not have been held in a cooperative spirit. By use of these visits, the company will be in a position to purchase customer loyalty by recognizing what is necessary to better meet customer needs. It can work with customers to better define needs and how to meet them. Meetings can be held with all the customers' functional heads, Purchasing, Engineering, Manufacturing, and so on.

Chrysler Corporation, during its turnaround, referred to itself in its advertising as the "New Chrysler Corporation," as if the company name had been legally changed, which it had not. This succeeded in conveying to customers that a fresh start had been taken. They could forget their complaints about Chrysler cars bought in days of old. The approach succeeded.

Something less than a name change, which can yield some of the same results, is to adopt a new upbeat slogan and heavily promote it.

When the name of the company has some positive value, its modification will probably be sufficient to psychologically convey the change. The "New Chrysler Corporation" is this sort of thing. Alteration of the name may be used to convey more than a fresh start. It could tell everyone of the shift in company purpose and strategy. To use a hypothetical example, let us look at a firm called Jones Machine Corporation, a maker of heavy machinery, which alters its name to Jones Technical Systems. Here, Jones could be telling the world that it has changed its strategy. It has undergone a metamorphosis from being merely a supplier of heavy machinery to being a state-of-the-art, customer-oriented systems supplier. As such, it will plan and sell entire systems—not just those elements of the system that it makes. It will handle the system integration and installation. It will be selling training services for its customers' maintenance people and will provide preventative maintenance programs. This is the strategic shift the company has had to make, and the name change announces it to the world, making it much easier to sell.

If a company wants to, or must, completely disassociate itself from its past, an entirely new name is an imaginative and effective way to do it at a manageable cost. A company must move carefully in this, however, to prevent confusing those whose continued loyalty is needed. A name change alone will usually not solve a company's problems. It can totally abolish a company's identity, which might be worse than having a disabled one.

4

PEOPLE ASPECTS

BUILDING TEAM SPIRIT

People are at the heart of a successful turnaround. This fact cannot be emphasized enough. People have to be treated like people, not like fixed assets. Things must be explained to them. They must be motivated and guided. Their willing co-operation must be achieved. They must develop a sense of urgency in carrying out their jobs and be inspired to act above and beyond the call of duty. Most important, they must develop a sense of confidence and pride—confidence in themselves and in the ability of the organization to restore profitability and guarantee the survival of the company.

The employees of a troubled company or division are usually disheartened and fearful of losing their jobs. They have to be inspired and their confidence in upper management has to be restored if they are to fully contribute to the turnaround effort. Openness, frankness, and truthfulness concerning the state of the business will help to bring credibility to management statements. People need to know just how bad things are. If they aren't told, they will believe things are even worse than they are.

For example, the employees of Danly Machine Corporation were assembled, early in the company's turnaround, to hear a state of the company address. They were told that the company intended to stay in business and survive, with their help. In talking with a number of individual employees afterward, it was learned that many people expected the speech to be an announcement that the company would close down, causing 1,300 persons to be unemployed. People believed the situation to be worse than it was.

A company's employees will act appropriately if they are made to understand what determines the success or failure of the business and its governing economics. They need a clear perception of their role in the turnaround.

A specific and continuing communications effort is invariably required to make people feel that they are part of the company team and develop in them a sense of urgency. All significant facts and events should be continually brought to the employees' attention.

The company should say nothing to employees that is not absolutely true. If something isn't known or hasn't been finalized, there is nothing wrong with saying we don't know or the matter hasn't been decided. People must learn to believe that what the company tells them is the truth—and it better be. What people are told won't only be the type of things they will want to hear. For example, at Danly Machine Corporation, with hundreds of employees on layoff, the company vastly increased overtime instead of recalling laid-off employees. When people asked why, they were told the truth: it was cheaper to pay overtime than to recall employees.

Destructive false rumors must be immediately squelched. There will always be rumors. But in times of stress the number and seriousness of the rumors will escalate. Many of these false rumors will be destructive to morale. Example 1: The plant will be closed. Example 2: Older employees will be fired to make way for younger, less expensive employees. Example 3: The major product line will be abandoned and all people associated with it will be fired. Destructive rumors generally involve job security. The way these rumors should be squelched is by debunking them head on. At production meetings, foremen should be told unequivocally that the rumors are false and to say so to their subordinates. At office staff meetings the problem should be handled similarly. The communications program, described in another chapter, should be used as a tool to stop destructive rumors. In time, as the turnaround begins to show signs of success, the level of rumors will decline.

Building a sense of common purpose and urgency among the employees must be accomplished among *all* types of employees: upper management, middle management, salaried professional, salaried nonexempt, and hourly. People must feel they are part of something—a team. While the communications program is a major element in team building, it cannot be the only element.

Visibility is another element. Upper management must be visible to all employees in order to communicate their concern. Frequent letters mailed to employees' homes and frequent walks through the manufacturing plants will help show this concern to production workers. You should initiate contact with employees on the plant floor and at all operational levels. The management must actively solicit employee input, and not merely passively accept it. If a worker stops the president, or any other member of management, with a question or request for help with a company problem, he should be satisfied that he received appropriate attention. A test of whether or not this strategy is working is when people do stop you with company problems they could not get satisfactorily resolved through normal channels. When they do this, it shows that they care enough to take it higher. When you listen, it shows that you feel what they have to say is important—you are both on the same team.

Three examples from Danly Machine Corporation are good illustrations of this. Example 1: While walking through the Cicero plant, a worker rushed up to me, saying that a circuit breaker box on the wall had what he thought was a short circuit, but no one would take care of it. I called Maintenance, and an electrician corrected the problem within ten minutes. Example 2: During the coldest part of winter, when the outside temperature was below zero degrees Fahrenheit, a worker stopped me in an aisle and led me to his machine. He showed me a broken window that he had been unable to have repaired that was allowing a cold blast to blow onto his machine. The worker was promised help. Before I could get back to my office to arrange it, the grapevine had gotten word to the Maintenance Department. Immediately a plastic cover was put over the broken window, to temporarily fix it until warmer weather would permit a proper repair. Example 3: A second-shift employee believed that his machine tool, which he had run for ten years, was improperly repaired and maladjusted. He telephoned me. Everyone said that this employee was just a troublemaker. I met him at his machine, with the head of the Machine Repair Department. The man whipped out a copy of the machine manufacturer's instructions, which he had obtained somewhere, and convincingly proved that the machine was improperly adjusted. The repairs were started at once. News that management cares about people and how they do their jobs travels fast. It builds good will and personal involvement. You must listen, be open, and take the required action.

Developing a sense of community and employee participation requires you to eliminate minor irritations and nondemocratic distinctions that would diminish the sought-after feeling of "we are all in this together." Hierarchical forms of visible distinctions, as an example, assigned parking space, with higher ranks being nearer the door, must be eliminated. Rules that safety goggles must be worn in manufacturing areas must be equally applied, from the president on down. The same applies for a rule that a company badge must be worn by employees on company premises.

Developing team feeling makes people more willing to give their all for the company's survival. A good team feeling-builder is to have the cafeteria staff deliver hot coffee and cold drinks, free of charge, to people working in manufacturing areas, say, twice a day; office people may have them as well. It is an inexpensive way to show that the company cares; it also allows better control of coffee breaks.

The conduct of all executives, and particularly that of senior officers, must be above reproach. No personal tasks for executives must be performed on company premises. There is a tendency in small manufacturing operations (and previously family-owned operations) for officers to use the manufacturing shop facilities as their personal workshop. Even if the actual costs involved are trivial, the negative effects on morale are substantial. It creates a "noble and peasants" atmosphere.

No use of company property or personnel that might be considered an abuse of position should be countenanced. It destroys the community feeling that so much effort is being expended to obtain. It also undermines the spirit of self-sacrifice needed at this time. Never think that people won't know—news of this sort travels fast.

Another undesirable but similar practice is for executives to use company employees after hours in their homes for repair or other projects. Even when these people are paid out of the executive's own pocket, it still raises suspicions of a type that cannot be permitted.

The Employee Relations/Industrial Relations/Human Resources Department will be receiving many questions from anxious employees during this time, and it must be capable of giving fast and accurate answers. In fact, special attention must be paid to promptly answering all questions. It is a matter of common courtesy, as well as representing the company's attitude toward its employees. Telephone calls should be returned (by the appropriate person). Letters should receive a written reply and, if answered by someone other than the addressee, should state that Mr. A forwarded the letter to Mr. B for reply.

The organizational ability to respond to questions must be examined at the outset to see if it is up to the task that lies ahead. If not, it must be immediately strengthened. Otherwise, the lack of response will subvert the accomplishment of the objective of developing a sense of community, a team spirit.

Employee communications must be a two-way street. People should be encouraged to ask questions. At Danly Machine Corporation, for example, employees are provided with postage-paid envelopes and cards so that they may ask questions or make suggestions. Some of these letters have raised matters that no one could have known needed to be ameliorated. For example, one woman felt that female cafeteria workers served female employees smaller portions than they served male employees. Now that employees are convinced they will be listened to, they come to see, or telephone, top management with important problems. This privilege has not been abused, showing that people use good sense in such matters.

As the staff becomes confident that the new management knows what it is doing and intends for the company to remain in business, its members will begin to contribute to the turnaround effort. Often they will be painfully aware of specific problems and some of the staff will be capable of contributing meaningful corrective suggestions. It is necessary to inspire people to offer these suggestions.

One example of an employee inspired to do his job better was the traffic manager at Danly Machine. He was responsible, among other things, for authorizing payment of freight bills. There were about 1,500 freight bills per month for Danly's eleven U.S. facilities. He had been using a book of freight rates, a time-consuming task. He found that by buying an Apple computer and peripherals for less than $3,000, and subscribing to a TRW freight rate service, which supplied the needed data on floppy disks for about $200 per month, he and his assistants could spend far less time on freight bill verifications. They also managed to find errors, averaging $22 each, in 2 to 3 percent of the freight bills.

A company should support efforts of people who wish to be able to do their jobs better. Buying low-cost personal computers and software, for use in department scheduling, that would allow work to be done faster and better is an example. A full-tuition reimbursement policy, on completion of courses that are either job related, or lead to a degree that is job related, is another example. These types of company support show people that the company cares about how well they do their jobs.

People have to be made to feel that they are all part of the same company. Barriers between departments and groups must be broken down. That is the only way a company can achieve lower costs and faster response to business and customer changes. Engineering, Manufacturing, Sales, and Finance must work in concert and have continuous dialogue. Toward this end, general staff meetings and individual department staff meetings must be held regularly to deal with important questions. Multidepartment task forces must be created to solve major problems, in a timely way. No one should be able to comfortably say, "That's not my problem."

STAFF ASSESSMENT, RECRUITMENT, AND REPLACEMENT

Having the right people is essential to achieve a successful turnaround. They must be right in ability, right in knowledge, right in experience, right in perspective, right in feeling a sense of urgency, and right in the number employed.

The strategic concept adopted for the revitalized company and its complementary business plan, including its manufacturing plan, engineering plan, purchasing plan, sales plan, cash-raising plan, and the like, will conceptually establish the types and number of employees needed. The troubled company, at the outset, will have a different mix of people. There will be a mismatch between the skills needed and the skills on hand.

An early task, then, but a continuing one, is to identify and justify the need for hiring people with these missing skills. The gaps will exist at all levels. Looking toward the top, the heads of Manufacturing, Finance, or, say, Purchasing may occupy these positions for historical reasons and not be sufficiently knowledgeable, experienced, or capable to handle these duties in the manner now required. If so, replacements will need to be recruited.

Looking at middle management, you may find a department led by a man who worked himself up from the shop floor. This executive may lack the breadth of knowledge and facility with analytical approaches and financial analysis needed to do the job in the manner required. If so, a new head for this department will need to be recruited.

Do not rush to replace people. First find out what they can do and what they cannot do. Perhaps, with your coaching and suggestions, they can learn to do their jobs the way you feel they must be done. Replacing someone takes a long time, is expensive, and may result in another unsatisfactory employee. This is why caution in replacing executives is called for.

The company needs some management continuity. Some long-term executives are needed to act as cultural intermediaries, helping to explain the changes being implemented and assisting long-term employees to adjust to those changes. Those executives who are found to be competent and are retained by the company will fulfill this need.

Looking at individual professionals, you may find that entire areas of vital expertise are missing. As an example, Danly Machine Corporation had no professional graduate welding engineer to make certain that welding was done in the most up-to-date, cost-effective manner. Yet it does a great deal of welding of heavy steel plate, employing as many as 150 welders. A well-educated, experienced welding engineer had to be added to the staff.

There is a great reluctance to add staff in a turnaround. At the same time, key skills are found to be missing. The solution to this dilemma is to ask yourself whether or not adding this person is important to reducing costs. If it is clear that cost reduction will be the end result, proceed. You are making a trade-off to add some cost in one area in order to eliminate much more cost in another.

Repeating, for emphasis, people will have to be recruited to bring missing skills to the company. A troubled organization is usually missing important skills of all types (engineering, purchasing, financial, labor relations, etc.) needed for the company to improve its effectiveness in carrying on its business and decrease its costs of doing business. These new employees will have to be highly qualified and experienced individuals—the company doesn't have the time and ability to upgrade existing employees or recent graduates. If the company is to attract these experienced employees, it will have to pay premium salaries, which will often be higher than those of current employees. Some companies make the mistake of trying to recruit these skilled employees while offering submarket salaries; that is, they try to maintain their current salary structure while recruiting. The usual result is an inability to attract needed people, with much lost motion.

The skills and abilities of executives must truly be appropriate. To make an analogy, it would be difficult, if not impossible, to pull off a bypass surgical procedure, no matter how good the hospital, the nurses, the anesthesiologist, the equipment, or the lighting, if the "expert surgeon" turned out to be a chiropodist.

Selection of executives, of all levels, and staff must be done with a critical eye. What is the individual's education (types of degrees, from what institutions); this may indicate receipt of the appropriate education. What is the person's work history—what companies employed him, where, in what capacity, with what responsibilities, with what reporting relationships, doing what, with what accomplishments? Thorough evaluation of a potential new hire is important. It will tell you if this person has the knowledge, skill, level of previous responsibility, and record of achievement commensurate with the company's current need.

This information should be verified by reference checks. For high-level executives, there should be follow-up luncheon or dinner interviews by selected executives who would be his peers. In this way the company will be able to judge whether or not the candidate is suitable, and if he could probably fit in with the rest of management. A number of qualified candidates should be identified for all positions, to permit some freedom of choice.

In recruiting people, it is important to look at more than their technical expertise. You have to consider whether or not they will be able to fit in to the company culture or locale. For example, if the company has a lean, self-starting environment, someone from a large, bureaucratic, heavily departmentalized organization, with much supporting staff, would probably be unable to cope. If the company is in a rural area and is considering someone who is (or whose family is) used to a big city, or vice versa, trouble is predictable. Relocation expenses are considerable, so the company should be certain that the new employee will stay before it hires him.

Many times a current employee will learn of an opening at a higher level and ask to be considered for it, even though he or she clearly doesn't have the right background or sufficient experience to be considered. In such instances it is usually best to hear the employee out and then explain, in detail, the needed qualifications and why that employee cannot be considered.

When you have found what seems to be the right candidate, you must do more than make him an offer. You must convince him of the worthwhileness of joining the company, a troubled company. No one wants to uproot one's family and move to a strange area in order to join a company that may go bankrupt or close down. The candidate must be convinced that, although things are bad, a sensible survival strategy has been implemented, of which he will be a part. It should be explained that the company has strong financial backing, either from its owners (if it is a subsidiary) or from its lenders, and its cash-raising efforts are being quite successful. New orders are up. By making these explanations, perhaps half the people who would have been expected to accept offers will do so. Without selling the company the offer acceptance rate would be far less. The same sort of reluctance to join the company holds true if a company is on strike.

For key executives of the high caliber a turnaround requires, you may want to offer severance agreements to mitigate their risk in case the turnaround does not succeed. This should be done only in unusual cases, as you need people to be fully committed to achieving success.

How does a company find executives and professionals with the necessary skills? This is often a difficult and expensive question. Word-of-mouth recommendations, advertisements (in the local newspapers, *Wall Street Journal*, *Sunday New York Times*, and professional magazines), employment agencies/contingency search firms, and retainer executive search firms are the usual means. Someone has to orchestrate and control these activities. It is easy to wind up with each department doing its own recruiting when there is no efficient, timely, centralized professional and managerial recruiting activity within the Employee Relations/Human Resources function. This is a bad situation because effort is duplicated. Simple activities, such as preliminary screening, can take up the time of people who have other commitments for their time. Recruiting costs can skyrocket. However, if the Employee Relations Department is not sufficiently staffed to do this well, managers must realize that they have no other choice but to do their recruiting personally—the task must get done. In the process, care must be taken not to make bad first impressions that turn off difficult-to-recruit employees.

A balanced approach to recruitment is needed, with the most difficult-to-obtain skills acquired by means of executive search and agencies and less difficult-to-obtain skills by means of advertisements. Relying solely on fee-paying approaches is an expensive route to follow, although it reduces the pressure on the firm's ability to recruit.

If a significant number of high-level executives need to be recruited, then it may be desirable to select a single, unusually competent executive search consultant. This recruiter will come to understand the needs and special perspectives of the turnaround effort and its leader and will measure people against these requirements. This will reduce the burden on the turnaround leader, as the search firm's prime focus will be finding the right people, whereas the turnaround leader must treat recruitment as a secondary responsibility.

New employees joining a troubled firm will have to receive good salaries and good relocation assistance. The higher the position, the better the relocation package, which, in general, must be reasonably broad, including reimbursement of real estate commission, mortgage points, temporary living and moving expenses, and the like. A troubled firm, lacking people with the appropriate skills and needing to acquire good people rapidly, cannot have a hard-fisted relocation policy; that would be self-defeating.

Some of the management and staff of the troubled firm will be incompetent. This cannot be permitted to continue. Once the deficiencies are apparent, replacements should be put into their positions either by internal transfer or by outside recruiting. A troubled firm is frequently thin on talent, which means that most of the replacements will have to come from the outside. This can be disturbing to a company whose culture has been one of promotion from within. There is no alternative. The existing culture cannot be allowed to constitute a barrier to the firm's survival.

In many cases a longtime employee who is incompetent in his present position could be both useful and necessary in another position, possibly one that needs to be created to meet an important unmet need. An effort should be made to identify such situations, as it helps the company to run better (you could not recruit this company-specific experience from the outside) and preserves or improves employee morale. An example of this was one firm that moved its unsatisfactory Purchasing head into a new position planning and managing long-range production planning, which he did admirably.

No "sacred cows" can be tolerated. If an employee is no longer useful, he must be terminated (or early retired). Carrying dead wood destroys the sense of urgency and fighting for the company's survival that you are trying to communicate. The company cannot afford unproductive employees, either financially or psychologically. It must also guard against transferring these employees to other departments that don't really need them.

You may be able to meet some of the gaps in the organization through reorganizations. This is less expensive than recruitment and may lead to much needed reductions in overhead.

Significant reductions in the salaried staff, once decided on, should be quickly carried out and be done at one time, if practical. A slow, drawn-out process of continual firings debilitates an organization. Fridays can become a day of staff paralysis as people await the news of who will not be back on Monday.

Termination benefits should be carefully thought out and consistently applied. This will avoid unnecessary troubles.

COMPENSATION

Hourly Wage Earners

Hourly labor is a purchasable service and should be examined on a local-market basis. The firm has to determine what the market is paying for the types of labor it is buying in the same market. This requires an analysis of the skill levels the firm really uses and the relation of this to area wage survey data, which is generally available on a sufficiently up-to-date basis. One can supplement this data by, say, talking to a couple of dozen other firms in the area who have labor requirements similar to the company's.

In 1977 a wages and benefits expert was recruited by Allegheny International, Inc. (then Allegheny Ludlum Industries, Inc.). He discovered that the *average* pay to secretaries in their Pittsburgh general office, of which there were a great many, was *over* $20,000 per year. This was much, much higher than the Pittsburgh area average. He discovered that many years before, a survey had been conducted on pay to secretaries by steel companies. This was used to set pay levels. With each succeeding steel industry union contract, the secretaries' pay scale, which was not covered by the contract, was upwardly adjusted by the terms of the steel industry contract. No one had ever stopped to consider whether or not this was reasonable. Needless to say, turnover among Allegheny's secretaries was almost nonexistent. Allegheny International's solution was a wage freeze for overpaid employees. This true story illustrates what can happen when a firm ceases to look at labor as a purchased commodity.

If a study shows that the company's wages are significantly higher than they need be, the firm can act accordingly. If the manufacturing operation is nonunion, the choices include:

- freezing the wages of those who are overpaid until, over time, wage levels rise to this point (popularly known as "red circling");
- creating a dual wage scale whereby new employees are paid at a lower rate, reflecting real market conditions;
- lowering wages to market levels.

As a practical matter, the ease of implementation is in the same order. If the workers are unionized, wages and benefits are subjects requiring negotiation. This can necessitate a company taking a strike, which is discussed in a later chapter.

Benefit containment is usually psychologically more palatable than wage reductions, although the end result is the same. Elimination of some paid holidays and a cap on the amount of paid vacation are the easiest changes to institute, with an explanation that this is part of the company's job-saving survival strategy.

Reduction in medical benefits, or putting some of the cost onto the employees, is an important item, owing to today's high cost of medical care. Its significance should not be underrated.

Salaried Exempt Employees

In looking at the salary structure of a troubled company, you may find that salaries are either too high or too low, or completely inconsistent. There also may be variations among departments within the company, with some departments being either too high or too low. You need to learn what exists before actions can be planned or taken.

What is learned has to be compared with area salary data and national salary surveys for various professions (e.g., engineers, electronic data-processing personnel), taking into account education, experience, and management level. Employees tend to read the same surveys, so the company cannot assume that its employees don't know what salaries are being paid elsewhere.

There is no reason to pay people alike. Equal pay for equal work is an economically dangerous concept to a troubled company because it implies paying everyone at the highest possible rate. Pay differences should exist based on differences in competence and market forces.

Different compensation policies can and should be applied to the tasks of retaining employees and attracting new employees. Retaining long-term employees usually requires a salary level no higher than a little below market rates. Changing employers involves risk and inconvenience, as well as the loss of important pension benefits, which is probably the basis of this situation. If salaries fall significantly below this level, a real danger of losing key skills will arise.

Many fringe benefits are dependent on salary level (e.g., vacation pay, pension payout), so the beneficial effect of effective salary controls will be magnified.

Don't let pay levels get in the way of hiring the right people needed for the turnaround. Having the right people is essential to the success of the turnaround.

Overpaid employees whose salaries become frozen may develop a desire to leave. However, they will find it difficult to obtain new positions with salaries sufficiently larger to warrant leaving. A troubled company must not be allowed to avoid coming to grips with excessive compensation for fear of losing employees.

Flexibility must be maintained on compensation questions. If a much-needed employee can be retained only with more money, then pay it if the amount is worth retaining this person's contribution.

After appropriate head count reductions have been made, the company may also have to consider temporary salary reductions for its existing staff, as a means of reducing its operating costs. This action may be psychologically acceptable to employees as a temporary move needed to help the company survive and, therefore, as a means to preserve their jobs. Many troubled firms institute 5 percent or 10 percent salary reductions, which, depending on operating results, may be in effect for one or two years. Usually a salary freeze (except for promotions) accompanies these cuts. It is important that salary cuts and freezes apply equally. High bonus payments to upper management while the rest of the salaried work force is under a salary freeze will be destructive to morale; it will destroy the sense of team spirit and eliminate the willingness of many employees to achieve cost reductions.

New hires are another story. Paying market-based salaries for new professional and managerial employees, instead of the existing salary structure, is the way it has to be if they are to be successfully recruited. There is no reason to hide this fact or make general salary increases because of it. This can't be afforded in a turnaround. Once these people have been hired, they must come under any wage freeze then in existence. You cannot give the new employees raises, after some period of time, and not the old without causing a civil war.

One troubling aspect is that sometimes new subordinates will be making close to or the same as their superiors. This can be talked through with the superior and explained as a manifestation of the strange actions needed for a turnaround. It should be looked on as a temporary matter until more normal times return.

The combination of reducing salaries that may have been submarket in the first place and hiring new employees at market salary levels does create tensions and ill feelings. Management must respond to this by promising to reexamine the situation and act in a responsible manner once the company's financial position improves (with no firm timetable for action).

CHANGING THE COMPANY CULTURE

A corporate culture consists of shared values among the employees, procedures for running the business, and preprogrammed responses to business events and crises. It represents the way top management believes the business should function, and all levels of management, descending from the top, should and must share this culture. New employees become quickly acclimated to it. People who have lived for many years in a given corporate culture, some for their entire working lives, usually see no need for major changes.

It is almost impossible for a cultural change to be made without an agent for change who is not beholden to company tradition—a new top manager. This is one of the reasons a company turnaround usually requires a change in top management. The new man carries no historical and psychological baggage for why these changes, no matter what they might be, were not instituted before. The new top manager is also presumed to know what he is doing, even if what he want to do seems strange. Employees believe that is why he was selected for his position—he knows what needs to be done. If the old management tried to make the very same changes, there would be suspicion as to their desirability and workability, as all would know that the instigator of the changes had no experience with such things.

The new company culture must include creating and instilling a sense of urgency. It must automatically allow people to properly set priorities.

You may ask how one actually accomplishes a change in the company culture. The answer lies in realizing that a corporation is not a democracy. Just as a good parent knows what is right and wrong and is both firm and vocal about such things with his or her children, so, too, should the new management be firm and vocal with the company's staff. Good table manners in children don't come from heaven. They come from monitoring actions and scolding departures from what is expected, almost incessantly. Good customer service in a company is arrived by the same process. After a while it becomes natural, meaning that a cultural change has been achieved. Perhaps a coach and his team is a better analogy than a parent and child. A coach of a sports team must continually impress on his players his game plan, which is how the game will be played.

Customer service is but one example, however, not a trivial one. The point is that you must first decide what is the preferred way to run the company and then insist that it be run that way, making an example of departures from what is preferred. The form of example usually need not be more than a series of questions tinged with incredulity and criticism. People will react to the negative feedback arising from pursuing obsolete cultural norms. The reason they will promptly react is that the new norms come from the top, and everyone will instinctively perceive that it is dangerous to employment security to not adopt the new conventional wisdom.

Positive reinforcement should also be used. Public praise for an action consistent with the new cultural values that significantly benefits the company will be a signal to others. An example of new emphasis on cost would be someone finding an outside vendor to make parts at a price substantially below their internal manufacturing cost and that person being publicly praised for doing this. This will encourage others to do likewise. Cultural values are held by people, so the cultural change process must be people oriented. The people you hope to influence must be personally involved in the process if it is to succeed in a timely manner. In a turnaround, cultural changes must be achieved fast.

Four of the ways cultural change will be accomplished are these: First, recruitment of new executives. As incapable managers are replaced, one criterion used in the selection of their successors is having the right corporate cultural values. The new executives will be expected to pass these new values on to their subordinates.

The employee communications campaign will be another means. It will influence individual behavior by identifying the correct cultural values. For example, quality. If slovenly attitudes were previously allowed and poor quality was the norm, then extolling the need for perfection will convey the concept of this cultural change. Disciplining workers for not complying with the new quality values will not, therefore, be a surprise and will probably not be met with much resistance.

Training of supervision, particularly manufacturing first-line supervision, will be another key step in getting the general's message to the troops. Much higher productivity, through elimination of late start, early quit, and maintaining a consistent work effort, can be achieved in this manner. Almost no one objects to the concept of a fair day's pay for a fair day's work, and this can be understood as a means to insist on obtaining the latter.

Last, staff meetings should be held, not only of the heads of all company departments, but hierarchical staff meetings as well, in which each department also has its own staff meeting. For large enough organizations, weekly meetings should be held at even a further level down. The interactions at these meetings are important for the company to do its business, but they also convey the new cultural norms. Two examples of changes in cultural values that can be propagated in this fashion are (1) the need for prompter collection of receivables and (2) the need and willingness of the company to accept technological change in its product designs and in the methods used to design its products.

There is usually a need to convey the change in corporate culture to outsiders, customers, say. These people have negative feelings toward the old values and can be expected to react favorably once they believe that the new values genuinely exist. An example of such a changed value is the timeliness and responsiveness of Danly Machine Corporation to customer repair/replacement parts needs. These items, frequently needed right away, often took months to be delivered (and sometimes were never delivered if the paperwork got lost). As part of the new culture, everyone was made to understand that repair/replacement parts had priority one. If Danly Machine's own plants could not manufacture the needed part fast enough, an outside specialized machine shop would be found that could do the job faster. Special tracking procedures were adopted to make certain that the repair part was on schedule and would be completed as promised. The customers, through actual experience, became convinced that Danly Machine would give them good service and gave much more of this type of business to them. Previously, with Danly considered an untimely supplier, the customers had other firms duplicate the needed parts, often with undesirable consequences.

EMPLOYEE SUGGESTIONS AND CANDID INFORMATION FLOW

Companies in a turnaround need employee suggestions. They don't need the type put on a one-page form and dropped in a suggestion box, to disappear for months at a time. What is needed is employee involvement in the need to make changes in the products, in the manufacturing procedures, and in the company's operating procedures—changes needed now to reduce cost and increase the ability of the company to survive.

People have to be motivated to propose changes because they think that these changes are right, not because they expect to receive an additional check. They must feel that proposing improvements is both their right and their duty. It comes with their being part of the company team. A series of actual examples from Danly Machine Corporation will illustrate this point. In none of these cases was additional compensation paid.

Example 1: A reorganization. An Industrial Engineering Department prepares shop routings and time standards needed to manufacture parts in the Cicero plant. Their work then went to the Keypunch Department for further processing. The manager of the Industrial Engineering Department realized that the two activities could be combined, thereby eliminating three positions at first and another two positions within six months.

Example 2: Adoption of software. The manager of long-range production planning laid out long, complicated production schedules for the building of complex machine tools. It was very time-consuming. He investigated software packages that would fit the capabilities of his Apple microcomputer and found one that substantially reduced the time required. It also produced a much easier to read graph.

Example 3: Product redesign. A welding engineer was developing improved procedures for welding a complex box section with internal stiffeners. By a leap in insight he saw that the complex design was needless. It could be replaced by putting together two commercially available rectangular box members and joining them with minimal welding. He didn't improve the welding procedure, as assigned; he replaced the design with one needing little welding, thereby cutting the cost in half.

Example 4: Hourly worker initiative. An assembler, an hourly worker, was given the task of assembling a hydraulic manifold. He realized that this particular unit was overdesigned. He sketched a simpler alternative and personally went to see the chief engineer, who gave it his blessing. This act saved the company $1,200 alone in the value of the eliminated parts.

These four cases show employees at all levels—manager, professional, hourly worker—taking the initiative to make the company run more effectively and achieve lower costs.

Most people are reticent to come forward with their ideas; it's human nature. So the company must find ways to take its program to them. One such way is to have a team, consisting of a product design engineer and a manufacturing engineer, visit with small groups of employees right in their work area. If the group is kept to about a dozen persons, it is large enough to encourage discussion without being so large that people won't have sufficient opportunity to talk. Everything should be fair game for the discussion. In a sense, it resembles a military debriefing after a mission. Long-accepted practices are often found to be wanting. For example, for many years at Danly Machine, covers were screwed onto machines, after predrilling both. The inevitable mismatch of some holes caused additional effort and cost. One worker wanted to know why Danly didn't use self-tapping screws to simplify matters. Two days later this was made the company's standard approach.

One particular reservoir of underutilized know-how is often a company's servicemen. Sometimes what they know to be fact and what a company's engineering staff believe to be fact are quite different. By arranging special meetings between groups of servicemen and the product engineering staff, all sorts of things are revealed. For example, special features that the product engineers are quite proud of, and design into every machine, are learned to be troublesome, unreliable, and frequently disconnected in service. The servicemen are also able to make comparisons with competitors' products, which they see operating as well as being repaired. These comparisons can lead to changes that decrease manufacturing cost or increase product reliability. One may ask why hadn't this gold mine of information been mined before? The answer is simple. There was previously no organized mechanism to accomplish it, and when an individual serviceman made a complaint, there was reluctance to accept what he said.

Another good way to obtain valuable employee suggestions is the use of consultants. The firm may have industrial engineering consultants already talking to people, trying to discern ways to improve their effectiveness. At the same time they could be on the lookout for all manner of good employee suggestions. A more straightforward way is to retain consultants to specifically go through the organization once, to uncover product, manufacturing, and organizational improvements. In practice, this approach will also uncover a good many things that are being done wrong that no one as yet realizes are being done wrong.

5

FINANCE

BUSINESS PLAN

A turnaround is a process to ensure the survival of a troubled company. To properly manage this process you have to quantify how bad things are and know what to expect in terms of losses (or profits) and cash flow on a month-by-month basis for the foreseeable future. Planning and information are needed in conducting the turnaround. You have to know if the company is likely to become insolvent, and if so, when; how much additional cash the turnaround will require; when the company is likely to return to profitability.

A business plan is a necessary tool in managing the turnaround. The achievement of results that follow the business plan will foster bankers' and other lenders' confidence in the turnaround management. This confidence is necessary to obtain their support at various critical moments. Dealing with bankers and other lenders is discussed in greater detail in the chapter on communications.

The first element in a meaningful business plan is preparation of a reasonable sales forecast. The sales forecast must realistically look at the near-term market, what influences its size, and the company's market participation and its controlling factors. The sales forecast must not be a wish list. It must be what the Sales and Marketing Departments realistically believe will occur. It should address both volume and price. Unfortunately, developing a good sales forecast requires a degree of knowledge and competence that may be sadly lacking in a troubled company's marketing function. This aspect is discussed more fully in the chapter on marketing.

The next step in preparing a business plan is carefully estimating the cost of goods sold. This must be arrived at by a multistep process, which includes input from Purchasing, Engineering, Manufacturing, and Accounting. It must not be only a Sales Department estimate.

Purchasing, for example, will impact the estimated cost of goods sold by striving to obtain better prices for raw materials, components, and the like. An estimate of purchase costs, including, where possible, reductions in purchase prices from recent prices, will need to be developed. If items will be subcontracted through a make/buy decision process, these savings will need to be estimated as well.

Estimating manufacturing cost will necessitate a manufacturing plan; what is to be made and where (for multiplant operations), and what is to be subcontracted.

The cost-reduction program being implemented has, no doubt, a timetable for achieving various levels of cost reduction. Improvements in manufacturing hourly labor productivity will probably be one element of this program. Reduction in product costs, owing to product engineering design improvements, can be another major element. Putting these elements together with estimated savings obtained by better purchasing allows a meaningful plan to be created for cost of goods sold versus time.

The combination of estimated sales by month and cost of goods sold by month will yield an estimate of gross margin by month. You will also have to analyze the needs for inventory and accounts receivables by month—important elements of cash flow. Selling costs, required to achieve the sales forecast, have to be estimated. Perhaps these costs can be reduced from historical levels, but not necessarily. General and administrative costs also must be estimated, taking into account whatever reductions are being implemented.

Then a variety of extraordinary costs, arising from the fact that a turnaround is in process, will need to be estimated and included in the financial projection. A partial list of some of these costs would include the following:

- Communications and public relations expenses (particularly fees for consultants needed for help with employee communications)
- Employee severance and termination expenses
- Recruitment and relocation expenses of new executives and skilled professionals
- Close-down costs of facilities that are closed or partially closed (which may require funding of not fully funded pension plans of employees in closed-down operations)
- Write-downs of overage and obsolete inventories
- Legal fees (including those of labor attorneys who may need to spend much time on union negotiations)
- Employee training expenses (e.g., first-line shop supervision)
- Capital investments (which should be of a compelling nature)

Putting all things together will create a monthly profit plan and cash flow plan. This is what performance will be measured against. The monthly statements will tell how well events follow projection. When a serious miss occurs, it will compel corrective action.

The product cost and sales/administrative cost reduction plans are important in their own right and should be tracked monthly as well. It is from these specific activities that much of the company's improvement in financial health will derive.

The estimated cash flows and the debt repayment schedules of the company will, together, tell how much additional cash will be needed. This must be viewed against available cash-raising opportunities, such as available lines of credit, sales of unneeded assets, sales of product lines, reductions in inventories, and the like. These are examined later in this chapter. Can bankruptcy be avoided? The study of projected cash sources and uses will do much to answer this question.

A prospective outlook, with measurement of results against plan, is important in the relationship with the company's financial sources.

Whether you are dealing with a parent corporation as a financial source (in the case of a subsidiary) or with financial institutions, there is a need for understanding and agreement on how the turnaround will be financed and how proceeds from asset sales will be used.

A troubled company cannot be managed by the "back of an envelope method." Knowledge must be the basis of action, and a turnaround requires many actions. Formal business planning, therefore, is a necessity.

CASH FLOW

Cash is the lifeblood of a company. In a troubled company, becoming illiquid is a real threat; preventive steps must be taken. The situation of a freestanding firm is much more precarious than that of a troubled division or subsidiary of an otherwise healthy company. The troubled subsidiary/division can usually rely on the resources of the parent company, thereby making its cash situation much less critical. The freestanding company does not have this recourse.

Both freestanding and subsidiary companies need to look at methods for reducing their operating cash needs, including ways to borrow money more cheaply. They must look for ways of providing additional cash by freeing up cash tied up in nonproductive uses and by obtaining it through other means. The freestanding company must look at defensive moves to increase and protect its cash reserves while it is still possible to do so. These might include the following:

- Selling new equity or long-term debt; this can be hampered by legal requirements for full disclosure.

- Acting now to draw down unused bank lines, negotiate new credit, and extend loan guarantees

- Obtaining relaxation of existing restrictive loan covenants

- Opening deposit accounts in nonlending banks to reduce the likelihood of banks seizing balances as offsets to troubled existing loans

The company must look at operational approaches to raise cash and improve its usage. This applies to non-freestanding firms as well. Cost reduction steps described elsewhere in this book will help the company to reduce its cash needs. Some of the more straightforward ways to raise or free up cash include the following:

- Sale of land and buildings not currently needed. Many companies have assets they used in a previous time that they hang on to in the hope that the business will someday come back, or that they acquired for use in a possible business expansion. The urgency of the current situation demands that realism be used in viewing these assets. Owning land and buildings costs money (e.g., taxes, maintenance, heat, guard service). Selling them will both reduce expenses and free up cash.

- Sale of product lines that are unrelated to the core business. This will provide cash while freeing management from time spent on what are distractions from the major management problems. The Burgess–Norton Manufacturing Company, as an example, had a primary business of manufacturing O.E.M. (Original Equipment Manufacturer) metal parts for sale to engine and farm machinery builders. It also had a minor tungsten carbide product line of whitewall tire grinding wheels and woodworking tools, involving eight direct production employees. These products were totally unrelated to the core business. The tungsten carbide product line (i.e., designs, trademarks, limited inventory, and customer lists) was sold for $400,000, most of which was profit.

- Sale of entire operations unrelated to the core business. Minor unrelated operations have a way of taking up much management time while having minor useful impact. Their sale is usually even more useful than the sale of minor unrelated product lines. Westinghouse Electric Corporation, by way of example, owned a commercial air conditioning operation, headquartered in Staunton, Virginia, that had ceased to be part of a core business. This operation had little market share and continuously lost money. An internal assessment concluded that it might, at best, be sold for perhaps $12 million. To everyone's surprise, McQuay–Perfex bought the operation for $23 million.

- Sale of leaseholds no longer needed. When Allegheny International, Inc., acquired Chemetron Corporation, it gained Chemetron's long-term lease to prestigious office space in Chicago. The value of prime office real estate in Chicago had appreciated over the years, allowing Allegheny to sell the leasehold for about $750,000.

- Reduction in inventory. Improvements in the management of purchasing and a change in its perspectives toward obtaining faster vendor deliveries should allow the company to run with less inventory, that is, to increase its inventory turns (for the active inventory). Disposal of slow-moving or obsolete inventory will provide some cash, reduce inventory carrying costs, and provide tax benefits from the write-downs.

- Sale and leaseback. Building and machinery can all be readily turned into cash in a sale-and-leaseback arrangement. This action provides significant cash now, when it is needed, thereby possibly overcoming an immediate crisis. The trade-off is increased operating costs in the future, at which time the firm, presumably, will be better able to handle these costs. The purchaser gains a number of tax advantages, which reduce the overall cost of this approach to the seller. The arrangement also allows the seller the continued use of the assets it needs to remain in business. The sale of major assets may require the consent of the company's lenders, as it may potentially violate existing loan covenants. Prevailing interest rates must be considered at the time of leaseback.

- Discontinuance of the pension plan. Depending on the state of the securities markets, firms can discover that their pension plans are overfunded. When this occurs, the plans may be discontinued, with annuities bought to replace the previous coverage. New plans can then be started for future years, perhaps on a defined contribution basis. The effect of this is to allow the reclaiming of the overfunding. Sometimes significant sums can be regained this way.

- Delayed cash payments, including slowed down payment of bills. In effect, the company is borrowing money for short periods, interest free. The payment of bills may be slowed down from, say, forty-two days to sixty days, and sometimes more. This is frequently done without a supplier's consent, but if possible, an understanding and consent should be sought. Care must be taken in doing this, but it is a classic and well-proven technique.

- Improvement in the collection of accounts receivables. Troubled firms often let this get out of hand. It is often a result of the Sales Department having responsibility only for obtaining the sales order and not being involved in making certain that the company is actually paid, and on time. To improve collections, accounts receivable must be carefully tracked. Table 5–1 shows a typical simple form used by one firm to focus attention, on a weekly basis, on slow-paying customers. Credit must be selectively withdrawn; for many firms this is psychologically difficult to do. A customer who doesn't pay his bills is no customer. A special effort to improve collections and reduce the number of days outstanding would include telephoning the customer a week before payment is due to ask if everything is satisfactory and whether the payment will be made on time; a call when payment is due to verify that a check is on the way; and frequent calls after the due date to urge payment. Pests have a greater chance of being paid by slow payers.

- Lock boxes to receive collections speed up the process and are well worth the cost.

- Paying from banks in distant locations that will generate greater floats, say, the Chase Manhattan Bank in Syracuse, New York, or the Bank of America in San Francisco, California, also has benefits and is becoming widely used.

- Obtaining extended payment terms from vendors. Sellers don't like to lose customers and market share. If the Purchasing Department approaches all significant vendors, explaining the situation and asking for extended terms, a good many vendors will grant them. Chrysler Corporation, in its turnaround, used this technique to great advantage.

- Borrowing from or issuing special stock to employees and others who have an interest in the company's success. One condition of this type of action will be a limitation on the right to receive interest or dividends, which provides for such payments only after the firm reaches certain levels of financial performance. Many firms, Eastern Airlines, for example, have tied this into employee wage reductions, thereby immediately reducing the company's operating cash needs.

- Cash can be obtained by developing foreign opportunities. Standard–Thompson Corporation is the leading independent manufacturer of automobile engine thermostats. When it was nearly bankrupt, it made good use of its technology to raise cash by obtaining foreign license fees and helping to set up offshore joint ventures to manufacture and sell engine thermostats in all important foreign markets (including Japan, Germany, Italy, England, and France), for which it received equity participations in the range of 25 to 45 percent for its know-how.

- Sale of research and development (R & D) tax shelters. The cash needs of new product development can be off loaded from the current operations of the business onto the shoulders of R & D limited partnerships. This is a new, but growing, approach. In 1984 the total investment in R & D limited partnerships passed $1 billion.

This list, which does not exhaust all possibilities, shows that there are many ways to contribute to the cash needs of the company. They are usually not in conflict with one another and simply represent the types of management perspectives that must permeate a turnaround.

Also, senior management must set an austerity image: no first-class airline tickets, no limos, no private company airplanes, no corporate retreats, no boondoggles, no Ritz Carlton hotel suites, a questioning of club memberships, and the like.

If the entire thrust is to decrease cash needs and make more cash available, often by one-time actions, great caution must be shown in pursuing any course that will increase the need for cash. If strategy dictates actions that look as if they would absorb cash, then alternatives that do not require as much cash, but allow the objectives to still be met, albeit less efficiently, must be examined.

The troubled company is frequently faced with a debt repayment schedule and additional cash needs for operations that it simply doesn't have the cash to meet. Technically, the firm is insolvent, although it may be viable in the long run as a business. The financial problem is to find a way to stay in business. The fifteen cash-raising actions listed above are ways to overcome an immediate cash crunch.

The proper management of cash flow is essential if the management of the turnaround will have time to succeed.

Once the financial health of a business begins to improve there is a tendency to give this area reduced emphasis; this has to be guarded against. It could be like eliminating antibiotics before a patient is truly well, thereby incurring a consequent relapse. Many of the cash-raising approaches can be used only one time, so there had better not be a need for a second time.

An almost obvious implication of this discussion is the need for an astute and experienced financial executive as a member of the top management team. Many troubled companies do not have this caliber of financial executive. If this is so, one should be recruited—and fast.

COST ACCOUNTING

The accounting system has to be a key tool in providing vital data needed in cutting costs, pruning product lines, making pricing decisions, and the like. A company in trouble usually doesn't know its costs. In most cases it has an accounting system that obscures rather than reveals true costs.

Table 5-1.
Jones Machine Corporation Accounts Receivable—October 1

NAME	TOTAL	CURRENT	1-30	31-60	61-90	90+	COMMENTS
Acme Steel	86,836	6,480	9,594	8,248	5,835	56,679	New Financing due 30-60 days.
Universal Ind.	139,083	17	(32,947)	(3,740)	(6,412)	182,165	No news on the payment plan.
United Screw	394,250	-	-	-	8,814	385,436	Tranfer of funds to be made any day now
Ropley Corp.	69,464	4,208	3,837	15,711	17,182	28,526	Mailing ck on 9/28-trying for $27,000
Thomas Ind.	28,096	-	1,721	6,188	5,815	14,372	Supposed to send $4,000 by end of month
Jackson Pump	52,555	17,604	11,088	7,235	11,008	5,620	Still working on 61-90 and 90+ figure.
Consolidated Dist	21,858	-	37	3,355	1,004	17,462	Still working on securing a payment.
B.J.Q. Corp.	20,400	-	-	389	98	19,913	Schedule: $7,500 out 9/22 $6,805 on 10/5; $5,400 or $5,900 on 10/12.
Sklar Corp.	1,280	-	21	1,259	-	-	All current
W-M Ind.	17,181	990	1,786	1,367	1,531	11,507	C.O.D. against bal.
Jensen Tool	54,594	1,619	1,837	775	18,202	32,161	Was trying for $27,000 by end of month.
Smith Co.	21,108	1,922	-	7,139	2,811	9,236	Progress being made to reduce 90+.
Metalsmith	42,623	-	-	-	-	42,623	Progress being made to reduce 90+.
Sonar Corp	1,244,520	14,620	33	208,780	36,668	984,419	Per meeting worked to clear up $752,363 by end of month.
LeMay-Jones	53,399	-	-	-	-	53,399	Chapter 11 filed-possible suit pending.
Pemex	35,251	-	-	(1,489)	-	36,740	Gov't. freeze-program initiated to reduce bal.
Hi-Tex	374,452	-	-	-	-	374,452	Potential write-off. Reserve set-up.
	2,656,950	47,460	(2,993)	255,217	102,556	2,254,710	

Some of the important questions to ask when viewing the adequacy and accuracy of the accounting system are as follows:

- Are outside purchase items, such as raw materials, represented in product cost by actual prices paid, or by some type of "standard" cost, or by prices paid at some earlier time, or by an old price multiplied by some broad inflation factor?

The wrong answer to this question can have several negative impacts. Understating costs means that the company can be losing money on a product and not even know it. The company can be trying to build increased sales for a particular product, when doing so will create an increased loss! The company can be dragging its feet on increasing price, when this action is desperately required. Overstating cost may make your pricing uncompetitive, causing a sharp reduction in sales and market share. One company, as an example, almost put itself out of business by using $600 per ton for steel plate in its cost estimates, when steel plate was being discounted by steel makers to about $400 per ton.

- Are the quantities of materials represented in a product cost, such as steel or other purchased items, based on actual experience, or merely surmised?

The quantity of material required may be in error, owing to a variety of factors. It may have been misjudged in the first place. If you weigh the actual parts and then figure in the probable scrap, you will know if the material use standard is correct. A simple paper exercise that can be used as a check is to take the weight of the finished parts and compare that with the material use estimate; the amount of material in the product cannot exceed what you start with. Once, in looking at the cost of making axe heads by the True Temper Corporation, it was found that the die wear permitted in their forging dies led to steel usages that were 50 percent above estimate.

- Are specific services, important in assessing the costs of specific products, actually recorded and directly applied, or is a broad allocation system used that applies these costs to the product indirectly by, say, a percentage of sales?

Broad allocations are a guaranteed approach to masking true product line profitability. A requirement for a high degree of inspection, for example, can mean that an item costs far more to manufacture than is assumed. Engineering support, quality control, technical and field service, and selling costs are all major cost elements that are frequently understated when using broad allocation schemes. One must unbundle these costs among the various products to the maximum extent feasible; it is well worth the effort.

- Are outputs per hour of each manufacturing step recorded and compared with an estimated value? It makes a big difference in unit labor costs if a machine is actually producing, say, 80 parts per hour rather than a hypothetical 240 parts per hour, or a furnace is heating 300 pounds per hour rather than a hypothetical 600 pounds per hour.

Standard cost systems can usually identify variances from established standards in output per man-hour, but they cannot identify differences between actual output and theoretical equipment capacity, for example, furnaces whose standard is set at only 50 percent of their actual processing capability.

- Is the degree of detail in data collection sufficient to allow costs of specific suboperations to be determined? If not, it becomes difficult to identify those suboperations in which the greatest potential for improvement exists.

- Is the data available when it is needed? It does little good to have excellent data made available well after the time it is possible to take advantage of it.
- Is the data available in a truly usable form? Thick computer printouts are seldom of use to anyone. Data must be presented in a concise, user-friendly format that provides a basis for action. If something is wrong or out of control, this should be readily apparent.

It is important to know costs, by individual product, in great detail. Whenever there is a difference in selling price between products, there should be a distinction shown in the cost, based on specific information. This is not to suggest that selling price is necessarily determined from cost alone. The data should identify those items for which selling price does not cover cost and that, therefore, should be considered for abandonment or repricing.

In the initial phases of a turnaround, one normally has neither the time nor staff to fully overhaul the cost accounting system. However, steps must immediately be taken to properly reflect the true costs of important items and generate this information on a timely basis.

Sample measurements should be taken, for some of the more important products, of the amounts of materials used in a batch of production and of the outputs/productivities of the various manufacturing steps/operations. In many instances the information gained in this manner will be quite different from what had been generally believed. Probably some products that had been thought to be profitable, and thereby emphasized, will be discovered to be unprofitable. Sometimes the reverse situation is found.

In addition to knowing cost and profit margin by product, it is important to know cost and profit margin by customer. Some customers will require costs that render them economically undesirable as customers.

Commonly, a small portion of sales may be responsible for a disproportionate share of costs. Elimination of these sales can bring a significant operating profit improvement.

ELECTRONIC DATA PROCESSING

Electronic data processing (EDP) is usually placed under the financial function, as its original and primary use is handling financial data. Sometimes EDP is as much of a problem as it is a solution. People forget that before 1955, large companies existed and ran without having computers.

EDP becomes a problem when it prevents needed information from being available in a timely manner, or in a form needed for it to be acted on. This frequently happens when a grandiose management information systems (MIS) plan is implemented and expensive, complex standardized software has been purchased from a systems vendor. The software, intended to integrate all locations and/or operating aspects of the company, is unable to do this because it was ill chosen, not recognizing its incompatibility with different types of operations or the incompatibility of different businesses in using the same standardized data-processing formats.

What is needed in the turnaround is to abandon the half-completed long-term project and have each location or operation use a simpler system, parts of which may be manual. Those parts of the original comprehensive MIS plan that are installed and working well should be retained, at least in the short run. The firm needs something that can produce timely results, and right away. These various systems need not fully integrate, but their outputs shouldn't be incompatible.

In most cases a multiplicity of simple, cheap, fast to bring on line, effective data systems for the various locations and businesses will meet the company's needs. A huge, complex integrated system that doesn't work will not. The wait for the big system, and the vacuum that exists during the wait, can be particularly damaging.

Data processing should be oriented to creating systems that provide common data bases and allow the elimination of redundant personnel, that is, systems that improve the responsiveness and cost-effectiveness of related activities, such as accounts payable, purchasing, material control, production control, receiving, stores, and materials movement. These things should tie together, for they have common and dependent needs for information: Do we have it? How many? Where is it? When will it arrive? How much should it cost? Have we paid for it? Do we need to order more?

A common reason for lack of MIS effectiveness is lack of specific goals and priorities in its systems development activities. Every firm has a multiplicity of groups demanding service, and each has a myriad of projects it wants done. Without a consistent set of priorities, the MIS group will handle too many projects at once and respond only to the latest crisis, leaving most projects uncompleted. The consequence is much effort expended with little to show for it. In other words, data-processing resources are frequently consumed by largely fruitless studies or projects, initiated by middle managers, that do not receive top management backing and are ultimately abandoned.

Less than ten years ago it was easy to show that abandoning EDP systems for well-thought-out manual systems might save much money and improve efficiency. The personal computer has changed that. IBM or Apple equipment, with much available inexpensive software, is often superior in cost and performance, in doing simple tasks needed by only one department, to either manual or mainframe systems. Troubled firms need to use more of these microsystems. They are often inhibited in buying them by the, say, $3,000 price tag per set-up. This attitude is penny-wise and pound-foolish. The paybacks of these little systems and their software are almost instantaneous. The microsystems can coexist with a mainframe system for general accounting, or CAD/CAM. The can reduce the needed size and cost of mainframe systems, or at least impede their growth.

The EDP Department and the MIS function represent a significant operating cost, one that continues to grow. These activities can either improve management's control of the company or be an important hindrance to the gaining of control. This is why they must be effective. If they are not, a change in the leadership of this area is required.

6

OVERHEAD

STAFF COSTS

A troubled company must control and reduce its costs. This is a matter of survival. An important type of cost that you must come to fully understand, justify, and control is salaried staff expense. Some staff overhead is vital—control and cost management would be jeopardized without it. Other staff overhead does not return its costs by decreasing other costs or by increasing profits elsewhere. These unnecessary costs must be quickly identified and eliminated. A sense of urgency must pervade this task.

In troubled, large, multidivisional firms, the chief executive officer must communicate cost reduction objectives and priorities to each division head. The division heads must then critically review their organizational structures and staffing with the view of obtaining significant head count reductions.

The location of staff functions within the company organization is an important element in overhead efficiency. The examination of organizational location is a route to overhead containment.

Multidivisional concerns are usually organized using some form of profit center concept. Each profit center normally has control of its own manufacturing, purchasing, and marketing and is responsible for orchestrating these profitably. The individual plants or subdivisions may, in turn, be treated as semi-independent profit centers.

The head of each profit center has a natural tendency to create staff in order to control or understand the major influences on profit. The net result of applying the profit center concept at sequential levels of an organization is a duplication of cost estimating, accounting, employee relations, and other staff functions. This duplication can add substantial costs. Usually it is best to carefully define what the profit center is and organize the staff functions at this level.

The problem of sequential layers of overhead was one of the basic causes of the lack of profitability of D.A.B. Industries, Inc., an automotive parts maker. It had a variety of subdivisions making different types of automotive engine and power train parts, all aimed at the same set of end customers—the automakers. Each operation had its own cost estimating, accounting, and other support functions. A large central headquarters staff, comprising about 125 persons, was superimposed on top. This headquarters staff was largely superfluous. It was a major element in the company's lack of profitability. D.A.B. Industries was never able to come to grips with this problem.

Head count control is a simple but effective approach to staff overhead containment. Each operating division of a decentralized company, or a centralized company, should have imposed on it head count maximums for each of its functions (i.e., marketing, engineering, finance) commensurate with the level of sales. Each functional head would be forced to eliminate employees in order to stay within the function's assigned maximum. In this way Blaw Knox Corporation eliminated more than 100 salaried positions in its various divisions, for an annual savings in salaries and fringe benefits exceeding $3 million.

Many times it is possible to limit the headquarters of a multidivisional company to a small size, depending, of course, on the scale of the firm. An extremely large headquarters staff for a decentralized company is a clear indication that head count is out of control. Corporate staffers have a need to justify their existence; they often retard rather than assist division operating improvement.

The large centralized firm needing to reduce its overhead can take a classic industrial engineering approach. In this approach an industrial engineering team would perform the following tasks:

1. Analyze department organization.
2. Collect transaction volume data (i.e., examine workload).
3. Conduct time/activity analysis by interviewing personnel.
4. Analyze systems and procedures.
5. Review data to determine opportunity for:
   - discontinuing activity
   - using outside services
   - improving methods
   - consolidating groups or functions
   - improving systems
   - reducing staff

By examining what tasks are performed, the methods and procedures used, the staffing, the interactions between people and between organizations, and the like, industrial engineers can recommend simplifications, the end of duplication, organizational improvements, and position eliminations. Sales, Engineering, Accounting, and so on can all benefit from this approach. The need is to run better and leaner. Leaner often means better because it means fewer persons have to be involved to accomplish something, so processing time is reduced.

For a reduction in staff to accomplish its aims, the functions performed by the displaced employees have to be either eliminated or accomplished by others with improved procedures and systems. Simply eliminating jobs and expecting the remaining employees to carry the increased workload will seldom work. As an example, one company eliminated 90 percent of its staff for material control and was then surprised to find that it had lost control of its inventory; 600 tons of steel couldn't be found at the annual inventory taking. This steel probably wasn't stolen; rather, meaningful records of material usage had ceased to exist. The firm had to restaff the material control function, and lost much information and incurred extra costs.

A careful review may reveal that there are far too many office employees per dollar of sales, but these employees are all necessary and working hard. Typically, this situation exists when a company is using outmoded manual systems. Mountains of cards or ledgers have to be moved, have entries made and rechecked. Each function may have its own systems, and duplication of data-based activities may be occurring in Purchasing, Material Control, and Accounts Payable, to name a few. In this situation, common data bases have to be created and systems instituted to replace the people-intensive manual systems.

Instituting or creating new systems and new common data bases is expensive and usually takes one to three years. This is a time horizon beyond that of the turnaround itself.

Some companies adopt electronic data processing (EDP) systems while retaining manual systems in parallel, particularly if the EDP system has problems. The need here is to force the EDP system to work and eliminate the manual system and its staff.

Overhead containment must be looked at from the perspectives of where, organizationally, the function should be carried out in order to eliminate duplication; how well the function is done; and if it can be done by fewer persons. Another, commonly ignored perspective is whether or not the function should be performed at all. You should determine whether the overhead cost adds to the value of the product, or is required to support some function that adds to the value of the product. If it does not, you are probably dealing with image overhead.

In turning a company around, image overhead can seldom be afforded. You must ask whether or not a customer would think a particular overhead function is essential to the value of the product. The metals industry, for example, has been particularly prone to the image overhead problem. For many years International Nickel Company and Allegheny Ludlum Steel Corporation, as examples, maintained superb staffs of product technical specialists who answered any and all questions on products using their types of metals and on how to process metals into end products. There was no connection, however, between a customer receiving this help and placing an order. The common situation became a customer receiving the help and then purchasing on a lowest-price basis, usually from one of these firm's competitors.

Allegheny Ludlum Steel Corporation has quite prudently timed its customer technical support activities. An example from before the time this change was made helps to illustrate this type of problem. Allegheny Ludlum spent much time and money helping General Motors Corporation perfect the use of a low-cost type of stainless steel, grade 409, for making structural members for a new-design transit bus. Grade 409 stainless steel is much more difficult to form and fabricate into structures than more common, higher-costing alloys. The development program succeeded and the new bus went into production. General Motors took the unusual step of allowing Allegheny Ludlum Steel to use pictures of the new bus in its advertising—something General Motors seldom permits suppliers to do. When it came time to buy production quantities of this steel, however, General Motors placed its business elsewhere.

Another useful way to approach reduction of staff overhead costs is to look into the possibility of subcontracting the activity to another firm. Essentially, this means applying the logic of a make/buy decision to services instead of goods. Other companies may be specialists at providing the particular service that the troubled firm is currently organized to provide only to itself. By buying the service from specialized firms who achieve greater productivity because they are doing this function as a business, you can eliminate the relevant internal manning and achieve lower costs. The preparation of payroll checks is a common example. Many vendors are in this business, making the pricing quite competitive. Plant or office cleaning is another likely subject, particularly in high-paying manufacturing firms where the cleaning staff tends to be paid according to the norms of manufacturing, rather than to those of service industries. A third area is plant security. At Danly Machine Corporation, by dissolving the Plant Guard Department and hiring a capable guard service, the quality of plant security improved enormously. At the same time the yearly plant security cost went from $650,000 to $350,000. Ingersoll–Rand found that by giving up its own truck fleet and using a contract carrier, it was able to reduce its costs, per running mile, from $1.25 to $0.95. This saved $300,000 per year. Real savings can be obtained by subcontracting internal services. It is easy to accomplish and should be given some priority.

Some types of professional services that are needed sporadically are better provided by outside firms on an as-needed basis. This would include, as a minimum, such areas as legal, compensation studies, market studies, and public relations.

To achieve the lowest overall costs, companies shouldn't minimize staff overhead. This is a common mistake. They should attempt to optimize the level of overhead, making trade-offs in which increased overhead leads to significantly decreased total costs. Adding the overhead of a make/buy function, for example, can lead to significantly decreased total costs. Common sense must be the guide.

FIXED COSTS AND OTHER COSTS

When looking at fixed costs and general and administrative nonstaff costs, there is no such thing as a stupid question. Every item should be examined, even those that seem above question.

Real estate taxes are a good example of this. They seem to rise every year and can reach considerable levels. This circumstance is based on taxing methodologies that make assumptions about the value of real estate and its usability. Is the taxing assumption true? Has the value of the real estate truly risen? Many consulting firms exist that will survey the actual conditions of your land and buildings and relate this information to recent real estate transactions. On this basis they will formulate a cogent argument for a real estate tax reduction and pursue this with the taxing authorities, in return for a percentage of the savings. Danly Machine Corporation used one such firm for its major Chicago area plant. When this consultant reached the limit of what it could achieve, Danly engaged a second consultant to obtain significant additional savings, which it did. All this was done in a strictly aboveboard, straightforward manner.

Sometimes buildings that are old and unneeded are located in an area where there is a permanent glut of such real estate on the market; that is, they are just about unsalable. They still bear real estate taxes, however, which probably are unrealistically high, require maintenance of their sprinkler systems and roofs, and must be heated and patrolled by guards, to prevent their use by vagrants. These represent a significant continuing cost. The solution is to bulldoze the buildings. Demolition companies, which recover various scrap values, can do the job for a reasonably modest cost. This will eliminate upkeep and drop the real estate taxes dramatically. The payback from demolition will probably be six months or less.

Utility costs are another usually ignored area. Utilities do have some leeway on their rate levels. They won't do anything to reduce their charges to a company unless the company knows where it stands and insists on an adjustment. Avondale Shipyards, Inc., in Louisiana, for example, did this and was able to negotiate a considerable electricity rate relief. Avondale realized that a rate reduction was possible, which is the important first step. Similarly, two divisions of Blaw Knox Corporation—Blaw Knox Rolls Division in West Virginia and Duraloy Company in Pennsylvania—learned that the public utility commissions of their respective states had established special lower electricity rates for troubled companies and each managed to take advantage of the opportunity.

Utility costs can also be brought down by carefully examining your usage pattern and altering it accordingly. Power factor, peak demand, and other use aspects should all be looked at. If a manufacturing step that uses much electricity, say, resistance welding, can be done exclusively during an off-peak part of the day, the savings may be considerable. For the typical manufacturing plant, electricity and fuel may constitute 1.5 to 3 percent of total manufacturing cost. This is a considerable expense, and thus deserves some attention.

Office space needs a critical examination. Is the amount of office space occupied by the company really needed, or is its size excessive? If major staff reductions occur, leased office space should be looked at for reduction and rationalization (e.g., fewer floors in a building, fewer locations). Is the location of the headquarters of critical importance? Saxon Industries, headquartered in New York City, found that by moving to a less prestigious office building, about one mile south of its current address, it could keep its rental costs per square foot the same, while selling its old lease for $1.8 million.

This also illustrates that sometimes a profit can be obtained from giving up leased office space. If the space was obtained on a long-term lease at a rate much lower than current market values, and has a reasonable life left, the space can be subleased at a profit. Allegheny International, Inc., after acquiring Chemetron Corporation, disposed of the former Chemetron offices in Chicago in this way, at a considerable profit.

Some companies that previously maintained a separate headquarters location have moved their headquarters to a major plant that had sufficient available unused office space. The cost of using this existing space was usually negligible. Moving can be expensive, but the savings from giving up the office lease costs may mean a rapid payback.

Purchased services should be scrutinized for possible cost reductions. Is the service provided by the vendor as timely and accurate or well done as it should be? Can better service be obtained for less? For example, insurance claims processing. If the firm is self-insured, it is probably using an outside service to process the claims. If the arrangement is of long standing, a market test is called for to ascertain whether another firm can give equal or better service at a lower cost.

Policy changes on company cars and air travel cost often need to be made and can have a twofold effect. First, a significant cost reduction can be realized. Elimination of eligibility for a company car and downgrading of the type of car for those few that remain can bring significant savings. Tightening up on travel cost and requiring coach only for domestic flights can also yield substantial savings. Attention to discount air fares and promotion fares is well worth the effort. You can negotiate with car rental companies to receive higher discounts. Second, implementing policy changes on company cars and travel creates desirable psychological benefits. It focuses people's attention on the need for operating economically.

Every item in your company's list of overhead accounts should be subject to question. The fact that a practice is of long standing is not an acceptable reason to continue that practice.

7

INVENTORY

Royal Little, in his heyday at Textron, used to tell people that managing inventory is "working where the money is." This statement emphasizes the truth that inventory ties up much of the capital and is the origin of many of the costs of any manufacturing business. The cash needs of the company will be highly dependent on how well it is managed.

Inventory is the basis of a number of significant costs: interest costs; real estate costs resulting from the need for space to store it; costs of obsolescence and product degradation; material handling costs; inventory-taking labor; and protection services. As inventory involves both cost and capital, its management is particularly important in achieving a company turnaround. Inventory mismanagement is a common characteristic of a troubled company.

In looking at the subject of inventory, one has to examine the questions of what kinds to have and how much to keep.

Troubled companies invariably have obsolete inventory, so this is one place to start. Obsolete inventory has to be recognized as such. Products or raw materials in storage, unlike wine, do not improve with age. If something has been held for six months or more, and a near-term use is not in prospect, it should be disposed of. Troubled firms hesitate to do this because their managements do not want to show the resulting loss on their financial statements. It is better to show the loss and recover some cash than to continue to incur the needless costs of maintaining this inventory, and to have capital devoted to an unproductive use. Once inventory is deemed obsolete, regardless of how briefly it has been held, it should be eliminated and the capital it represents freed for more productive use. Unrecorded losses in obsolete inventory can be an important element leading to insolvency.

If the obsolete inventory contains purchase items, still in good condition, provided by a supplier you are still doing business with, there may be a good opportunity to return them. Although the entire purchase price may not be refunded, a significant portion of the original cost may be recaptured.

An interesting alternative exists to scrapping obsolete products, replacement parts, partially finished goods, and the like—dealing with a "rebuy" warehousing company. There are always items that have a remote possibility of being needed once again, and this excuse is frequently used to prevent disposing of them. A rebuy warehousing company will buy these goods at nearly scrap value but retain them in a warehouse, available for resale back to the firm, for a considerable period, say, ten years. According to one typical agreement, a firm can buy the goods back at any time at 90 percent of the stated book value or variable cost at the time it sold the goods to the warehousing company, multiplied by a time escalation factor of about 6 percent per year. This amount would probably be less than the cost of making or obtaining these goods sometime in the future. It would provide the company with immediate cash and eliminate the numerous expenses incurred in holding inventory. Not enough firms realize that this alternative to scrapping goods is available.

Many accountants, who are usually unfamiliar with the rebuy approach, may object to it improperly on tax law grounds. The U.S. Supreme Court, in Thor Power Tool Company versus Commissioner, ruled that only if inventory is sold with title transferred, scrapped, or physically abandoned, is a corporation entitled to a current deduction for the loss realized equal to the difference between its tax basis in the inventory disposed of and the amount, if any, it receives on disposition. Legal opinion concerning the impact of this ruling indicates that for the customer to sustain a deduction in this context, it is important that the sale clearly pass title to the inventory out of the hands of the customer. In determining whether a taxpayer is required to include merchandise in inventory for federal income tax purposes, a great deal of emphasis is placed on who has title to the merchandise. Under the rebuy agreement, and in view of the fact that the material is stored on the rebuy warehouse's premises, there is a clear transfer of title. The transaction must have some element of economic risk for the customer to sustain the deduction. The element of the economic risk is present for the rebuy warehouse, since it assumes the risk that it will not be able to resell the inventory at more than scrap value, balanced against the potential profit it will realize on items that it does resell to or through customers, as well as the risk of occurrences such as fire and theft. The risk from the point of the customer, on the other hand, is that the inventory will not be available for repurchase if and when required.

A hypothetical example illustrates the benefit of the rebuy approach for the remote-need type of inventory:

Inventory cost basis		$500,000
Estimated scrap value @ 2%		10,000
Loss on sale of inventory		
Book value	$500,000	
Selling price	10,000	
Loss		490,000
Tax reduction @ 50%		245,000

Therefore, the company realizes the following first-year cash savings:

From income taxes		$245,000
From carrying costs @ 24%	$120,000	
Less 50% tax	60,000	
		60,000
First-year cash savings		$305,000

Usage over time needs to be examined in determining whether or not goods are obsolete and in establishing their proper inventory levels. If, for example, a certain type of casting or electric switch hasn't been used or sold in, say, three years, then it is time to decide whether or not this item should remain in inventory. If something is used at an average rate of 1.5 units per year, and the normal order quantity is 15 units, then the size of the normal order quantity needs to be reassessed.

Raw materials inventories are often excessive in firms not managed to achieve tight control of cash flow. Purchasing will have to give improved emphasis to obtaining faster delivery, which will decrease the size of needed buffer stocks. These are often too large, owing to excessive conservatism in their estimation. Operations must be forced to work with shorter lead times, relying on the supplier of the material to make it quickly available. In almost any industry there are suppliers who will place material on consignment, or at least store it for immediate customer requirements.

It is usually better to experience some loss of business than to pay the economic price of overstocking, giving up your potential profit through incursion of inventory costs of approximately 24 to 28 percent per annum.

The level of finished goods inventory (and some raw materials and work-in-process inventories as well) must be consistent with the firm's strategy concerning customer service. If rapid response to customer needs has been adopted as part of the business strategy, inventory levels and types must be set and managed to support this strategy. If they are not, the inconsistency will doom the success of the strategy.

A strategy calling for higher inventory levels must be well justified by a cost benefit analysis. It cannot be adopted on the premise that a higher level of sales is intrinsically desirable.

If the firm maintains inventories of the same types of finished goods at a number of locations, this can lead to another common problem—inventory suboptimization. This is when each storage location manages its inventory level independently of the other locations. In this situation a company is not managing its finished goods inventory as a whole. The result is inventory bloat, with each location stocking the same slow-moving items. Unless transportation costs are high compared with inventory item values, it is probably best to coordinate the inventory stocking levels of the various locations, having slower-moving items kept at a reduced number of locations.

Excessive work-in-process inventory is often observable in walking through a poorly managed plant. Boxes or pallets stashed here, there, and everywhere indicate a lack of proper scheduling. The consequence is enlarged work-in-process inventories. A reduction of this excess, by better manufacturing management, will free up needed capital and reduce work-in-process inventory carrying costs.

If a business must be able to respond to surges in demand, and insufficient time exists to make the product from scratch, an alternative frequently exists to stocking the finished goods. A careful analysis of the manufacturing sequence will reveal at what stage of completion the least value will have been added to the product, while necessitating the least time to complete the product. This optimum, if carefully chosen, can possibly lead to meaningful inventory reductions and lessen the problems associated with obsolete goods.

To reduce inventory, the company has to be able to use whatever inventory it has to its best advantage. Inventories often bloat when information is either undependable or unavailable. Ask oneself these questions: Does the company really know, specifically, (a) what items it has, (b) how many are in stock, and (c) where they can be found? These questions cannot be answered yes if receiving inspection doesn't ensure an accurate count of purchased material; stores are not closed to make it impossible for items to be taken for use without the transaction properly recorded; and material movements are not tracked in real time, establishing that an item has *arrived* at a certain place or manufacturing plant work center (rather than establishing that it has left a certain location).

When something cannot be found because it has been moved to the wrong place, or is unlabeled, or is misplaced in a store room, it will be either repurchased or remade. When the missing item surfaces weeks later, it may become excess inventory and then just sit gathering dust.

Getting control of inventory takes people and systems. This isn't accomplished without cost. Much labor may be needed in sorting and relocating a substantial amount of current inventory. Items will have to be identified and labeled. Easy access to items ranging from simple bar stock to completed subassemblies will have to be eliminated. This will entail instituting paperwork to draw these goods, installing fences and locks, and assigning people to the check-out and check-in functions. Unless these things are done, inventory reduction will consist of much talk and little action.

Going through these efforts will often cause people to come to the conclusion that inventory is being kept in too many storerooms. Usually the excessive number of locations were developed over time as means to achieve convenience. They do achieve convenience, but at a huge carrying cost. If the number of storage locations is reduced, this will allow further reductions in inventory levels and will, in turn, possibly reduce the need for storekeepers.

Putting in on-line real-time, accurate inventory records will help solve the question of whether or not enough of a certain stock item is available. People won't need to go to the shelf to count for themselves. Cathode ray terminals can be put wherever they would be useful to permit people to check an inventory item at any time. The resulting greater certainty in inventory availability will reduce manufacturing assembly and shipping problems, improve customer service, and possibly allow for reductions in the size of inventory buffer stocks.

These goals will be defeated if the inventory records are not truly accurate. For example, Amphenol Division of Allied Corporation maintained inaccurate inventory records on their computer, with the consequence being that people would physically go to double check if the items were actually there.

Firms use a variety of criteria for selecting order quantities for goods that go into inventory. These include a fixed number of weeks of expected sales, a fixed number of units, or the level at which one obtains a vendor's price break. The most rational way is to use the economic order quantity (EOQ). This is the quantity that provides the minimum cost from both manufacturing/purchasing and carrying cost points of view. The usual formula for EOQ is

$$EOQ = \sqrt{\frac{2AS}{I}}$$

where A is the annual usage in dollars, S is the setup or ordering cost in dollars, and I is the annual inventory carrying cost, as a decimal fraction.

The use of this formula can be found in any production control textbook.

The EOQ needs to reflect the changes in inventory consumption patterns. The value of A in the formula cannot go unexamined for many years. The value of I, the carrying cost, needs to be realistic, which means something like 0.30. If a company has cash flow problems, then it must be set much higher, say, 0.45 or 0.50. EOQ needs to be reexamined, for purchased goods, when there are quantity discounts, to see if the lower prices are offset by higher carrying costs.

How should one judge the proper level of inventory? Every business is different and the company must be able to respond to customer demand. This question relates to inventory turnover, that is, sales divided by inventory. Various businesses have normal values for turnover. If the troubled company has an inventory turnover significantly below this value, the reason has to be ascertained and corrective action taken. It may be obsolete goods that haven't been disposed of, or excessive buffer stocks of raw materials, or finished goods kept in too many locations.

Inventory levels need to be reviewed and adjusted in terms of the general state of the economy and its place in the business cycle. A company going into a period of high demand with firm prices can let inventory levels drop if its customer has little choice but to wait for reasonable delivery. On the other hand, if demand is low and prices weak, maintaining a greater inventory, to permit quick delivery, will be required to obtain many sales orders.

Just-in-Time, or KANBAN, production and inventory systems are receiving much attention as a means to achieve lower costs and reduce working capital needs. They are applicable only under special circumstances and will be examined in the chapter on manufacturing.

8

PROCUREMENT

Procurement has broader and wider meaning than that usually ascribed to the word purchasing. It goes beyond merely satisfying a company's material requirements by introducing strategic elements, such as *how* the company will meet its materials needs. Will it make or buy? Will it satisfy its needs domestically or abroad? How will these decisions impact and support the overall business strategy? The following sections deal with these aspects.

PURCHASING

Purchasing is a key factor, and sometimes "the" key factor, in the profitability of a company. To assess the relative importance of Purchasing and how much emphasis it should receive in the turnaround, look at a ratio of total purchases to total sales. If this ratio is greater than about 0.20 to 0.25, then it has to be a major area of concentration. Regardless of the value of this ratio, Purchasing should be looked at as a potential source of important savings and managed to ensure that it will achieve them.

Many times the relative importance of Purchasing isn't understood. For example, two troubled fabricated metal products companies, Tube Turns, Inc., and Alloy Rods, both had materials purchases constituting 60 percent of sales and direct labor amounting to 8 percent of sales. This meant that a 10 percent improvement in purchase prices, which was within the realm of possibility, was equivalent to a reduction in direct labor of 75 percent, an impossibility. Yet both companies focused almost all management attention on increasing labor productivity, assuming that purchase costs had to remain at current levels. The subject of Purchasing never arose when these companies' managements reviewed ways to improve profitability with their parent corporations. This lack of understanding of the true importance of Purchasing is common. A small reduction in purchase costs can often have a greater effect than large reductions in labor costs.

Purchasing has strategic dimensions that need to be understood. It controls an important portion of the cost of your manufactured product. Purchasing represents a possible alternative to a company's own manufacturing cost. By its ability to have the product made by another manufacturer, it may be able to drive product costs down. Purchasing is able to deal in a global marketplace. By sourcing abroad, it may be able to counter a present cost advantage of foreign-made products. Purchasing may be able to obtain needed technology quickly, through product purchases, with little investment. Purchasing may also be able to provide foreign market opportunities in countries in which it is obtaining goods by the relationship it develops with firms within these countries. Much of the world outside the United States does business on a reciprocity basis. These are far broader considerations than the common purchasing perspective of merely ensuring that production doesn't run out of raw materials or parts.

Consequently, Purchasing needs long-range, as well as short-range, perspectives. Long-range supply relationships must be carefully built. A step-by-step process is often needed with a supplier in order to develop the supplier's ability to supply goods with the quality needed, at advantageous prices. Another long-term goal can be a reduction in service costs through reducing warranty expenses.

The Purchasing function should be value oriented. Purchasing needs to review its procedures and establish new goals, such as buying more value and productivity, rather than just buying a physically described product. One way to do this is for Purchasing to invite vendors to view the manufacturing process and make recommendations on ways to add value by changes in processing and product design, and offer suggestions regarding outsourcing.

Most troubled operations do not give the Purchasing function the status it deserves and do not staff it with top-caliber people. The Purchasing staff normally sees its function as making certain that materials, components, and so forth are reliably delivered to the quality required so that production will never be impeded. Price is considered less important, as long as it is acceptable. New suppliers are considered only reluctantly, as this introduces questions of delivery reliability and quality. In a turnaround this approach to doing business needs radical revision.

A Purchasing function with a poor-quality staff will not promote change—it will be afraid of change. People with the right skills and experience are needed to head and staff the Purchasing function. If the company doesn't have them, it must replace the current staff with people who do have them. It is penny-wise and pound-foolish to have anything but a first-rate Purchasing function, staffed by first-rate, experienced people. Remember, this small group of people may control between one-quarter and one-half of the company's total costs.

The Purchasing function may be doing a terrible job and be completely unaware that this is the case. Purchasing must have specific objectives that support and complement other objectives in the company's business plan. It must have cost reduction or containment targets whose achievement will have a significant impact on profitability and cash flow. In a troubled company it often has none of these.

Poor purchasing commonly results from improper organization, poor operating procedures, and a lack of integration into business plans. The following remarks will look at some of these aspects.

Do the same buyers have continuing responsibility for the same types of items? If steel is bought by one person, electrical fittings by one person, bearings by one person (with one person possibly having several commodity responsibilities simultaneously), then a sense of the market develops. Varying who buys each product prevents this expertise from developing. Product and commodity responsibilities should be clearly defined.

If product assignments within Purchasing have not changed in a long time, a sort of comfortable staleness may prevail. Suppliers will not feel a competitive necessity to quote their lowest prices. You need to change product responsibilities, in this case, to break up relationships between buyers and vendors, and instill a new sense of competition to the buying process.

How much buying do buyers do? If you make a survey of how buyers spend their time, it may show something like only 18 percent of their time is spent on buying analysis and negotiation, their most important tasks, with the rest of their time spent on clerical chores. This situation is more common than people realize. If this is the case, then the clerical tasks must be unloaded onto clerical assistants, or reduced by greater use of mechanized systems, to free the buyers to do the needed purchasing analysis and negotiation.

Part of the problem of buyer ineffectiveness may be due to antiquated procedures. If a manual system is still in use and many types of items are being bought, the paperwork may become strangling. One useful alternative is for a buyer to have a computer, which allows him to instantly call up the previous purchasing and pricing history of the items and the experience had with the vendor. The emphasis of the buyer must be buying, not paperwork preparation.

For smaller companies it may not be practical to install a mainframe computer-based system. Here, good purchasing planning, blanket contracts, and efficient manual records can provide the same information. Few companies are too small to make use of microcomputers as an extension or evolution of a good manual system.

Important questions to ask are whether or not a sufficient number of quotations are normally obtained for making a purchase decision, and are purchasing decisions well documented? Is it easier for buyers to simply place an order with someone they are used to doing business with, rather than go through the effort needed to obtain the lowest possible cost? A good check to see what is actually happening is to select purchase orders at random and examine their back-up files, to see if they exist.

Vendor identification and qualification can be hard work. Visits must be made to potential new vendors to see that they have the right equipment, people, and operating procedures. This may require adding staff. Quality assurance people should also be involved in all of these visits, to verify that suitable quality can be expected.

Another question you have to examine is whether there are too many active vendors for similar items. If the firm is buying castings, for example, and has patterns at fifteen foundries, this may be necessitating large amounts of paperwork with no commensurate purchasing savings. By concentrating the business at a small number of vendors, you may become a more important customer to them, with resulting benefits.

You must determine if an analysis of purchase requirements has been made, with resulting decisions on where to concentrate attention for greatest probable impact. If such an analysis has not been made, minor and major items are receiving similar attention, with the consequence that major items are receiving insufficient attention. For minor items, blanket orders by category are prudent, with the vendor selected by comparison of a representative market basket of items. From time to time a fresh market test will reveal whether or not it would be advisable to change vendors.

Approval levels should be established for various dollar levels of purchasing approval. This will help to maintain discipline, honesty, and adherence to policies.

Specific targets should be established for vendor price reductions and cost containment. Buyers need to be made responsible for their results. Vendor price increases should not be accepted at face value. Justifications should be required and negotiations on their amounts and timing should ensue. We sometimes forget that price increases cannot be unilaterally instituted by a supplier. Prices are matters arrived at by mutual consent. If a supplier wishes to make a price increase, require a procedure that makes the sellers justify the increase and then negotiate with them. As a last step, negotiate the timing of the increase; a wait of three additional months constitutes a type of discount. At Danly Machine Corporation, which went from accepting price increases to negotiating them, a supplier request for a 5 percent increase was turned into an 8 percent decrease.

Negotiation should include communicating an understanding of the impact of a price increase on the company and the challenge this poses for the vendor.

Purchasing needs the capability to negotiate with other companies. It is not merely a clerical function. Better prices top any list of negotiation objectives, but other important aspects need to be negotiated as well. These include a supplier reserving capacity for your needs, developing product enhancements in support of your business objectives, the exploitation of market opportunities, and the obtaining of better quality.

In buying foreign goods, trips must be made to identify, qualify, and negotiate with foreign suppliers. The foreign supplier may not be represented by domestic middlemen, and when they are, this can be an unaffordably expensive convenience. The Purchasing Department must add expertise in foreign purchasing, if this is lacking. It must also know how to negotiate ocean freight costs and forward buying of foreign currencies. The rest of the company must back up Purchasing's efforts with proper support in Engineering, Quality Assurance, and Manufacturing Engineering.

The question of domestic versus foreign suppliers has many nuances. The advantages of domestic sources include much less transit time, lower coordination costs, no currency risks, and ease of communication (i.e., U.S. telephone system, fast mail, same language).

Foreign sources, however, often offer potentially lower costs. Against these you must weigh the negatives of the preceding attributes of domestic sources, plus the potential that currency exchange rate changes will negate the currently favorable prices (this can be handled in the short run by buying currency futures to meet the payments for current orders). Frequently some mix of domestic and foreign suppliers will turn out to be the optimum. This mix must be constantly monitored, as it is liable to change quickly.

Buying foreign products is now in style as an approach to solving company product-cost problems. Foreign buying can be used, however, to mask basic deficiencies in the management of the Purchasing function. One leading U.S. manufacturer, extolling the benefits of foreign purchasing, provided the following example. As recently as August 1984, they bought all of their requirements for 2–1/2-inch thick, type A36 steel plate domestically. They were paying $550 per ton and have reduced this cost considerably by buying abroad. Apparently, their Purchasing function didn't realize the same steel could be bought domestically, at that time, at a price of $410 per ton. This example shows that sometimes incompetent Purchasing management may be the real problem when foreign buying looks unusually attractive.

Domestic suppliers who have normally charged the firm according to a price book on raw materials and commodities may lower their prices significantly when told that there is now competition and that supply capacity exceeds demand. Once better prices are received, it is sometimes advisable to have the purchasing agent negotiate further—in buying specialty steel, for example—to demand another 5 percent off. In the specialty steel industry it was observed that the lowest prices didn't necessarily go to the largest buyers; they went to those with the most vigorous and aggressive purchasing agents. Purchasing negotiations should be tough-minded and include careful explanation of strategic considerations facing the company; they should not be threatening. The final agreement should include mutual benefit and understanding. The company's negotiating position must include a caution that present and future market conditions be carefully assessed. If the market becomes tight, consequences of antagonizing suppliers may include late deliveries, poor quality, and other indications of the supplier's displeasure.

Terms and conditions of sale are worth fighting over. Terms of sixty days or ninety days, compared with thirty days, represent a hidden discount. The additional time represents the value of foregone interest on the size of the transaction for this period. In effect, time is money.

Ask for goods on a consignment basis. Sometimes you can get it and this frees up working capital. Many companies fail to explore this avenue.

What is the supplier's necessary lead time? If they are nearby and can ship on short notice, this is another way to reduce the level of needed inventory. Some suppliers, say, steel companies, are willing to make and hold inventory earmarked for specific customers in order to allow for fast delivery. Purchasing should try to develop such situations. They are worth a special effort. Remember, inventory has carrying costs of 25 percent and more per annum. Not having to carry inventory is equivalent to achieving a significant price decrease.

Transportation has now become a purchased commodity, subject to competitive pressures. Substantial cost reductions are now feasible, but their achievement requires effort and negotiation. If transportation costs are a significant portion of total costs, it may be advisable to place the Traffic function under the Purchasing Department. In any case, Purchasing should be responsible for obtaining lower transportation costs.

Consultants called in to review a troubled company's organization and procedures almost invariably recommend going to a Material Requirements Planning (MRP) system. In this arrangement, Purchasing, Production Control, Material Control, Traffic, and any other material-related activities are brought together within a single organization headed by a director of materials. This is frequently a bad idea and must be assiduously resisted, unless the nature of the business makes a compelling case for MRP. It may submerge Purchasing within a group of interacting activities. In a turnaround, Purchasing by itself may require particular attention. Only with this type of attention will it improve its procedures quickly, restaff with the caliber of people it needs, and obtain the lower prices the company usually desperately needs. The company may also need timely delivery and better quality.

Purchasing must be made sensitive to matters of malfeasance. Many industries that are large purchasers of a few items are prone to graft, say, the steel industry's purchase of refractories and grinding wheels. This potential problem deserves special attention, principally focused at the plant level.

Short-weighing and short-counting by vendors can also be a continuing problem, unless specific procedures prevent it. Does a freshly arrived fifty-five-gallon drum of solvent, hydraulic fluid, or lubricant contain fifty-five gallons, or forty-nine gallons? Does anyone check? This information should be recorded and communicated, both to Accounts Payable and Purchasing (which should remove such suppliers from its approved vendor lists).

Your company will probably find that it has both excess and obsolete inventory. You need to dispose of these items to free up cash. You also want to receive the best possible price for these goods. The Purchasing function can be useful in this task. They can often convince vendors to take back goods at little or no discount, as an implied condition of a continuing favorable relationship.

Purchasing is a key area in the management of a company turnaround and must be treated as such. It must be staffed with a sufficient number of capable and highly experienced professionals.

MAKE/BUY

Make/buy decisions can be made for a variety of reasons: economics, investment, labor relations, capacity, technology, and lack of organizational resources. Make/buy decisions usually have major beneficial cost and capital impacts. The subject, however, must be approached with a thorough understanding of what is entailed in making these decisions; otherwise, major risks may be inadvertently undertaken.

Troubled manufacturing companies usually do little subcontracting and have minimum experience in make/buy decisions. The reason is that Manufacturing managements want to keep their plants busy and work force employed. Little thought, therefore, is usually given to the possibility of reducing cost by purchasing something outside that is currently made inside, as this would lead to reduced employment. Considerable savings are frequently realized if make/buy decisions are systematically pursued. These actions will reduce working capital and possibly allow the sale of no longer needed plant and machinery. Through subcontracting a company can gain a needed technology with less investment and time delay, and take advantage of a market condition.

A particularly bad example of a company making something it should have been buying was observed at Toledo Scale. Two men were assigned to make ball bearings needed in making scales. This may sound like an incredible example, but things like it occur every day.

Occasionally a company's trouble comes from its subcontracting too much. This usually arises when a company provides little added value to its product in a competitive market where most of the company's competitors provide the majority of their manufacturing content.

Instituting a make/buy decision is sometimes complicated by a labor union agreement "contracting out" clause. This is a prohibition on a company subcontracting work of a type previously done by employees covered by the bargaining agreement. Even where these restrictions exist, there can be considerable leeway that allows one to justify the action on technological or other grounds. The contracting out clause frequently is invoked by plant management to prevent work from leaving their plant, whether or not the contract prohibition is truly controlling.

Make/buy programs should be ongoing, independent activities. They should constantly look for alternatives to internal manufacture of goods that are either low in margin or high in fixed asset investment requirements.

Conceptually, the make/buy decision can exist at two levels, which may be termed the incremental level and the activity level. Both levels require good cost data for proper analysis. The incremental level is when one compares the incremental cost of making a specific item or doing a specific manufacturing step against its outside purchase. But what constitutes incremental cost? This is the cost the firm would not have if it didn't make this particular batch of this item. People often confuse the issue by looking at costs including various factory burdens and overheads. You cannot do this and stay within the meaning of the word incremental. A fear is often expressed by manufacturing managements that buying something at a lower cost than its incremental cost will not allow them to cover their factory burden expense. As you can see from the definition, buying something below incremental cost will allow the company to cover its burden expense as well as it does by making the item itself.

Cost comparisons at the incremental level pertain when a manufacturing plant is operating below capacity. However, if the manufacturing plant is at capacity, the management choice changes from making it inside versus buying it outside, to buying it outside versus not having it at all. At this point the appropriate cost comparison is the purchase price against the fully burdened manufacturing cost.

If a company has well-paid manufacturing employees and makes a variety of types and sizes of products with widely varying popularity, then it is a certainty that some items can be bought outside at a price below the internal incremental cost.

The activity level approach to examining the make/buy decision is when the firm considers giving up the activity as a whole and buys the item or service outside. At this level, substantial fixed cost can be eliminated as the entire overhead associated with operating a department, plant, etc. disappears. For example, buying all forgings outside and closing down the company's own forging shop. Many items that looked attractive to retain for in-house manufacture, when considered individually, on an incremental basis, are collectively best suited for outside purchase; hence the need to analyse at the activity level as well as at the incremental level.

If significant manufacturing-cost reductions are being successfully achieved, the implementation of a make/buy program may have to take some additional factors into consideration. The first of these is the desirability of operating the plant with a steady workload. Wide swings in workload, either up or down, tend to adversely affect manufacturing productivity. If the home plant has capacity problems, this ceases to be a factor. If it does not, the savings from subcontracting must be worth their effect on plant productivity if an unsteady workload is foreseen.

The second factor is the possible disruption of the development of cost-reducing product design changes on the items being sent outside. To make the improvements, Manufacturing Engineering needs to be working with batches of actual production. These design changes normally evolve over a relatively short period, so, at worst, the make/buy decision is only delayed.

Having passed the conceptual hurdles of the make/buy decision process, how do you implement it? The first task is to decide who runs it. Purchasing is one likely place; they are used to dealing with vendors but lack insight into internal costs and scheduling impacts. A branch of the Manufacturing organization, such as Production Control/Material Control, is already experienced in deciding which items to route to Production and which to Purchasing and knows about scheduling impacts. However, they lack both the objectivity needed for make/buy decisions and the systems needed for dealing with vendors. In many companies make/buy decisions are the responsibility of Manufacturing Engineering. This function is used to looking critically at internal costs and has the know-how needed to assess whether or not a potential vendor has the equipment and skills needed to properly make a product. Probably the most pragmatic solution is to have make/buy administered by someone in Purchasing, as his specific responsibility, with oversight and coordination from a Make/Buy Committee composed of representatives from Purchasing, Manufacturing (Manufacturing Engineering, Production Control/Material Control), Quality, Engineering, Labor Relations, Finance, and Sales (if customer approval is required).

In administering a make/buy program, just as in developing new suppliers, Purchasing needs expertise and manpower to evaluate potential suppliers (to an even greater degree than normal); it may have to rely on the expertise of the Manufacturing Engineering function. Potential vendors, domestic and foreign, must be identified and visits to them made in order to ascertain the existence or availability of the following:

- Suitable equipment in type and quantity
- Sufficient labor with suitable skills
- A quality control system that will meet the requirements
- Management resources of the depth required
- Business conditions that will allow for a long-term relationship. You don't want to work with a firm that will be using your orders only for a short-term fill-in, considering the magnitude of the effort you will expend in order to work with them.
- Scheduling and tracking systems sufficient to ensure on time, reliable delivery
- Adequate financial resources
- Negligible risk that by this arrangement you are, in effect, creating a future competitor

Purchasing will need a staff of expeditors to visually check on progress, identify problems, and help develop solutions to those problems. Analysts will also be required to evaluate vendor price quotations and factor in related aspects, such as freight costs and customs duties. They will also have to look for errors in vendor quotations, such as misstatements of material costs, which may imply improper understanding and communication. The performance of these functions will necessitate additional staff.

The company will also need systems adequate for the task of tracking the status of all the subcontracted items. Otherwise, delivery problems will not be discovered before it is too late to take meaningful corrective action, or to ensure that the vendor does so. This lack, unless corrected, can have serious consequences.

Assuming suitable items are discovered for subcontracting, the company will need quality assurance and inspection resources to check production in progress and at completion, for suitability. This means sufficient people, gauges, and travel budgets.

Sufficient analysts, tracking procedures, and quality assurance resources are needed by Purchasing in its normal activities without having a significant make/ buy program. A make/buy program will greatly increase the requirements for such resources.

By subcontracting, the firm must be careful not to create a future competitor. Signed proprietary information and noncompetition agreements by themselves may not be enough, particularly when dealing with foreign firms. The potential threat of this happening is related to how much information has been provided. It is more prudent for the subcontractor's efforts to be compartmentalized—that is, by doing the task each one is still missing key information needed to make the whole product—than to have someone make the product in its entirety. A possible exception to this is having an existing foreign licensee make production for you, under your name, with the understanding that there may be no customer contact.

Troubled companies usually have little experience in make/buy decisions. Make/buy decisions can bring significant benefits and may be, in fact, an important element in achieving the turnaround. To be successful, however, the company must be organized to make them, think through the various business implications, and provide the effort with sufficient staff resources.

9

MANUFACTURING

Manufacturing is the heart of a manufacturing company. A troubled manufacturing company invariably requires significant improvements in the management of this activity.

Most of the key aspects of manufacturing are of a professional nature. The manufacturing organization's key executives must be well educated and have broad experience. A manufacturing organization led and primarily staffed by men who worked their way up from the shop floor is inappropriate today. If this is the case, it may be one of the company's problems.

Except in the smallest of companies, an effective manufacturing function requires the performance of complex manufacturing and staff activities. These must be well coordinated and timely. A "one-man show"-type of manufacturing management becomes impossible when annual sales pass a threshold of about $15 million.

Good manufacturing plant supervision and skilled hourly manpower, no matter how well intentioned, cannot produce good manufacturing results if a capable manufacturing staff organization is absent. Manufacturing has grown too complex for that. The manufacturing staff organization must be properly staffed in terms of manning level and appropriate skills. This is needed for the company to achieve reasonable production costs and consistently meet production schedules.

Some of the necessary manufacturing staff activities include the following:

- Routings Preparation/Industrial Engineering. This group lays out the sequence of manufacturing steps and chooses the most appropriate manufacturing equipment for each step.

- Labor Standards. This group predetermines how much time each manufacturing step should take, providing a basis for labor cost control.
- Material Control/Inventory Control. This group ensures that the needed materials will be available when they are required.
- Manufacturing Engineering. This group develops improved manufacturing methods, selects new equipment to be purchased, and designs tools and fixtures needed for production.
- Production Control. This group looks at capacity constraints on production and schedules use of the production equipment.
- Facilities Engineering. This group looks at plant layout for purposes of reducing material handling cost; it also manages the manufacturing site.
- Traffic. This group manages inbound and outbound freight movements and seeks to minimize freight costs.

Having a capable manufacturing staff organization will not, by itself, guarantee good manufacturing results. There must also be a plant work force with the required level of skills, good shop floor manufacturing supervision, an absence of restrictive work rules, appropriate fixed assets, and competent overall manufacturing management. Without all of these things, shipments will be late, quality will be poor, and product costs will be needlessly high.

Manufacturing must be conducted in a manner consistent with the company's overall strategic concept. It must be responsive to the company's strategy and cannot exist in a world of its own, making decisions contrary to this strategy. An example of such a situation arose at D.A.B. Industries, an auto parts firm supplying the major automakers. D.A.B. obtained an order for a railroad product—a diversification opportunity, similar to one of its automotive products. The product, a railroad bearing plate, could be made without any further capital investment. However, the plant manager, consulting no one, chose not to make the part. As a consequence, D.A.B. never delivered the goods and the diversification opportunity was lost.

ASSESSING THE CURRENT STATUS

Every type of manufacturing business has a more or less characteristic cost structure: of the total manufacturing cost, say, W percent for materials, X percent for direct labor, Y percent for indirect labor, Z percent for manufacturing staff and supervision, and so on. The troubled business has to be measured against this to learn if it differs from the norm in some significant way. The study of these differences leads to insight useful in discerning fundamental problems.

How do you go about assessing the current status of manufacturing? Remember, the further removed your source of information is from the actual event, the less likely the information is to be currently correct. There is no substitute for walking a plant—every aisle. Observing housekeeping, scrap, the work pace, the amount and distribution of work in process, which machines are actually in use, and the like often tells a skilled observer more about the status of an operation than a pile of reports.

It will also reveal problems not committed to paper, for example, an "early-quit" problem. This is the common, but never acknowledged, practice of production workers stopping working at some time before the end of the shift. In some plants this means the end of effective output after six or seven hours. A quick unaccompanied walk of the plant a half hour before the shift ends shows you whether or not you have this problem.

Dust or rust observed on inventory (including raw materials, finished goods, or work in process) may reveal slow-moving or obsolete goods. Piles of work-in-process inventory with special tags, stashed various places, could alert you to production process problems.

These are effects and not necessarily causes. They are classic and almost always appear when a company is in trouble. One must be careful to analyze and identify the causes, rather than just treat the symptoms.

In walking a plant a recommended technique is to count the number of employees in sight and then recount those actually performing meaningful work during your "still" snapshot. This will give you a rough measure of utilization, a component of productivity. Look for a ratio of 60 to 70 percent. Anything below 50 percent represents what may be a nearly fatal problem. The question such a situation raises is why are things this bad? Who is tolerating it? Does the plant have a lack of, or bad, production standards? Is plant supervision shirking its responsibilities for some reason?

The perspective so far has been that of a single business in a single location. What do you do when there are a number of plants, probably making different products? In fact, they may be different businesses. This is a far more complex situation.

Obtaining information relevant to identifying critical problems and needs in this case is similar to conducting industrial market research. First, you read everything you can about what has transpired, the problems, the situation, and what solutions have been and are being implemented. Next, you gather organizational charts and personnel records and learn who the players are and their backgrounds. Then you visit the various facilities, key players, and their subordinates, gathering their views and perspectives, as well as important facts. This includes exploring such activities as order entry, cost accounting, plant management, plant purchasing, plant industrial relations, maintenance supervision, product engineering, manufacturing engineering, and production control. You obtain copies of their monthly reports, lists, purchase orders, and so on.

Much of the information gained this way will be contradictory. You learn that a step, supposedly implemented with success, hasn't even started and is, in fact, irrelevant. Much of what is learned will be contrary to long-accepted views of "the problem" and how to handle it.

In these visits you must watch the various production processes from beginning to end. Unless you understand how things are actually made, you will not be able to put things into proper perspective.

The troubled True Temper Corporation hand tool operation (i.e., hammers and axes), which lost money year after year, was a good example of the need to do this. The long-held management view was that low productivity in the forging of axe and hammer heads was the main problem. The proposed solution was the investment of millions of dollars in new forging equipment. Investigation found this aspect of their manufacturing sequence to have a minor unfavorable cost impact. In studying every facility, a warehouse in Nashville was found to be filled with hundreds of thousands of abandoned wooden handles. Tracing this back to their handle factory, it was discovered that 30 percent of handle production was graded "C" after manufacture and practically unused, owing to brown streaks in the wood (which were cosmetic—strength wasn't impaired). The competition obviously produced a similar mix of handles, owing to the nature of the wood, but dipped them in brown stain and used them. The handle problem was unknown to upper management. It was discovered only through firsthand investigation. It represented a needless cost penalty of thirteen cents per hammer. To make matters worse, grade "C" hammer handles, which had cost thirty cents each to make, were being sold to Stanley Tool Works, their largest competitor, for ten cents each, in order to recover part of the cost. In effect, True Temper was subsidizing its competitor's products.

No manufacturing is without problems. Defective materials arrive, or good materials arrive late, leading to late deliveries. Customers change their specifications. Engineering makes design errors that are spotted after the fact, in manufacturing. Productivity is below what it should be. How well manufacturing management copes with the ever occurring problems is a test of their ability. If shipments are always late, quality problems are endemic, and production costs go up rather than down over time, there is a problem in manufacturing management.

MANUFACTURING STRATEGY

Companies need a manufacturing strategy—what is to be made and where. If the company has a number of manufacturing plants, the question often is which one to use. This is as important to established products as it is to new ones. If, for instance, the plant where the product is made has high labor rates, say, 25 percent higher than those of another plant, then moving the product line should be seriously considered. In time, major operating cost elements change: nonunion plants become unionized; different plants evolve different wage costs; relative labor productivities change; customer locations and purchased item sources change. These aspects should influence the manufacturing location strategy. If no thought is periodically given this question, the company may drift into unprofitability.

An illustration of such a situation was the True Temper Corporation's manufacture of hammers and axes. Their handles were made in a plant with an hourly wage averaging $6.50 per hour. These were sent to a second plant, organized by another union, which forged and finished the hammer and axe heads and then joined the handles to the heads. The average wage rate in the second plant was $11.60 per hour. About one-third of the workers in the second plant were engaged in assembly and packaging. No one had considered shipping the heads to the handle plant for assembly at the wage rate of $6.50 per hour, instead of their current practice of shipping the handles to the head plant, where the wage rates averaged $11.60 per hour. Including fringe benefit costs, this move would have resulted in an annual savings of $1.1 million. Moving the assembly operation required a one-time cost of only $300,000. This example is an exceptional case. Usually one-time costs associated with moving production have a much slower payback.

A move to an entirely new facility (frequently in the Sun Belt) may be another viable alternative. A good example of this is the move of the headquarters and manufacturing plant of National Lock Cabinet Hardware, Inc., from Rockford, Illinois, to Spartanburg, South Carolina. In 1982, just before the move, their cost of hourly manufacturing labor, including fringe benefits, in Rockford averaged $16 to $17 per hour. In 1985 their Spartanburg hourly manufacturing labor cost, including fringe benefits, averaged $8.04 per hour. The Spartanburg facilities have about 400 salaried and hourly employees.

The choice of proper manufacturing location should be influenced by factors other than labor costs alone. Costs of utilities and taxes may be important. Availability of the right skills must be satisfied. Proximity to raw materials or markets may be important considerations. The choice of where to manufacture a product must be based on optimizing all pertinent aspects.

Manufacturing strategy has dimensions other than selection of where to manufacture the product. These include make/buy decisions and the amount of vertical integration. Many times a product, or a component of a product, can be bought from a job shop specializing in this type of item for far less than it would cost a firm to manufacture the item itself. The decision to do this, and its impact on manpower and capital spending, has to be part of the manufacturing strategy.

The degree of vertical integration in a company's manufacturing should be the result of careful analysis, rather than of historical accident. Frequently, backward integration does not provide a return commensurate with the capital employed. In fact, there may be no return, if the product, or component, can be bought for less on the outside. The reason lies in the difference in competitiveness of items or manufacturing services bought in a competitive environment compared with those obtained from a captive source.

The additional question must be raised of how to manufacture. Manufacturing processes must be reexamined for their relative total costs. Many common cylindrical parts, for example, are made on automatic screw machines, which is a reliable production process. However, screw machines may require up to eighteen hours to set up for a change in part. CNC (computer numerical control) lathes may be able to make the same part, with a set-up of only one hour or less. These kinds of alternatives frequently exist. A failure to identify and address cost-reducing changes in manufacturing methods will, over time, degrade the profitability of a firm. The cumulative effect of this type of neglect may be a major factor in the current need for a turnaround.

Troubled industrial firms often have a weak or nonexistent manufacturing engineering capability. To properly identify and assess alternatives to current manufacturing processes requires having such people on staff. They must be allowed to travel to relevant trade shows and vendors. It is almost impossible to send manufacturing engineers to the biannually held International Machine Tool Show, for example, without their identifying a number of ways to significantly improve manufacturing processes.

PRODUCTIVITY MEASUREMENT AND CONTROL

Increasing the productivity of manufacturing operations requires us to face the question of what we mean by productivity. Basically, we provide capital, in the form of plant and equipment, and inventory. To this we add staff, management, and labor. We want to optimize the use of these inputs in obtaining the required production quantities. Too often companies in trouble cut back these inputs beyond what is reasonable, and thereby hurt productivity and raise product costs.

The "effectiveness" of the manufacturing operation, that is, the potential maximum output per unit of direct labor, depends largely on the manufacturing processes used and the equipment employed. This is directly related to the history and magnitude of capital investments (and process research and development). No matter how well a labor force is managed, the best that can be achieved cannot exceed the intrinsic "effectiveness" of the operation.

In a turnaround situation it is normally advisable to limit further capital investment for two reasons: (1) the capital may not be available and (2) considerable risk is attached to achieving a satisfactory turnaround. Therefore, the wish is to avoid the possibility of throwing good money after bad. In many instances the management responsible for the economic decline of a division will have claimed that the division's problem was obsolete equipment, which can only be remedied by substantial new investment. Seldom is this the primary cause of the troubled situation. A turnaround, therefore, largely focuses on making the best use of existing equipment, owing to the low availability of capital.

How well you use your labor force may be termed your labor "efficiency." Frequently people blame low efficiency (usually termed low productivity) on the work attitudes of the employees. This is only a partial explanation. After all, employees are told what to do and how to do it. The primary cause of low efficiency, probably 75 percent or more, is due to management. Examples: not providing the proper tools to workers at their work stations, making the workers wander around looking for them; not providing proper information to workers, such as a missing dimension on a blueprint; not properly scheduling the workers' activities or the order in which they are to do things. Low worker efficiency is really a management rather than a worker problem.

Sometimes labor "efficiency" is maximized by taking steps to keep people working at the fastest practical pace, with as little downtime/unproductive time as possible. One frequently successful approach is to underman production operations. Manning estimates are usually based on all machines being in working order and operating. In reality, some equipment is always down for such things as a sanding belt change, tool replacement, or drive repair. Foremen should be expected and required to immediately move production people onto backup production work when their regular task cannot be done. Making this a normal approach to management has frequently decreased labor costs by 10 to 15 percent. However, this approach is applicable *only* when meeting schedule is not of critical importance, for example, in manufacturing standard products to meet constant inventory levels, as in hand tools.

Another tactic in improving efficiency is to find and eliminate "early-quit" problems. This arises when production workers develop an informal consensus as to how much they should be expected to produce, and stop producing when this level is achieved. Occasionally this problem can increase the direct labor per unit of output by as much as 20 to 30 percent. Solving an early-quit problem requires forcing first-level supervision, foremen, not to let it happen. Employees who stop working before the end of the shift, and supervision who permit this to occur, must be disciplined. In the same vein, late starts, extra coffee breaks, wandering around, and other unacceptable uses of employee time may no longer be permitted by supervisors.

In resolving the problem of supervisory permissiveness in regard to the misuse of employee time, one must usually go back to basics. Are there published rules of employee conduct? If not, then management must publish and enforce them. It will also be necessary to conduct refresher meetings with foremen to reinforce their support of the company rules and review the proper procedures to discipline employees to make sure disciplinary actions are upheld.

Productivity is the combined result of "effectiveness" and "efficiency," as defined earlier. To avoid confusion in using these terms, just remember:

Effectiveness—doing the right things.

Efficiency—doing things right.

Improving productivity requires attention to these two separate areas.

The secret to improved productivity in the industrial environment is to look at efficiency in a new light. The machinist, welder, or assembler has little control over his efficiency other than to cheat. Approximately 25 percent of inefficiency is directly attributable to the operator; the responsibility for the rest can be placed directly in the hands of management. Therefore, emphasis must be placed on knowing, measuring, controlling, and reducing the various elements of management inefficiency, as well as operator inefficiency.

The key to obtaining greater efficiency in using direct labor is detailed monitoring of how labor is currently used. This means putting in a labor analysis system (usually manually, at first) that categorizes all uses as percentages of productive use. Items such as machine repair, plant transportation, idle time, store keeping, rework, and standard labor variance are presented as percentages of productive labor. This gives you a basis for direct action. If machine repair is averaging 35 percent of productive labor, you know this aspect is wildly out of kilter and must be corrected.

An example of this approach to controlling labor usage and improving productivity is the use of the weekly report shown in Table 9–1. Every use of labor other than achieving production at standard rates is shown as a percentage of standard direct labor. This immediately puts the data into a meaningful context, which would not occur if one looked at actual hours or dollars alone. This is an extremely powerful tool because any significant unreasonable use of labor stands out. The report can be prepared at a number of levels corresponding to the needs of the user: one for the company as a whole; one for each plant for the plant manager; and one for each section of a plant for the superintendent of that area.

Supervision, which is not hourly labor, has been included in the report of Table 9–1. This is a true cost of production and must be controlled in the context of the relation between productivity and degree of supervision. By presenting hourly labor and its supervision together, you are forced to face this issue.

Today, with computers, every company generates a great deal of data. The challenge is to organize the data into a useful management tool. The report of Table 9–1 does just that. The benefits deriving from a good labor usage reporting system is shown in Figure 9–1. This graph shows the actual improvement in labor productivity obtained at Danly Machine Corporation over a seven-and-a-half-month period—some 37 percent!

Troubled operations constantly have lower monthly shipments than forecasted, with the slip being discovered only near the end of the month. They need a real-time approach to monitoring their level of output that allows them to respond to problems (e.g., scheduling overtime, adding workers, subcontracting). A simple and effective method for operations using standard cost accounting utilizing labor standards is to record *daily* the standard hours earned. The very next day, management will know whether the output of the previous day was satisfactory.

Such an approach, which is applicable to almost any type of manufacturing operation, improves profitability by increasing monthly sales and decreasing the underabsorption of manufacturing burden. It also brings productivity problems to the fore, as low productivity can be a major reason for lower-than-expected earned hours.

The daily tracking of standard direct labor earned hours was adopted with instant beneficial results in companies as diverse as Blaw Knox Rolls, a process-type company operating large foundries and machine shops, and Blaw Knox Food & Chemical Equipment Company, a fabricator and assembler of special machinery.

Improvement in productivity is not an automatic result of accurately measuring

Table 9–1.
Weekly Comparison: Direct and Indirect Labor

TOTAL HOURS	4/08	4/15	4/22
STANDARD DIRECT LABOR	7484.6	7888.5	6391.1

PERCENT OF TOTAL HOURS OF STANDARD DIRECT LABOR

STANDARD DIRECT LABOR	4/08	4/15	4/22
Production	87.4	87.3	88.3
Setup	12.6	12.7	11.7
Total	100.0	100.0	100.0

NONSTANDARD DIRECT LABOR

	4/08	4/15	4/22
Variance : Setup (+)	1.9	2.4	1.9
Setup (-)	-3.1	-3.0	-2.7
Production (+)	16.9	15.5	14.7
Production (-)	-19.6	-19.5	-20.6
Rework	2.5	2.1	1.6
Added Operations	4.5	4.9	5.0
Regular Daywork	14.3	10.1	10.5
Delay: Nonproductive	2.6	2.1	1.7
Other: Nonproductive	8.0	6.6	5.4
Capitalized Repairs	5.2	4.1	4.3
Inspection	13.6	13.0	13.4
Customer repair	9.6	9.1	9.0
Total	56.4	47.4	44.2

INDIRECT LABOR

	4/08	4/15	4/22
Crane Service	7.3	6.6	6.8
Plant and Office Cleaning	7.9	8.2	7.7
Plant Transportation	3.4	3.2	3.5
Tool Crib	2.1	1.9	1.2
Press Store	5.1	5.0	4.8
Heat, Light and Power	4.5	4.3	4.9
Maintenance	6.6	5.8	4.7
Machine Repair	6.9	7.5	6.5
Tool Grinding	4.7	4.0	3.9
Indirect Helpers	6.6	5.3	5.2
Union Officials	1.1	1.0	1.0
Total	56.2	52.8	50.2

SUPERVISION	29.4	27.9	26.7

GRAND TOTAL	242.0	228.1	221.1

and tracking productivity. It is the numerous management actions that have to take place, based on the availability of this data, that improve productivity. If action isn't taken, productivity will not improve.

Another approach to productivity improvement is participative cost reduction. Implement a program of creative and motivational meetings, and encourage all members of the professional and management team to search out ways of improving costs. Every technique of value analysis, brainstorming, methods im-

Figure 9–1.
Improvement in Labor Productivity at Danly Machine Corporation over 7.5 Month Period

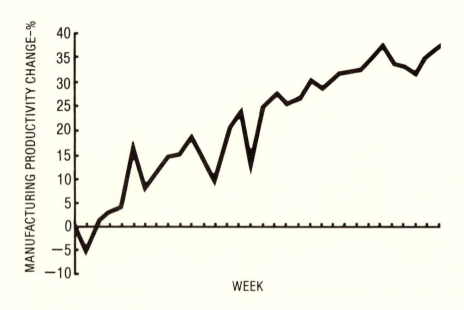

provement, tool improvement, quality control, make/buy analysis, productivity, simplification, and standardization should be used to attack costs. Most important, encourage everyone to be involved in the program.

As the program progresses, you should encourage the hourly employees to participate and, after some time, possibly reward them in some monetary form. The salaried employees should not be rewarded monetarily, since this is already part of their job. Management should, however, acknowledge their efforts with quarterly recognition dinners. Outstanding achievers could be rewarded with trophy awards. A well-run program not only provides significant savings to the company, but is also a real morale builder; employees feel that they are participating and involved in rebuilding the company.

What about nonmanufacturing labor—the productivity of the office staffs and professional groups? Substantial productivity improvements are obtainable if better operating procedures are used and organizational arrangements are improved. To accomplish this, classic industrial engineering approaches should be used by skilled objective parties; frequently consultants are needed because the necessary skills are simply not available within the company.

Interviews examining what people do, how they do it, why they do it, and so on lead to recommendations for work simplification, elimination of duplication of effort, job combination, faster response time, organizational improvements, and the like. This approach has been successfully applied to such functions as accounting, sales, purchasing, employee relations, engineering, manufacturing methods and standards, and others. Frequently professional groups say that what they do is different and not suitable for such treatment. Don't you believe it.

WORK RULES

For control purposes, and to maintain administrative consistency, manufacturing plants are usually operated in conformance with established procedures and work rules. In unionized plants these rules are part of the labor contract and can be changed only through negotiation. Frequently the work rules have become fossilized and represent a severe economic burden on the company. Unions are reluctant to agree to changes because they feel that every word in the labor contract was hard earned and fought for in labor negotiations. They want "make work." They want more employees on the payroll than are needed. They do not consider the profitability of the company to be one of their concerns. In achieving a turnaround, management must squarely face the work rules issue.

In general, the fewer work rules, the better—the better with regard to working environment and manufacturing productivity.

Managements are commonly found to have taken either a neglectful or a hopeless attitude toward plant work rules problems. A bad situation is invariably much worse than it has to be. Labor contracts do not require companies to employ workers who either are incompetent or have low productivity. The contracts, however, usually make it exceedingly difficult to fire such employees unless strict due process has been followed. First-level supervision (i.e., foremen) need to fully understand the grounds, procedures, documentation, and clarity of purpose needed to do so. Too often little or no training in these aspects has been given, and "support" from higher management comes in the form of criticism for a bungled confrontation. One or two bungled attempts, because of lack of know-how, to justifiably discipline an employee are usually enough to preserve an economically intolerable status quo in a plant.

Foremen must receive thorough training (e.g., at once-a-week dinner meetings held over a period of two to three months). A major subject of this training should be clarification of the actual terms of the existing labor contract. Frequently foremen have failed to act because they didn't know what the company's rights were under the contract, or the terms of the contract were misrepresented by union stewards and the foremen didn't know better. Foremen must be shown just what can legally be done within the limits of the labor agreement, and the proper way to discipline employees who do not conform. After a few bad apples have been fired, and the firings have withstood the test of a formal grievance procedure (and possibly arbitration), esprit among the foremen greatly improves. Things thought to be impossible under the contractual work rules begin to become possible. Morale significantly improves; after all, nobody likes to see rules being flouted.

Working to the limit of the work rules does not change the contractual obligations on work rules. These must be made the priority subject of the next labor negotiations, and the company must decide if this is a subject worth taking a strike over. Often it is. However, an effort should be made, before starting actual negotiations, to educate people with regard to the reasons and needs for changing work rules. Many companies have entered labor negotiations demanding changes in the work rules but, when the union refused to make these concessions, backed down, as they feared that a strike would put them out of business. Shortly thereafter these same companies often failed, owing to the losses incurred by not eliminating the unsound work rules. Remember, the risk of going out of business because of a strike (on the issue of work rules) may be no greater than the risk of going out of business from not satisfactorily resolving the work rules problems.

A strike does not mean that a company has to cease operating for the duration. Hiring new workers (frequently at lower wages) as ''economic replacements'' to work under your new, productive work rules is perfectly legal and becoming more and more common. It greatly reduces the risk and cost of a strike.

There are a multitude of unsound work rules, but here are some of the most damaging:

- *Fixed Manning/Crew Size.* The number of workers required is permanently fixed, whether or not this number is currently realistic. At a steel company, for example, an electric arc furnace crew may be set at seven men, whereas current methods require only four. The presence of firemen on diesel locomotives was another example of this type.

- *Excessive Number of Job Classifications.* In many plants balkanization of the types of work has evolved, with 150 or 200 job classifications. Each work element must be performed by someone in the right classification. Jobs that would be more efficiently performed by a single individual now have to be performed using a multiplicity of individuals. For example, if you want to move a heavy object using a crane, you have to permit the separate jobs of rigger (to wrap the lifting chains around the object) and craneman (to operate the crane), instead of the one position of craneman/rigger. I observed a particularly bad example at McDonnell Douglas. They used two technicians to run a simple test machine; one was the mechanical technician and the other an electrical technician, as it was a mechanical device having an electrical on/off switch. The solution to this problem is to combine the various job classifications into the smallest practical number.

- *Inflexibility in Work Assignments.* To be productive, you need the ability to make temporary transfers, that is, to assign personnel across classification lines briefly (say, two weeks or less), irrespective of seniority. Often you need something done temporarily, say, spending two hours grinding an item that has just been machined. It is costly and foolish to not be able to allow the machinist to finish the job instead of having to find/hire/recall someone else, with a resulting great loss in production time.

Inflexibility also creates unstable working conditions in which people are continually being laid off and recalled (which inherently hurts productivity). If a man runs out of work to do in his normal job, and you know that more of this type of work will be needed a week hence, and there is another productive way you could use him for the intervening week, then it is only sensible to be able to do so. The existing labor agreement may, however, require that the senior displaced employee, who used to perform the temporary assignment, be recalled. It may take forty-eight hours to bring in such an employee, by which time either the job has been completed (one way or another) or an undue delay has occurred.

• *Excessive Job Classification Bidding.* An excessive ability of employees to bid on changing jobs will lead to people continually bumping in and out of positions. Proficiency remains low, owing to the brief dwell time in each position. Administration of such a system becomes a nightmare. The solution is for job bids to be for an initial opening only, rather than for an entire series of different jobs. Contract language must provide that an employee remain in a classification of record for, say, six months before being eligible for the next promotional bid.

• *Equal or Lower Related.* Contract provisions for permitting downward-bumping employees to come into "equal or lower-related" assignments, rather than into their classification of record, leads to people being assigned tasks they are not completely qualified to do, which creates inefficiency on the shop floor. The solution is to eliminate "equal or lower related" from layoff and recall.

• *Time to Show Proficiency.* On a job posting with an employee having thirty days, or other long period, to demonstrate his ability to perform the task, this frequently becomes "a right to fail" process, resulting in the time and expense of further posting.

• *Paid Agenda Meetings.* Meetings held on employee grievances and incentive pay issues, if conducted on company time, are frequently abused and become a paid invitation for people to unnecessarily complain and avoid work. One commonly finds the company paying for the lost time of the grievant, steward, and committeeman that was spent in the initial and supplemental meetings. The contract should be changed in order to eliminate agenda meetings, grievance and incentive, from being conducted on company time.

• *Supervisors' Right to Work.* Many contracts have work prohibition clauses preventing supervisors from doing productive work. In situations where a supervisor supervises only a few persons (e.g., a foreman and three workers), it makes little economic sense for him to be unable to assist production.

• *Temporary Layoffs.* Companies need the right to make temporary layoffs without regard to seniority. If an employee is not needed for a few days, the turmoil and low productivity resulting from his bumping another employee into layoff status for these few days is economically intolerable, but common.

• *Call-in Pay.* If an employee is needed for only part of a shift, it is legitimate to make this subject to a minimum-pay provision, say, for four hours. But some contracts require a full day's pay for any amount of work, regardless of how little.

• *Multiple Machines.* Management must retain the right to extend the job scope to require machine operators to run machines in tandem, when this is technically feasible. This problem is illustrated by the Caterpillar Tractor Company plant in Montgomery, Illinois, where I once observed a row of fifteen or twenty identical numerically controlled machines, each with its own operator, who had little to do most of the time. It would have been easy enough to have each operator run two or three machines.

- *Production Standards.* Production standards are frequently frozen after a short period, say, ninety days, before it is realized that they are far too loose. The company should have the right, at any time, to change a production standard that is found to be inappropriate because the methods or conditions are not in accordance with those of the planned rate. This quick freezing of production standards prevents improvement in output. It also means old standards are never updated.

- *Outsourcing/Subcontracting.* Companies must have the right, at any time, to shift production from one company facility to another and to switch to purchase of an item or service previously the responsibility of its own employees. An inability to do this represents a rigidity in responsiveness to market forces. The consequences can be fatal for a company.

Looking over this list, the items are philosophically similar. They are all restrictions on management action that inflate the number and reduce the productivity of employees. They represent a bleeding of the economic vitality of the company. Work rules are a major subject that cannot be ignored in managing the turnaround of a troubled company. Far too often they are ignored because their solution may necessitate a strike. A strike should not be sought, but avoiding one at the price of retaining insufferable work rules is not the answer.

The union and work force must be confronted with these obstructions to continued operations. The options that exist should be honestly and directly discussed long before beginning labor contract negotiations. The message has to be clearly sent that the enemy is not management, but the competition, and the sooner management and labor join forces and start beating the competition, the better everyone's chances are of keeping their jobs.

PLANT MOVING AND CONSOLIDATION

Plant consolidation is a painful process that has to be considered when a company has permanent significant excess capacity (in light of current business conditions).

Apart from the direct product costs, each plant has a significant overhead intrinsic to its existence: personnel staff, guard service, lighting and heat, real estate taxes, and so on. Combining plants will have a significant initial cost, but thereafter, this duplicated overhead is permanently eliminated.

Combining may have another, subtler advantage. It forces you to look at which products to move and which to eliminate. It forces you to face the psychologically difficult task of pruning the product line. Underutilized plants have a tendency to retain manufacturing of products that are no longer profitable, in order to retain employees. If the manufacturing capacity of the combined plant will be less than that of the separate plants, the decision to prune marginally profitable products will be forced to happen.

A sometimes successful variation on the theme of plant consolidation is to reduce one plant to being a satellite of the other, with production limited to a single high-volume product. Almost all independent plant overhead is eliminated. The satellite plant needs just a few foremen and workers, with all staff functional needs met by the other plant. The cost of the limited product line made on this basis drops significantly.

The decision regarding which plant or plants are to survive and which are to be eliminated deserves careful analysis. There is a natural tendency to retain the new, large plant in preference to the older, smaller, less aesthetic plant. This may mean keeping the white elephant in preference to the truly economically productive operation. The analysis should look at all aspects and be as fair-minded as possible. Consolidating plants will have the same aspects as moving a plant if the product is strange to its new location.

Many operations have gone out of business as a result of a move. Careful planning and investigation has to be given the questions of whether or not employees with the right skills can be found in the new location, and whether or not needed support services can be found in the locale.

In the move of D.A.B. Industries' Detroit area stamping plant to the Sun Belt, the ability to attract a work force with the right skills was a major concern. The Fantus Company, using census data, matched all counties in "right-to-work" states less than a two-day drive to Detroit against a criterion of 0.3 percent of the labor force being engaged in metalworking manufacturing. This was their test of being able to find the needed skills in the labor market. The only counties to pass the test constituted the northern third of Alabama and adjoining corners of Mississippi and Georgia. The plant was finally located in Athens, Alabama, and came on-stream fast, owing to readily available labor with the right skills.

In moving a plant, a number of objective criteria should be considered:

- Availability of labor with the necessary skills
- Attractive area wage rates
- Right to work law
- Good work ethic (low percentage of work force unionization)
- Absence of unemployment compensation payments to strikers (which would eliminate, for example, New York, Rhode Island, and Illinois)
- Suitable land and building costs
- Ability to finance plant using low-interest industrial revenue bonds issued by a local governmental agency
- Low taxes (real estate, workman's compensation, inventory, franchise, etc)
- Good transportation
- Proximity to major airport
- Reasonable transportation costs of products to customers and of raw materials to the plant

- Quality of life for management
- Low utility rates
- Welcome attitude toward industry

Moves under contemplation contrary to these criteria deserve severe scrutiny. A move is always a great risk. Even moves that meet all of these criteria can end in disaster.

An unfortunately not infrequent result of a move taken to save the company by reducing labor costs is the production of products of unsatisfactory quality. It is usually underestimated how much special know-how is involved in making an established product in an old plant using longtime employees. Because of the poor product quality, customers are lost and the operation goes out of business relatively quickly. Two examples typify this sequence of events.

Eaton Corporation manufactured die springs in Ohio for many years. They moved the die spring operation to South Carolina and lost the ability to make satisfactory die springs. They left the business and sold their equipment to their main customer, which satisfactorily restarted the business in another locale (Chicago) that possessed a labor pool with the right skills. Today the restarted spring operation in Chicago is the leading supplier of die springs.

For many years Carmet Company supplied the tool and die and wire drawing industries with tungsten carbide parts made in an operation in the Detroit area. The operation was moved to South Carolina and, after a short period, had to close down because they were unable to make products of acceptable quality.

A frequent mistake observed in moving troubled manufacturing operations in order to obtain lower costs is the movement of obsolete machinery, production processes, and operating methods. Old machinery often requires special nursing to keep running, and long experience in doing so. Moves that don't include adoption of modern methods and processes (i.e., CNC, CAD/CAM, MRP, robotics, etc.) tend to have greater problems.

Another strategic question to be examined is whether or not the movement of an operation will actually overcome its poor performance. Westinghouse Electric Corporation performed a postmortem on eleven originally poor-performing operations that had been moved, largely to new Sun Belt locations, over a period of ten years. The study found that none of the operations achieved the projected results that were the basis for proceeding with the moves. On average, after five years, the individual operations were performing as poorly as they had been before the move. A partial explanation of this is that the new locations operated with the same companywide norms (i.e., administrative procedures, methods, compensation schemes) as used in the old locations. Perhaps a change in locale is not enough. The move should probably bring a change in management methods, approaches, and perspectives.

In deciding whether or not to move an operation to a new location, somewhere in the United States, there are several useful rules of thumb:

• Don't run from a union or labor problem; face it head on.

• Don't run for cheap labor because it is often not skilled, or unproductive (unless you need primarily unskilled labor).

• Don't move unless you install modern equipment, facilities, processes, and systems.

• Don't move unless all of the evaluation factors are significantly improved, including taxes and government assistance.

INCENTIVE PAY SYSTEMS

Incentive pay systems, in which additional compensation is paid for production exceeding a base level, in unionized plants, are an almost certain method of developing low productivity. Often these systems were installed with the belief that they would help to spur productivity. In practice, the opposite often prevails. Unfortunately, incentive systems are usually firmly embedded in a union contract, so change requires long negotiation, which is not necessarily successful.

The base for incentive calculation normally becomes out of date, owing to numerous small changes that evolve over time. These arise because of the normal inventiveness of man. It is impractical to resurvey every process routing for minor changes. Yet, over time, these minor changes add up to significant improvement. Another reason is that many union agreements prohibit resetting the base level unless the changes in manufacturing procedure are major. Incentive systems, therefore, may be an important contributor to high unit cost.

A prime example was the situation of coil handlers at Allegheny Ludlum Steel Corporations. Under an incentive system these men were paid additional compensation for loading coils onto trucks when the total weight loaded for the shift exceeded a certain level. When this incentive system was instituted, steel sheet coils weighed 2,000 pounds each. In time, customers wanted 4,000-pound coils. Then a market shift occurred to 8,000-pound coils. It takes about the same time to load any size coils, so by 1977 coil handlers were receiving wages of $50,000 per year. Negotiations with the steelworkers' union to eliminate this proved fruitless; they had no reason to give up this sweet arrangement. The incentive system, therefore, increased rather than decreased unit labor costs.

Incentive systems also lend themselves to abuse and must be carefully policed. In one plant the incentive applied only to machine uptime, so false machine downtimes were recorded. The actual production applied to the fictitiously reduced operating hours resulted in generous incentive payments, part of which were kicked back to the clerks who kept the records.

When a company is in trouble, its workers know it is in trouble. With everyone understanding this, a fresh attempt should be made to renegotiate union contract provisions pertaining to incentive pay.

One of the fresh approaches to the incentive question is group gain sharing (which goes by many names). Here the group as a whole, not individuals, frequently including foremen, participate in improvements in productivity compared with some reference time. The reference time becomes important. If it was a time of low productivity and significant improvements in productivity could be or were achieved through just good, normal management, then a payout is occurring for nothing and the initial objective has been subverted. You don't need a group incentive system in order to eliminate an early-quit problem. Warnings, suspensions, and firings will do it nicely. The second major question is how to split the gains. Many plan advocates urge fifty-fifty. Such a high value should not be necessary. Companies should be wary of too generous a split.

Group incentives may also lead to increased, rather than decreased, unit costs in comparison with those of competitors. This is seldom appreciated when installing such a system. The reason is that the employees' gains are usually forever; they don't phase out with time. Progress in manufacturing methods should be considered normal. Sooner or later, by movement of people, methods improvements become widely known and copied. If one company adopts changes in order to improve its productivity and pays its workers more, then in time the innovating company will have higher unit costs than the competing copying company.

SCHEDULING

Continually missed shipping schedules are a symptom of poor plant administration, production control, purchasing, engineering, quality assurance, or all of these. Usually a significant cost penalty is associated with the reason the schedule was missed. It is important to learn the reasons and if these constitute a general problem needing immediate attention. Usually they do.

Scheduling exists on at least two levels. First, the global level, which might be termed production planning and analysis, contains all the elements that have to be orchestrated to meet the customer promise date. These include engineering (if it is not a standard item), purchasing, and production control. The scheduling group has to interact with the various functions and vouchsafe the sales commitments or develop a new and feasible commitment. Much new, simple, cheap software exists to run on Apple or IBM PCs that makes scheduling to customer commitments much more practical, accurate, and timely.

Dealing with the schedule and its problems, what they are and why, gives great insight into general company problems that have to be solved as part of the turnaround.

Scheduling goods through the plant, production scheduling, is the second type of scheduling and is dependent on how effectively the manufacturing operation is controlled. In a turnaround it is not usually controlled enough. Goods are frequently lost track of until they emerge at various points in the system. Large amounts of time may pass between these points, and the bloated resulting work-in-process inventory level may put a strain on the firm's working capital capacity.

Fresh production scheduling approaches, frequently manual rather than electronic data processing-based, are often needed. Goods have to be tracked in progress if the schedule is to be compressed. Compressing what is often an excessively long processing time must be accomplished if customer response is to be improved and working capital reduced.

PLANT LAYOUT

Most U.S. manufacturing plants are laid out in a manner representing how they grew, with each machine in its original location, rather than in a production use sequence. This means that items are continually being moved between all sections of the manufacturing facility. This movement takes a great deal of time. In a typical production sequence, which might take eight weeks, five weeks may be spent in material handling among the different activity centers of a plant. All this handling is quite expensive. Someone is physically handling the transport of the goods time after time. The working capital needs of the firm are enormously increased by the long manufacturing process time (incurring additional interest costs on this capital as well). The flexibility of the company to react to the market is severely restricted by this long time.

The alternative is to carefully examine the flow of material and relayout the plant on this basis, so as to minimize material handling. Each machine should be adjacent to the next machine in the manufacturing sequence, rather than near its general relative (i.e., lathes with lathes, grinders with grinders). Of course, this won't be perfect, as some production that doesn't follow the most common sequence will exist and will need material movements similar to those discussed before. But it is far better to have this pertain to some of the production than to have it pertain to most of the production.

A frequently unanticipated benefit of relaying out the work flow is the elimination of much indirect personnel, in addition to no longer needed material handlers. Workers naturally take on additional tasks because it becomes convenient for them to do so. An illustration is the manufacture of a large turned part at Sturtevant, an industrial blower company located near Boston. Previously someone in the materials area would cut off the correct lengths of large-diameter bar stock and send them on to the lathe operator, who, in turn, would turn the part and send it on to inspection to be checked. Now, while one part is in the lathe being turned, the lathe operator himself cuts off the next piece of bar stock from the near-at-hand bar inventory and loads it into his lathe at the right time. While the lathe is cutting, he also has time to carefully inspect the last finished piece, eliminating the need to send it on to a separate inspection department.

Very large capital equipment can have installation expenses as high as its purchase cost. For this economic reason, such equipment must usually be kept where it currently sits. But this is an exception and can be looked on as such.

Relayout of manufacturing operations requires expertise beyond the skills of ordinary plant engineers; the question is not how to install it, but where to install it. If such professional in-house facilities engineering capability doesn't exist, obtain it. The savings will far outweigh the costs.

QUALITY

Quality costs are usually a sleeper-type of issue in a turnaround. Generally, the firm doesn't know what they are. As a rough guess, one may take the purported scrap and rework and field service costs and multiply this sum by four to arrive at an estimate. This is often a significant sum. Developing an understanding of current quality costs improves one's understanding of major operational deficiencies that require solution.

The troubled operation usually has a quality control function but no quality assurance function. Conceptually, this is important. Quality control is the system of activities whose purpose is to control the quality of product or service by verifying it against established specifications. Quality assurance, on the other hand, has the broader perspective of ensuring that the product or service will meet the needs of users in the sense of being satisfactory, dependable, and economic.

The first step in coming to grips with quality cost is to quantify current and recent quality costs. These costs may be organized into the categories of prevention, appraisal, internal failure, and external failure. Prevention includes quality administration, quality engineering, supplier assurance, maintenance (on equipment, machine tools, dies, jigs, and fixtures), and, possibly, amortization of dies, jigs, and fixtures. Appraisal includes manufacturing inspection and test, and supplier inspection and test (including incoming inspection). Internal failure includes scrap and rework owing to manufacturing errors, engineering errors and changes, sales-induced errors, and supplier errors. External failure includes warranty costs, field service costs, and product liability costs.

Having identified these components of quality cost, you can see that they may add up to significant sums. Making this analysis usually points out areas needing prompt examination and improvement. Doing so is worth the effort.

Reduction in quality costs in general, once you have identified them, requires a thorough effort to define your quality system specifications, train operating management to quality concepts, and establish a total quality assurance program plan.

Two cultural changes generally must occur to significantly reduce quality costs:

• Top Management must convey and show by examples and attitudes that quality is first; it can't be compromised.

• The management team must begin to become "intolerant" of defects. This intolerance of defects will filter down to lower management and hourly employees.

The cultural changes can be reinforced by placing quality awareness posters at strategic locations in the manufacturing plant and by instituting weekly quality problem meetings of top management and operating management.

Reducing quality costs also needs the existence of effective process control.

To obtain effective process control, particularly in process-type industries, the following elements are needed, as a minimum:

- Purchasing specifications are required for all raw materials. Receiving inspection should be instituted on a sampling basis.
- Process specifications and checklists are required to identify the critical parameters involved in each process. These parameters should be verified *and* documented by the hourly worker, the supervisor, or an inspector. This should assist in cause-and-effect analysis. In addition, guidelines should be given on process parameters that *cannot be deviated from.*
- Statistical analysis should be done on selected processes to provide a tool of control.
- The process control engineer should be given the authority to stop any process that will not give the desired results.

The pragmatic question arises of what to do before your total quality assurance program is in place, when too high a proportion of output consists of rejects. It is a natural tendency to continue operating while tinkering along the way; you don't want to miss delivery. This is usually the most expensive way to try to solve the problem. Admit that the shipping schedule cannot be met as promised. Stop everything and think through the problem. Then implement the solution. Usually production needs are more quickly met by doing it this way, and considerable losses are prevented.

JUST-IN-TIME PRODUCTION/KANBAN

Just-in-time (JIT) production, also called KANBAN, from the Japanese, is receiving widespread attention and being adopted by a number of companies. It may or may not be suitable for a particular firm, depending on a number of factors that will be discussed. Its adoption, when not truly appropriate, can have grave consequences.

The basic concept of JIT is to produce just in time for use and not before and, similarly, to receive purchase items just when needed and not hold them in inventory—no buffer stocks. That is, you receive what is needed, make the item; receive what is needed, make the item, and so on.

In achieving a JIT operation, the company works with its supplier, who must continually make small deliveries throughout the day. It must work with its manufacturing engineering group in order to devise ways to achieve rapid part-changeover. A changeover that once took ten hours must now take, say, ten minutes. A company must relayout its factory in order to achieve a direct man-ufacturing progression, without significant buffer or staging areas. If some operations must be slowed down to accommodate the overall pace and what would otherwise be considered excess capacity created, so be it. If additional equipment must be purchased to be now rendered single purpose in use, so be it.

The factory becomes a very different place. Work-in-process and raw materials inventories disappear and the space needed for them becomes unnecessary. The receiving area must be substantially larger than one is used to, in order to handle the greatly increased number of deliveries. Preventive maintenance becomes much more visible—breakdowns become intolerable.

What are the advantages of JIT production? Inventory costs significantly decrease, as there is so much less inventory. Less factory space is needed, which can save a considerable sum if a new facility is being bought. Much less time is taken to produce a product from beginning to end. Most of the time taken in production, perhaps 80 percent, normally is simply waiting as work in process for the next operation. By eliminating these dwells, a production time of three months might be reduced to three weeks. This allows a firm to possibly become much more responsive to the market. A substantial improvement in quality can possibly be obtained. Richard J. Schonberger has pointed out the following example (R. J. Schonberger, "Just in Time Production," *Quality Progress* (October 1984): 22–24):

Imagine a pure JIT operation—one piece production. Worker A makes a part and passes it on to Worker B, whose job is to join it to another part. But they do not fit. Worker B hands the part right back, telling Worker A that the part is bad. Worker A's reaction might be, "I thought the machine didn't sound right," or "I thought the raw material that we got from the new supplier was not good," or "I wondered how I was supposed to do it right—with no blueprints."

It is natural for such diagnostic thoughts to run through Worker A's head, because the *trail is still fresh*. Now consider the reaction if one thousand parts have been made, passed on as a lot to Worker B, found to be nonconforming, and sent back. Enough time would have passed that Worker A would have difficulty diagnosing the cause of the problem. The trail is cold. Producing in small lots enhances quality in the following six ways:

1. Large lots high in nonconformities are avoided.

2. The producer of the bad parts learns about it soon enough to diagnose the causes.

3. The cause sometimes is simple to cure on the spot by the worker and the worker's associates. They are quality controllers (and production controllers), not just makers.

4. Most data collected on the shop floor need not be kept very long, because problems needing attention surface soon after the causal events. Simple blackboards and clipboards serve well as data collection media. Since production workers are also quality controllers and need data to analyze nonconformities, they appreciate the need to record the data accurately.

5. Many of the problems and diagnoses require the attention of experts from Quality Assurance, Engineering, Maintenance, Purchasing and other staff groups. For these experts there is no hiding in offices, for they are continually summoned to the shop floor. They clearly pay their way by working on problems that tend naturally to set priorities for themselves according to their severity.

6. Blaming workers for bad quality is seen as folly, because the real causes—factors that are controllable by management—have a good chance to be discovered. In this

atmosphere, the worker is a partner in the quality effort, perhaps relishing the exposure of a problem rather than sweeping it under the rug.

With all these advantages, why is JIT a seldom appropriate and potentially dangerous manufacturing strategy? First, the company makes itself dependent on the reliability of shipments from its vendors. In Japan the vendors are often captive operations, located in geographical proximity to the customer. Is your supplier located within five or ten miles of your plant? Is your volume of purchases sufficient for him to make four, twelve, or sixteen deliveries per day? Usually neither of these conditions is met.

Second, you generally tie yourself to one vendor for an item, with great difficulty in changing vendors. You can't be assured that this vendor will provide his goods at the lowest price available in the market. The cost penalties in higher purchase prices you thereby incur may obviate the other JIT savings—that is, if all other things are equal. But they are not. The vendor has the cost of making incessant small deliveries. He may also have to bear (and pass on) the inventory costs that the company used to bear, for he may not have built a JIT type of plant just to serve your needs.

Third, adjusting your manufacturing methodology to JIT production, developing fast changeover methods, may take the time of a large number of skilled manufacturing engineers at a great total cost. This is money you either don't have or can ill afford in a turnaround situation. You may not have the time either.

Fourth, JIT does not allow you to use each piece of existing production machinery to the maximum extent of its capacity and capability. But the company can't currently afford to lose this capacity. It doesn't have the resources to replace it. As an example, imagine a blanking press in a stamping plant taking coils of steel and stamping out blanks to be fed into a number of press lines to make various products. It is fast and surrounded by large batches of different blanks (work in process) it has made. In JIT you would eliminate this inventory, and therefore have this blanking press servicing only a single stamping line. This means a need to buy blanking presses for each press line.

JIT production and inventorying has special requirements, in order to be appropriate, that make it suitable generally only for large, high-volume operations, such as automobile plants and consumer appliance plants. To try to implement such a changed way of doing business in a turnaround situation is courting disaster.

PROCESS INDUSTRIES

Process industries, such as metals/foundry, require special perspective in viewing their performance and potentials for improvement. These industries are investment intensive. They have high fixed costs. Fixed costs, for cast and machined rolling mill rolls, as an example, might typically be on the order of

45 percent of total product cost. It is usually the challenge of the turnaround management to produce greater salable output for the existing fixed costs.

If the end-use markets are soft (compared with industrywide capacity), an increase in the absolute production level may not be feasible, as additional production would be difficult to sell. However, reduced processing time and regular delivery to promise date are bound to improve a company's competitive position.

Troubled process companies usually have out-of-control production processes. Goods deviate from specifications, leading to much rework and sometimes remake. This means late delivery, high direct costs, and excessive occupation time of fixed assets.

Out-of-control production processes are not satisfactorily corrected by fire fighting. The basic problem is usually the quality system, that is, the forest rather than individual trees. A process company needs a total quality system. The first element in this system is the creation of and adherence to explicit written procedures for everything. No variance from procedure may be allowed without documentation of when and how. Thereby, when something goes wrong, one can immediately learn what was different this time.

By analogy, a successful baker makes consistently good cakes by having a good recipe and following it exactly, each and every time. The same is true for process industries.

Seat-of-the-pants manufacturing management, which substitutes thirty years of hard-learned judgment for adherence to a system of well-documented and strictly adhered to procedures, must be replaced and quickly. It is not a suitable substitute.

Let's consider a representative example. When a casting is about to be poured and the temperature of the molten metal is ten degrees below that called out on the process sheet, the metal should not be poured. Rather, it should be returned to a furnace for additional heating. By pouring at too low a temperature, a risk (of cracking) is undertaken in the mistaken belief that taking this risk saves money. The accumulation of numerous such lost gambles results in high cost and poor asset utilization.

Process industries invariably understate and misunderstand their quality costs. Many times they look at scrap and customer warranty costs, often low numbers, and do not realize that their true quality costs may primarily consist of rework and that these costs are frequently buried.

A product may develop a defect early in the production process that becomes apparent only after much more money has been put into it. This will lead to scrapping the item and making it over, or to salvaging the item through much additional rework. Rigid adherence to a comprehensive quality system substantially eliminates such situations. Other aspects of quality are discussed in the subchapter on that subject.

Maintenance/Plant Engineering is another area requiring special attention in a process industry. In a troubled operation this area is frequently mismanaged;

the Maintenance Department acts as a fire brigade, handling breakdowns on an emergency basis when they occur. This is expensive and fails to properly support the company's quality system.

The maintenance effort must prioritize and establish daily, weekly, and monthly schedules for its activities based on the impact of what is to be handled on the total business. Not all equipment is of equal importance and needs to be repaired or adjusted with the same urgency.

Effective maintenance management has other elements as well. A program of preventive maintenance has to be planned and installed, so that unexpected breakdown or departures in performance of key equipment is substantially lessened. Analyses of frequency of breakdown and the causes have to be made, so that needs to modify or replace equipment become apparent. Otherwise, incessant repairs are carried out on inadequately performing equipment with little to show for this expense. A total inventory listing of spare parts has to be compiled and maintained. Otherwise, expensive parts will be ordered without realizing that such parts are already on hand but out of sight—a common occurrence. To support effective spare parts inventory control, spare parts should be stored in controlled access areas.

Maintenance incurs substantial costs and, by affecting the performance of a plant's equipment, has a major impact on quality and other operating costs. This is why it needs effective management and a competent manager.

Underabsorbed burden is common in a troubled process-type company. To minimize this problem, shipments (whose manufacture absorbs burden expense) must be maintained at the highest possible level. The adoption of *daily* reporting of direct standard labor hours earned gives top management a direct real-time measure of manufacturing output (including work in process). When the figure is below forecast, this provides a basis for intervention. One knows how much production has fallen behind and can thereby implement corrective actions (e.g., overtime, additional people, subcontracting). One can also direct attention to learning why production is falling behind. Duraloy Company, a division of Blaw Knox Corporation, by use of this method, was able to stop missing its monthly sales forecasts, and thereby to achieve profitability.

Raw materials purchasing will possibly require special attention to ensure that the lowest possible prices are being paid. One high alloy foundry company was purchasing nickel at $2.30 per pound, when the same material could be obtained from other vendors, with bargaining, at $1.90 per pound. The possibility of such situations requires vigilance.

10

MARKETING

ASSESSING THE CURRENT STATUS AND COMPETITIVE SITUATION

Company and division managements usually believe that they are fully aware of the structure of their markets and how their market position compares with that of competitors. In the troubled company this is simply not so.

Companies become parochial and isolated when they fail to make a concerted effort to remain informed. Troubled firms are seldom well informed. They main-tain, as fact, perceptions of the market and their role in it that have long ceased to be valid. Often they believe that they are the product leader, when customers actually judge them to be no better than the rest of the competition.

An example of this was the Chemetron Process Equipment Division, which manufactured Votator food-processing machinery. Its president proudly stated that his equipment was priced 25 to 30 percent above the competition, reflecting its much higher quality. Interviews with purchasers of this class of equipment revealed their view that Chemetron had no better quality; it had obsolescent designs that were more costly to manufacture than the modern designs manu-factured by others. This is why so few purchasers continued to order Votator brand equipment. The reality is that markets change constantly and sometimes rapidly. Your product can become obsolescent without your knowing it.

To learn the actual current competitive situation, market research has to be done on a continuous basis. Initially this often necessitates using a market re-search firm. Market research can be simple, straightforward, and impressive.

For example, having determined who the current competitors are and obtaining catalogs and price sheets from each (sometimes using a third party), comparisons of these documents often reveal major differences in breadth of product line. These differences need careful scrutiny because there may be good business reasons why others have chosen to discontinue certain models that you continue to offer. Differences may also exist in the published terms and conditions of sale. Are your discounts more generous than others? Do you pay freight, while others price F.O.B. plant? Often differences are found that no one realized existed. This is because changes evolve over time, and no one had the interest or ability to detect these changes as they occurred. Generally, these changes are to the disadvantage of the uninformed.

A market research firm, protecting the company's anonymity, should be used to visit competitors and call on or telephone distributors and customers. This will reveal much about how the company differs from competitors, how it is perceived in the marketplace, and how the marketplace is structured. You must guide the market research firm in defining the specific types of information to be sought. It is important to know what customers really think of your company and what problems they have in dealing with it.

Obtaining market information must not be considered a "one-shot" affair. A continuing effort must exist to stay on top of the market and changes in it. This specific responsibility must be given to someone inside the company.

To properly assess the current marketing and competitive situation, the turnaround management needs reliable in-depth knowledge about:

- market structure, dynamics, and size;
- key competitors;
- product requirements;
- pricing;
- sales requirements/issues;
- distribution; and
- product positioning.

George W. Plohr, of Technomic Consultants, a competent market research firm, compiled the following useful list of aspects that need to be examined in order to clarify these issues:

Market

1. Market size for your product over the past five years

2. Segmentation by product type (or other important product characteristics), geographical region, price range, or other distinguishing factors

3. Factors—economic and others—that have impacted the growth of your markets over the past five years

4. Current and expected future market for your products

5. How future markets will segment (segment as in item 2)

6. Factors—economic or others—expected to impact on your business and the business of your customers between now and the end of your forecast

Competitive Environment

7. Competitors active in your markets or potential markets

8. Market share of each of your major competitors

9. Product and marketing strengths and weaknesses of each of your major competitors

10. Your own product and marketing strengths and weaknesses compared with your competitors, including relative manufacturing costs

11. Historical, current, and planned competitor strategies

Product Requirements

12. Physical or chemical properties or other attributes required for a product to be accepted in this environment

13. Attributes of quality in this market

14. Importance of each of the product characteristics to the successful sale of the product

15. Role/importance of guarantees

16. Price levels required to be successful

17. Terms of sale required

18. Prevalent discount practices

19. Distribution and delivery costs

Selling Effort

20. Trade factors to be reached to effectively serve your market

21. Call patterns required for success

22. Role of an inside sales force versus an outside sales force

23. Qualifications of salespeople active in these businesses

Channels of Distribution

24. Trade factors involved in your channels of distribution

25. Market segments by elements within the distribution channels

26. How distribution channels are expected to change over the next five years, and the rationale underlying the changes

27. How the channels of distribution used by your firm compare with the channels necessary for success in this market

Product Image/Positioning

28. Typical advertising and promotional messages used to reach your target customers

29. Trade associations that can be used to reach the important buying influences for your product

30. Trade publications expected to be the most effective media for reaching the important buying influences
31. Advertising and promotion programs and the sources required
32. Role of direct mail, trip programs, giveaways, and other techniques for reaching the important buying influences
33. Messages and benefits to be stressed in advertising and promotion

Compiling this information may tax the current resources of the troubled company. However, the task is important because some of the answers may lead you to focus on strategic considerations that are critical, but not obvious.

An example of the type of specific information you need to learn is how many competitors' products are carried by a typical distributor. In welding rod and many hand tools, for example, the typical answer revealed by market research was four competitors' products. This information is essential in evaluating the validity of the company's current market approach and in assessing the restraints on shrinking the present breadth of the product line. Another example is the customers' classification of the company's relative quality level and sophistication. If it is low, your company would have difficulty in switching to higher-quality, higher-margin areas of the market.

An understanding of the market and competitive situation becomes of paramount importance if a change in the type of product to be offered is under consideration. For example, Western Zirconium, Inc., decided to spend $2 million to convert some of its zirconium manufacturing capacity to the manufacture of titanium. They didn't evaluate whether or not the marketplace required another titanium producer. There was a glut of titanium capacity at the time. After they completed the conversion, they learned that they could not interest customers in buying titanium from them.

Another example concerns Komatsu, Ltd., the Japanese producer of construction machinery and stamping presses. They designed an entire line of small O.B.I. stamping presses for sale to U.S. automotive manufacturers. They proceeded to staff five U.S. sales offices to sell this equipment. They then learned that, in the preceding five years, U.S. automotive manufacturers had abandoned using this type of equipment; almost no market existed for this expensively developed product line.

Pricing is critical market information. How you are perceived in the marketplace is generally a function of your pricing approach. Frequently low price is equated with low quality, particularly in consumer goods. If you are not completely aware of current pricing, you may be giving important profit dollars away. Your low prices may be disadvantageous and creating a negative image of your product.

MARKETING AND SALES ORGANIZATION

The test of the appropriateness of the organization of a marketing and sales function is its effectiveness. Usually it must be made more effective in a company requiring a turnaround. Certain important marketing functions are usually poorly done, or are not done at all. This is particularly true of long-established organizations that have had little recent inflow of executives from the outside. As a general statement, the troubled company is not particularly marketing oriented and a degradation of the effectiveness of its sales organization has already occurred.

Most companies combine sales, which has direct responsibility for customer contact and order solicitation, with marketing, which is responsible for pricing, product strategy, advertising, and product promotion. Other, usually larger companies separate these two functions into sales and product management groups. Both approaches are usable in a turnaround. Because the sales function is important to the success of the turnaround, careful analysis of the relationship of the sales organization to the marketplace must be made.

The most important question is how many separate sales organizations should be maintained? Multidivisional firms often have a single sales organization for all their products. Sometimes each division has its own sales staff. The right question to ask is whether or not the duplication of overhead arising from having separate sales organizations is needed in order to effectively sell the various products. Combining sales organizations could allow substantial economies: elimination of separate sales offices, elimination of highly paid management positions, and fewer salespeople. One should make the assumption that existing separate sales organizations can be combined unless a good, convincing case is made to the contrary.

One convincing argument for separate sales organizations is the sale of a product with entirely different market characteristics than the primary products. Alloy Rods, a manufacturer of weld wire and other welding consumables, primary products are high-volume, low-value items sold primarily for Original Equipment Manufacturer (O.E.M.) use. It also has a line of low-volume, high-value products (Allstate brand hard facing and maintenance electrodes), which sold poorly. As a result, hard facing and maintenance electrode sales eroded over eight years from $6 million to $2 million annually. To solve this problem, a separate Allstate sales organization was established at a different location, with its own warehouse to provide faster delivery. Within two years sales climbed back to $6 million and were still climbing.

What are the important missing or poorly executed marketing functions in a troubled firm? Bear in mind that the sales organization is the company's primary source of market intelligence. Does the sales organization have effective marketing services, capable of collecting and analyzing meaningful data from sales figures? Does the firm really know in detail about changes in competitors' product offerings and market prices? orders won and lost at major customers—by whom? market share shifts? problems at customers that can be exploited? external effects that are likely to impact sales—how? If it does not, which is common, the company has a sales function but, in reality, no marketing function. The absence of a marketing services capability must be corrected.

Does the sales organization have contract administration and project management skills commensurate with the demands of the business? Lack of these skills is a common problem. Customer change orders can have major impacts on engineering schedules, purchases, manufacturing costs, and manufacturing schedules. They cause problems in cost recovery and create potentials for significant job profit improvement—which can be forfeited through oversight and carelessness. Project management skills are needed for complex contracts to make certain that all aspects of the order properly dovetail, and in a timely manner. Without an explicit project management function this may not happen and severe cost overruns may arise.

Repair/replacement parts orders can be the most profitable segment of any business, but they are, by definition, a separate business and must be managed as such. Explicit sales responsibility must be assigned for this part of the business. Not having separate responsibilities in this area can forfeit a golden opportunity. Pricing aspects of this business area will be discussed later.

A meaningful credit function must exist. The credit manager must be organizationally located in either Finance or Sales. Usually Finance is the best location, as it eliminates a potential conflict of interest. In either case, his responsibilities are the same: prevent the taking of undue risk. An insolvent customer who can't pay the bill is no customer at all. A troubled company is often so hungry for sales that orders are accepted that should be rejected. There must be a competent credit manager with sufficient authority to prevent this.

Sometimes sales organizations pick up extraneous responsibilities not normally found in this department. Invariably these functions are poorly done. Effective cost control is not part of the psychological makeup of salesmen. When extraneous responsibilities are found, they should be transferred to other organizations, where they will be managed effectively.

The Sales Department is the primary interface between the company and the market. A poorly organized sales function can never exist in a successful company and may destroy a troubled company. In a turnaround it needs priority attention.

SALES EXPENSES

What level of sales expense should be maintained in a turnaround? Is this an area to make deep reductions, or should even more be spent? To answer these questions, you must look at the specific business and determine whether or not salesmen and other sales expenses are truly the basis of obtaining sales.

Do most sales come from repeat orders from well-established customers? If so, the salesman is probably really not selling the product. Rather, he is maintaining good relations with the customer, showing that the company cares about him, and continuing to obtain his business. The salesman is also performing a customer service function, receiving complaints about quality, timeliness of delivery, and the like. But, most important, the salesman in this situation is not really responsible for gaining the business—the orders would have been mailed in anyway.

If the product is widely sold to a great many customers, the sales organization may be quite large and expensive. When no single sale is critical to the business plan of the manufacturer, the risk of a minor potential reduction in sales, which, in practice, usually doesn't occur, can be traded off to obtain a major reduction in sales expense. For a troubled company, selling standard products to repeat customers, the sales organization may be a luxury that can be severely curtailed.

Remember this: If the product is standardized and made by a small number of well-known firms, most current sales probably do not arise from the sales effort of your organization.

Two examples can give insight into this subject. Alloy Rods, Inc., recently spun off from Allegheny International, Inc., is the leading U.S. manufacturer of high-quality welding rod and wire. Alloy Rods was selling about $85 million of its products through 400 distributors and to about a dozen large O.E.M. customers. With the highest market share and the most efficient manufacturing plants in the business, its profit levels were still not satisfactory. Marketing expenses were significant. Sixty salesmen were thought to be required to service the large number of accounts. To reduce these costs, a different selling approach was adopted. A number of the large distributors agreed to become master distributors, substituting their large sales force for Alloy Rods'. As such, they serviced their nearby smaller distributors, in place of Alloy Rods' own force. This then allowed Alloy Rods to reduce its sales force to twenty-five persons, creating a substantial overall savings.

Another example: Allegheny Ludlum Steel Corporation is a leading producer of stainless steel. It is solidly profitable, in stark contrast to most steel companies. Over a ten-year period Allegheny Ludlum slowly closed out three-quarters of its sales offices, which were once located in all important markets. With each closure sales increased—the opposite of conventional marketing wisdom. An extrapolation implied that closing all their sales offices might overwhelm them with sales (no one took this seriously). This is another case of sales of standardized items to established customers where the business supported the sales effort, rather than the sales effort supporting the business.

Sales departments, besides their personnel and travel expenses, may run up high entertainment expenses. These, too, must be carefully scrutinized. Today customers buy on price, performance, and delivery. Business is more competitive than ever. High entertainment expenses are usually a relic of the past. Many steel companies, for example, stress expensive golfing affairs with their customers' top executives as part of their marketing approach. Everyone has a good time and much money is spent. No steel gets sold. For some years steel has been an item bought strictly on price.

Norms for travel and entertainment have to be developed and enforced; otherwise, significant costs will be needlessly incurred. The problem of the absence of such controls was typified by D.A.B. Industries, an O.E.M. auto parts maker.

This company had a salesman who was a "Good Time Charlie" on its money. Once, while visiting Ford's transmission plant, he scooped up eleven persons and took them out to lunch. Another time he and another like-minded salesman took twenty men out to a drinking-and-eating fest at a good restaurant, running up a mind-boggling bill. When questioned he said that the company expected him to entertain and hadn't specified which customers were important. Norms must be created and enforced.

If, on the other hand, the company wants to seek new customers who do not have a history of buying a particular product from them, these customers can be developed only with a significant sales effort. Direct person-to-person contact is essential. Failure to make this marketing effort will prevent such sales from materializing.

Sturtevant, a recently divested division of Westinghouse Electric Corporation, was a manufacturer of large blowers, used to provide forced air to power plants, coal mines, steel mills, cement plants, and the like. For many years they dominated the power plant niche of the market (i.e., 40 percent market share or greater) but had little penetration of the many other industrial market segments—market shares of 10 percent or less. With the decline in the early 1980s of new power plant construction, Sturtevant was faced with a bleak long-term business outlook. Their solution, outlined in their strategic plan, was to build up their market penetration in the non-power plant portion of the market. However, they hired no salesmen experienced in these other areas and spent inconsequential sums in marketing support. This resulted in no appreciable increase in non-power plant sales, and continuing losses.

The Blaw Knox Food & Chemical Equipment Company had a relatively large sales organization, needed for its highly engineered products that customers purchase infrequently. As a cost savings, its salesmen were prevented from traveling. For a typical month its airline travel costs were only $1,000. This was extremely foolish. Why have salesmen if you won't let them visit customers? The policy was reversed, with salesmen ordered to be on the road three or more days per week. Almost immediately the level of incoming orders increased.

In a turnaround a review of sales expenses is mandatory. Usually a reduction in these expenses will not cause harm in the short run and will focus attention on the need for economies. In addition, they will directly benefit cash flow.

PRICING

Pricing may be the most difficult of all subjects to manage. Setting prices too low may be a significant contributor to unprofitability. Setting them above what the market will accept will lead to a precipitous decline in orders, which can put the firm out of business.

Pricing decisions must reflect the competitive situation, the uniqueness of the product, and alternatives available to the customer. This implies a need for good competitive information and a full understanding of the market and the company's position in it. Most troubled firms possess none of these things. Many times decision are based on limited and faulty information. In a mature market, where the number of competitors and buyers is reasonably small, it is possible to develop an understanding of the competitors' costs and likely bidding behavior. Not having this market information has frequently led to serious underpricing for fear of losing the business. The direct consequence is often sales volume without profit.

As an example, D.A.B. Industries, the O.E.M. auto parts maker, underpriced Imperial Clevite by 25 percent on an annual order bid to retain Ford Motor Company's business for engine bearings. Imperial Clevite was surprised. Underpricing them by 5 percent would have been sufficient. Imperial Clevite didn't understand how D.A.B. Industries could make any money at this price level. They were right; D.A.B. Industries didn't make any money on this business.

If purchase items constitute a significant portion of total product cost, this area must be given more than the perfunctory attention it usually receives in setting prices. The ability to forecast the cost of purchased items at the time they will be bought is important to properly making quotations to customers. This methodology is termed NIFO pricing—next in, first out. It was the key step in improving the profitability of Special Metals Corporation, a specialty metals producer whose raw materials prices varied widely over time. NIFO pricing is especially appropriate in a high-inflation environment. The limitation of this method is that competitors with less understanding of their costs will tend to underprice the product. This forces you to face the agonizing decision of whether or not to price yourself out of the bidding, knowing that you will lose money if you acquire the order at the lower price.

Kentucky Electric Steel Corporation was able to devise an ingenious approach to this problem. An automotive spring manufacturer wished to order a considerable quantity of automobile spring steel, but only on the basis that the price be attractive and Kentucky Electric Steel be willing to hold this attractive price for a year. What was Kentucky Electric Steel to do in view of the volatility of steel scrap prices, a major cost element? Kentucky Electric Steel arranged for their major steel scrap supplier to sell them a year's worth of scrap now, holding it for them, thereby fixing the cost, adding in the interest expense to the scrap price. This permitted the spring manufacturer to quote a firm, for a year, price to its automotive customer.

Another approach, used by a milk company in quoting annual buys of school districts, was to give the customer a choice. Because the cost of milk could change during the year, the buyer could choose either a higher, but fixed, price or a lower price with an escalation clause.

A classic example of a company needing to make a decision when a competitor demonstrates that it doesn't understand its costs was the competition between Douglas Aircraft Company, the DC–10, and Lockheed Corporation, the L–1011. Douglas initially priced the DC–10 at about $16 million, estimating that it would have to sell 200 airplanes to break even. Lockheed proceeded to reduce the price of the L-1011 to about $14 million. Douglas matched the $14 million price, realizing that this would destroy the potential profitability of the product. Both Lockheed and McDonnell Douglas continued to lose money on these products as they made them over the years.

Return on investment (R.O.I.) should be an important consideration in pricing decisions. When a variety of products can be made using the same equipment as in, say, the metals industry, looking at margin per ton, or a similar broad measure, masks the economic utility of the equipment. Relating the profit margins to R.O.I. on the assets used allows for better pricing decisions and indicates whether or not something is wrong with the current product mix. It also gives guidance on which products to emphasize. Amsted Industries, based in Chicago, is an example of a company that has been particularly effective in using this emphasis on R.O.I. as a management tool.

Escalation clauses, based on changes in major costs, should be included in all pricing for future delivery to the extent the market will tolerate it. The only way to know whether the company can do this is to go ahead and include escalation clauses and see what happens, being prepared to back down if necessary.

Without escalation, major cost increases in important cost inputs will not be recovered, sometimes leading to serious losses. If, however, the market won't tolerate escalation and a major raw material input is a commodity (i.e., copper), then the purchase of futures contracts can arbitrage future price movements. In order to use this method, you must be able to estimate future needs relatively accurately.

The length of time that a bid price holds and control of this aspect can have long-term consequences. When a market becomes soft and prices are at low levels, a major customer may issue requests for quotations for long-term delivery. Once the customer actually places orders, this by itself will change the industry's capacity utilization situation and may, thereby, drive prices up. The customer may come around a second time to try to buy even more at the low prices quoted in the first quotation. This would not be good for you as the supplier. Whether or not this can happen, locking your company into further long-term profitless sales, will depend on whether or not the initial favorable quotation gave the customer a limited time frame to place additional orders. Careful wording in the quotation, to control this possibility, is often overlooked in its preparation.

Sales departments will invariably recommend against raising prices, protesting that market participation will collapse if you do. If you cannot afford to continue to sell products at current prices and have no way to reduce costs, then a price increase will let the market decide. It will either restore profitability or force the company to cease participation in an unprofitable product. To continue making an unprofitable product indefinitely, with no change in prospect, is an untenable situation.

Terms and conditions of sale are another element of price competition that are frequently ignored by sales departments. Alloy Rods, the welding products manufacturer, used to pay for freight. They changed to F.O.B. plant and lowered their prices to reflect the corresponding decrease in cost. The true benefits, however, were greater than this. Some customers ignored freight costs in making purchase decisions, which made Alloy Rods' prices seem even more attractive. Also, Alloy Rods' internal administrative costs were reduced. Furthermore, they no longer had to be concerned about adverse impacts on profit margins of changes in freight rates. Another aspect of the terms and conditions of sale that could be changed is the warranty (e.g., length and coverage).

In addition to information on demand and supply for your class of product, pricing decisions require you to have a good understanding of your own costs. This, in turn, demands a cost accounting system adequate to provide this understanding. This aspect is discussed more fully in the chapter on finance.

A company has to know its contribution margin. It has to know the minimum price it can set for a product and not lose money on an incremental basis. A break-even analysis should exist for every product. If a price level is set below this, then the more volume, the greater the loss. This happens frequently when costs are not well understood, particularly when any sort of transfer pricing is occurring. This knowledge is also essential in setting a lower limit in an intensely competitive bidding. An item being sold for less than the value of the steel that is needed to make it is a recurring example of this problem.

Can a sales volume increase result from a decrease in sales price? This question is not asked often enough. If the product is price inelastic, the size of the market will not change, and with competitors likely to meet a price decrease, the net result will only be lower operating margins. As an example, look at zirconium tubing. A drop in price from $22 per pound to $18 per pound would be unlikely to increase the industrial demand for this product. Many products, however, are price elastic. A drop in market price level would lend to much greater volume. Just look at how airline passenger traffic increases with a decrease in air fares. The real economic question is whether or not the increase in volume arising from a price decrease more than offsets the decline in margin on each transaction. A company needs a good understanding of its costs and margins when making pricing decisions.

An understanding of costs, and, more important, the probable costs of competitors, must exist before price leadership is attempted. In general, a troubled company should avoid leading the market to lower price levels. Once the price level has been lowered, restoring it is a difficult task. If the troubled company lowers prices and is not the lowest cost producer, it will be in worse shape than before, with even greater losses, as competitors quickly match its lower prices.

A troubled firm selling products on a quotation basis often doesn't know when its pricing departs from the general market level and exceeds it, with a resulting sudden drop in its market share. This is a serious situation, for it can ultimately lead to the failure of the company. Market share must be known and monitored. If it has dropped because of pricing policy, then the firm must quickly decide if it can price at a new, lower level and make changes in the way the business is run to be profitable at this lower price level. Costs usually depend on the level of business activity, so a decline in market share may drive up product costs. This is another reason to price to protect market share.

Sometimes a company deliberately maintains a pricing policy that overprices its products in the marketplace, thereby significantly lowering sales, which, in turn, causes underabsorption of overhead. White Consolidated Industries required many of its subsidiaries/divisions to price their products with a minimum margin of 36 percent, regardless of market conditions. In time, this policy turned healthy businesses into troubled ones. A major element in reviving these troubled businesses was the abandonment of this pricing policy. A company must always price at market, and learn how to live with that price level, if it is to stay in business.

Competitors who can't keep their inventories in balance tend to have all-too-frequent "fire sales." If your firm matches these prices, it would destroy the market price structure. If it doesn't match them, it may have a major loss in market position. Faced with such perils, you must carefully examine the specifics of this particular event and not act precipitously.

Chemetron Process Equipment Division was a money-losing operation that had once been solidly profitable. Its annual sales were about $20 million, and its prices were 25 to 30 percent above those of competitors. Fifteen years before, and for the entire interim period, its annual sales were typically $20 million. No one seemed to realize that $20 million in sales did not represent an equilibrium. It represented a continual decline in market share. The firm had evolved into being a marginal supplier.

A contrasting example is the experience of Danly Machine Corporation. Danly Machine had been the leading supplier of large mechanical stamping presses to the U.S. automotive industry. The globalization of this industry and entry into the U.S. market of Japanese and German manufacturers during 1981–83 caused the general price level to decline by 25 percent and Danly's market share to nearly collapse. In the fall of 1983 Danly adopted a policy that it would not, in general, be undersold and priced its presses at the world level—a price decrease of 25 percent. It adopted a technology-based cost reduction program intended to reduce product costs by 32 percent within eighteen months. Within nine months Danly was, once again, the leading U.S. supplier to the U.S. automotive industry, and its bookings actually exceeded its manufacturing capacity. It also achieved its cost reduction goals.

REPLACEMENT PARTS AND SERVICE

The pricing of replacement/repair parts can be a key element in a company's profitability. When markets become competitive in the pricing of new equipment, the business takes on the aspects of a "razor and blades business." That is, you find new equipment being sold with little or no profit, while replacement parts for this type of equipment command high margins.

The reason for this dichotomy in pricing is that the customer psychology and competitive situation facing replacement parts are utterly different from those facing the sale of new equipment. The customer buying new equipment may not be sure that he wants to buy the new equipment, and if he does, he has a great variety of choices. Once he owns your equipment, the situation is radically different. His choice of suppliers is greatly restricted, and each further purchase is small compared with the value of the equipment itself.

If the customer's equipment is down, that is, unable to function, and the repair part order is of the rush breakdown type, the situation is even more favorable to the supplier. In this instance the supplier is psychologically not being looked on as a goods supplier. Rather, it is viewed as a service firm and being measured as such, with the customer's ability to return quickly to production as the major criterion.

When it comes to repair/replacement parts and rush breakdown pricing, the supplier has to keep these perspectives at the forefront. Rush breakdown orders can allow for a surcharge above normal replacement prices, for example, justified on the basis of the special handling required.

Chemetron Process Equipment was a profitless company. It had a large installed equipment base, owing to its many years of manufacturing food machinery. It was proud of the low prices it charged customers for replacement parts. Yet its customers were extremely displeased. They didn't need low prices; they needed fast service. Four weeks to get a simple part to allow a food machine to run again was not acceptable. If Chemetron Process Equipment had doubled its prices and cut the repair part lead time to one week or less, it probably would have enjoyed a much better profitability and a higher level of customer satisfaction.

Troubled durable goods manufacturers are frequently found to substantially underprice their repair parts and to provide poorer customer service than this market requires.

A company must have a means to actually accomplish providing good customer service. Often managements simply don't know how. The key element is instituting a tracking system. The typical company has too many transactions going on to properly monitor them. An electronic data processing-based system needs to be created to look at the three very different types of parts whose coordination is needed to meet the customers' requirements.

- *Special Parts*. Parts that have to be made to order, by the company's factory, to properly fit into the customer's equipment. Making these parts will often necessitate engineering review, special routings, and breaking into and expediting normal manufacturing sequences.

- *Standard Parts*. Parts of the company's design that the factory normally makes in economic order quantities as stock items. If the company is out of inventory, then a special or expedited run may be necessary.

- *Purchase Items.* These are components or elements provided by outside vendors, and special efforts will be needed by the Purchasing Department to achieve timely delivery.

The status of all three of these types of parts will have to be simultaneously monitored to ensure that the promise dates are met and to develop flexible solutions when they are not met (which, unfortunately, is not infrequent). A special replacement parts group will usually be needed to do the expediting, hand-carry paperwork through the organization, and drive to vendors to make sure things are progressing properly. This group has to have the authority and ability to subcontract items when it finds the factory unable to be timely.

The sale of replacement parts can be made into a profit center, with its own special characteristics. These would include closer attention to inventory stocking levels, special expediting approaches, and, possibly, a separate marketing structure.

In addition to needing replacement parts, customers often need service. They need your serviceman to install replacement parts, to guide the installation being performed by their own employees, or to find out what is wrong with the machine. They need your people to train their maintenance and machine repair staff to properly maintain and repair your equipment. They need a preventive maintenance program prepared by you. All of these activities can carry a high profit margin.

Customers tend to respond to good service. If your efforts are truly helpful, timely, and competent, customers can often be readily convinced to expand the scope of their service purchases. Besides being profitable in its own right, service sales usually lead to increased sales of replacement parts bought by the customer, on your serviceman's recommendation, for stocking purposes.

Many troubled equipment companies treat their service business as a nuisance, rather than as a business in its own right that deserves to be nurtured.

PRODUCT LINE BREADTH

Many companies and their marketing departments like to boast that they are a full-line supplier, or to say that they have the broadest product line in the industry. Such a situation can be the basis of excessive costs. The lowest-volume items in a product line frequently have disproportionately high manufacturing set-up and changeover costs per unit. As production requirements dictate a minimum batch size, slow-moving items often cause disproportionately high inventory costs, owing to their low turnover. Significant accounting and paperwork costs also accompany these items. Therefore, the lowest-sales-volume products of any product line should always be candidates for pruning.

Two questions must be answered before a product line is pruned: Does the company have to be a full-line supplier to be successful, and does the profitability of the slow-moving items, by itself, warrant their continuance? Looking at your competitor's product breadth often gives insight. Sometimes you will find that larger, more profitable competitors have a narrower product line, possibly having pruned theirs long ago. Carrying slow-moving, not particularly profitable items is usually *not* necessary to protect your market position for faster-moving items *if* your customers are buying from several sources. Inexpensive customer surveys can be taken before making a decision.

One possible approach to eliminating slow-moving items is to apply a R.O.I. test to these products. This method would be a good indicator of the inappropriate products in your offerings. As a result, you may choose to selectively increase prices to meet a minimum R.O.I. as an alternative to immediate pruning.

The time to prune the product line is now. The sooner, the better. If finished goods exist that will be dropped from the product line, an analysis should be made whether or not to let them dribble out of the system, to sell them off all at once at a reduced price, or to scrap them.

In looking into the True Temper Corporation's hand tool operations (hammers and axes) some years ago, they were found to have a large catalog containing many slow-moving items no longer made by the much more profitable Stanley Tool Works. In some cases Stanley bought these items from True Temper, on a private label basis, for resale, thereby gaining the best of both worlds.

Makers of equipment spanning a wide range of sizes, capacities, and so on may have their manufacturing plant and its machine tools best suited to one end of this product spectrum. By offering goods at the other end of the spectrum, they may be incurring either actual losses or profitless sales (which, nonetheless, require extensive working capital).

Most products follow the well-known "product life cycle." Over time the number of competitors and the degree of price competition change. A product that once was a profit maker need not still be so today. But people seldom think about this. There is an inertia in companies inhibiting the pruning of product lines. It is important to ascertain whether or not the product is, or can be, manufactured economically. If it cannot, purchase/resale or offshore procurement may be viable alternatives that would permit the product to be continued to be marketed (if that is deemed important).

Danly Machine Corporation's manufacturing of mechanical stamping presses is a good example. The company is best known for its custom-designed, high-tonnage presses (which range in size from 500 tons to 5,000 tons capacity), sold primarily to the automotive industry. These presses are normally made in quantities ranging from one to ten for a given design. The company also made small O.B.I. presses (25 tons to 150 tons capacity), which were of a standard catalog design. The manufacturing operation, its machine tools, procedures, and overhead structure, was geared to manufacturing small numbers of large presses. Hence it could not be cost-effective on making large batches of small presses, although the company had offered them for years. An analysis of the actual cost experience on the last six orders for small presses revealed total costs averaging 180 percent of sales price. The decision was made to no longer manufacture the small presses.

Virtually no troubled company should feel that remaining a full-line supplier is an important consideration.

This logic applies to job shops as well. Many operations can be classified as a type of job shop, that is, an operation that makes customized parts or assemblies for others. To be successful, a job shop must understand its niche in the market; it will have its strength in some areas and its competitors will have greater strength in others. If it tries to maintain competitive prices in all areas, including those outside its niche, it will incur excessive costs that will tend to make the entire operation suffer. A job shop operation must, in its pricing, avoid seeking business outside its niche. Burgess–Norton Manufacturing Company, a leading powder metal products producer, as an example, accomplished a turnaround by, in effect, rejecting business for fifty parts it was currently making that didn't fit its market niche of making usually precise and difficult-to-manufacture parts. Profits improved thereafter, reaching twice the industry average for return on sales.

This discussion has, so far, looked at the breadth of the product line from the point of view of prudently contracting it. But there is another direction whose dimensions must be understood—broadening the product line. It is a natural reaction to think that adding products to the product line, and thereby generating additional revenue, will improve the health of the business. Unfortunately this is seldom so. Broadening the product line may actually exacerbate the firm's operational and financial problems. The paramount task in a turnaround usually is cutting costs. Cost reductions can't be achieved in new product introductions, where costs cannot be accurately forecasted.

Broadening the product line puts a strain on the firm's existing staff resources and increases overhead costs as well. Product engineering efforts will be required, even if the additional products are simple extensions of existing ones. Manufacturing and process engineering will be needed to create or perfect the ability to manufacture the additional products. Significant marketing and sales expenses will be incurred in introducing the additional products to the market. Purchasing may have to buy items it might otherwise not have had to spend its time on. All these efforts represent a diversion of staff resources from the main product lines, which need all the attention they can receive. Financial strains will be created and inventories will have to be established, manufacturing fixtures built, and so forth.

All of this will occur before any meaningful level of revenue is realized. The troubled firm will be taking on something it probably can't handle properly and most likely can't afford. What you usually find is a desperation play with little chance of success.

An example is a money-losing zirconium metal operation that decided to overcome its problems by adding titanium to its product line. Much more staff time and cost were incurred than anticipated in converting its process equipment to the additional product. It took significant effort to be able to make titanium satisfactorily to meet market standards. When all was said and done, sales of titanium failed to develop.

Another common approach to broadening of the product line is to add complementary products, on a purchase/resale basis, figuring that the firm already has the marketing mechanism, and this is a way to easily generate additional profit. Because no product engineering or manufacturing is entailed, it is assumed that this is a simple nondemanding endeavor. Actually the demands are similar to those arising from any new product endeavor—a market introduction effort, the need to provide sufficient inventories, and so on. The usual result is losses. A troubled firm is one that has demonstrated that it can't properly run its business. Directing the attention of key management people away from the main problems of the business is not desirable. Adding the complexity of new products to an overloaded system is not a solution, but the addition of more problems, whether it be on a purchase/resale or other basis.

PRODUCT STANDARDS

Firms may adopt product standards that differ from their competitors but have no particular basis in actual customer preference or utility in use. If using these product standards costs more than using the standards of the competition and doesn't provide a competitive advantage, a reassessment is certainly called for. A case that illustrates this aspect concerns the grade of wooden handles used in nail hammers manufactured by the True Temper Corporation. True Temper graded its handles A, B, and C, based on wood color and aesthetics, in sorting the handles after they were made. A-grade handles were very white, whereas C-grade handles had brown streaks. C-grade handles, which constituted 25 to 30 percent of production and were functionally sound, were seldom used. They were either stored indefinitely or sold to jobbers and competitors at distressed prices, typically at 25 percent of cost. Their major competitor, Stanley Tool Works, which had a larger market share, simply stained such handles dark brown by dipping them into stain, at an insignificant cost, and used them with no ill effect on sales.

Beware of the lowering product quality, as perceived by the customer. During the 1970s U.S. automakers "economized" to the point of driving consumers, in large numbers, to seemingly more reliable Japanese products. Acceptable quality is ultimately defined by customers, not by a manufacturer.

No two firms have identical manufacturing equipment and manufacturing processes. A firm should always try to slant its product standards to take maximum advantage of its manufacturing capabilities. If a minor design change will make a product better suited to the manufacturing equipment, with no deleterious effect to the customer (or unwanted aesthetic aspect), and not be in violation of customer purchasing standards, then such changes should be sought and implemented.

Similarly, standards detrimental to the firm should be fought tooth and nail. A good example occurred in 1977, when the metrication madness had its heyday. The U.S. government was pushing the adoption of a standard width for steel coils of 125 centimeters (49.21 inches). This would have suited foreign steel producers. Only most U.S. steel mills had hot strip mills built to produce sheet to the standard U.S. size of 48 inches wide. At the stroke of a pen the adoption of the new metric-based standard would have dealt a severe blow to U.S. steel companies without providing the consumer any benefit whatever. The new standard was opposed and never adopted.

When a firm has sufficient market power to make its own standards, it must realize that this is the case and act on it. It must also be realized that a voluntary standard that customers don't really care about when purchasing is no standard at all.

Often standards can be capricious and arbitrary. Specifying engineers tend toward overkill. Specifications in materials, surface finish, metal gauge, and dimensional tolerances can usually be redirected in negotiation toward cost-effectiveness and profitability if you share the savings with your customer.

DESIGN OBSOLESCENCE

As industrial equipment evolves, it usually becomes more compact and lighter weight for the power transmitted, or has increased capacity, for the same size, for the function performed. In an economic sense this means a decreasing relative real cost. Designs of capital goods unchanged over decades tend to become uncompetitively priced. When it reaches this point it is time to copy the current leading designs and forget pride of initial innovation.

A food machinery company, Chemetron Process Equipment, which hadn't changed its major designs significantly in forty years, for example, offered equipment that weighed 30 percent more, and cost 30 percent more, than competitors'. They called it higher quality. The customers felt that the quality was the same; just the price was higher.

When the company's designs are obsolescent, the choices are either to update them or to prune the product line. Usually market share has been significantly eroded by this time, so rebuilding market share, even with state-of-the-art designs, will be no easy matter. It will take much time and money. This is a task suited only to a healthy company with other nonobsolescent product lines. It is usually beyond the capacity of a company requiring turnaround. For such a company to attempt it would probably result in the company's spreading itself too thin and squandering its limited resources. Pruning the product line in a turnaround is discussed more fully in the section on product line breadth.

Design obsolescence and product obsolescence are not the same thing. A design may reach the limit of its perfection, only to have the product itself superseded in the marketplace by a successor product, say, automobiles replacing horses, or solid state elements replacing vacuum tubes. When the product itself becomes obsolescent, the company must react by either abandoning the no-longer-profitable business or devising a strategy to run the business as a specialty niche with very different dimensions. Those companies that were still manufacturing vacuum tubes in 1987 are profitable at doing so.

ADVERTISING

Advertising is important to introducing significantly new products to the market or entering new market niches. A turnaround company, however, is not usually faced with new product introductions. Rather, it is typically struggling to sell its long-established products.

The PIMS data base, reflecting much collective experience, shows that, in companies with low market share (in a mature product), profits from new business created by increased advertising fall short of the cost of that advertising. Of course, there are exceptions, such as the spectacular turnaround of Remington Shaver. But these are uncommon and one cannot manage a turnaround on the anticipation of a remote possibility. Substantially reducing advertising expenditures is usually the prudent action if your market share is low.

An almost classic illustration of this type of situation occurred at Jacobsen Manufacturing Company, the lawn mower manufacturer, in 1979–80. The firm had been doing poorly for years. Its new president, a marketing man, thought the solution to be a large, costly advertising campaign. With only a 3 percent market share, experience indicated that the advertising might attract potential customers to stores where they would then buy the competitors' products. Sure enough, Jacobsen's increased margin from the greater sales did not equal the expanded advertising cost. The firm lost even more money.

If you wish to change the marketing focus, reorienting your efforts to reach a group of customers other than your normal customers, you have no choice but to advertise. If no one has heard about the company or its products, the company cannot expect to generate customer inquiries.

Advertising is a communications tool. It communicates the existence of a supply to meet the existence of a demand. Demand is difficult, or impossible, to create. However, it can be redirected. For example, a young woman's quest for beauty can be manipulated to any number of products. You must make sure that demand for your class of product exists and determine the size of the potential market. Advertising uses economies of scale. A small market doesn't benefit from thirty-second commercials on television prime time. For example, most of the engine bearings used in the United States are bought by three automobile manufacturers. Advertising is not the best way to influence this market.

Advertising must be managed with attention to cost/benefit justification. The content must be scrutinized to ensure that it motivates potential customers to buy the product.

Great caution should be shown in spending money on what may be considered "image advertising." If the company has been supporting an image type of advertising for a long time, it must face the fact that this is no longer affordable. This applies to company publications given away free, as well.

CUSTOMER CHANGE ORDERS

Customer changes in orders already received impact all areas of the company. Because management of customer interface is primarily a sales responsibility, it will be discussed here in the chapter on marketing. This is frequently a critical problem area in a turnaround.

There is no such thing as a customer change that doesn't affect cost and schedule. If proper procedures do not exist to track and control these impacts, two common consequences occur. The additional costs aren't recovered; something the company can't afford. The customer's delivery schedule is missed, creating ill will on the part of the customer, even though it is his action that caused the miss.

The first problem arising from customer changes is that various elements of the company (e.g., Engineering, Manufacturing, Purchasing) may not know these changes are about to occur, or have occurred. Communication on this subject must be mandatory and rapid.

How do changes occur? Many ways, often informal. A customer's engineer, discussing the design with one of your engineers, will suddenly conclude that an electrical control box should be mounted on the left side, rather than on the right side, and your engineer agrees and marks it so on the drawing. The company has a change implemented that no one knows about, for which no additional charges will be paid. This must not be allowed. However, the company must remain flexible and attentive to its customers.

Figure 10–1 shows one means to gain control of the change process, by use of a form and a procedure. The form is initiated from wherever the proposed change enters the company (Engineering, Manufacturing, Sales, and so on) and is sent to the responsible party in the Sales Department. The form clearly states the request, who made the request, and when it was made. An assessment is immediately made as to whether or not work on this order should stop or continue to proceed, until the matter of the change is settled. All of the various impacts are defined and estimated:

- How much additional engineering time will be required, its cost, and what this does to the engineering schedule.
- The same process exists for manufacturing.
- The disposition of obsoleted production and purchased items.
- The total cost and delivery schedule impact.

Having done the above, a rational price change can be arrived at for the proposed change. This may have a very different profit basis than the initial bid.

Figure 10-1.
Customer Change Request

CUSTOMER CHANGE NO.	JOB NO.	DATE

___ REQUIRES A STOP WORK NOTICE

AFFECTING--

1. ___ DRAWING

2. ___ MATERIAL

3. ___ SHOP ORDER

4. ___ ROUTING

5. ___ TOOLS

6. ___ ACCOUNTING

7. ___ FINAL CONFIGURATION

OTHERS:_____

_____

CHANGES REQUESTED - Attach Sketch If Necessary.

CHANGE REQUESTED BY _____
                              Name

ON _____
        Date

Submitted_____

PROCEDURE REQ'D. TO EFFECT CHANGE

1. Change to Engineering Schedule _____

_____
                                    Signed   Date
                                    (Engineering)

2. Estimated Change in Mfg. Hours _____
                                    Signed   Date
                                    (Manufacturing)

3. Changes in Purchased Material Cost & Delivery _____

_____
                                    Signed   Date
                                    (Purchasing)

4. Estimated Change in Cost _____
                                    Signed   Date
                                    (Sales)

5. Changes in Manufacturing Schedule _____

_____
                                    Signed   Date
                                    (Manufacturing)

6. Other (Including Disposition of Stock)- Semi and Finished Parts _____

_____
                                    Signed   Date

7. Price Change For This Revision Accepted By _____ On_____

Getting the initial order was probably the result of a competitive process, and the estimated profit margin may be negligible. Customer changes are essentially noncompetitive bids and can be priced as such. Many troubled companies fail to realize this and underprice customer changes, or fail to price them at all.

The customer is presented with the price addition and impact on delivery and has the choice of rejecting them, restoring the initial situation, or accepting or negotiating them, with the consequence that the purchase order is properly amended.

Unless the purchase order is amended for the price change due, the system isn't working. No changes must be allowed to happen without cost recovery and profit margin.

Each customer change needs to be numbered and tracked. A complex project may generate a series of numbers.

It is not a favor to the customer to have a haphazard change-order system, for this leads to confusion about what will ultimately be delivered and when. It also creates a billing nightmare.

In the turnaround of Danly Machine Corporation, one of the most pressing needs was for the creation and adoption of an effective change-order control system.

DISTRIBUTION

For every product there is more than one possible approach to distribution. No one approach is necessarily permanently the right one for all circumstances. It takes insight to reexamine a long-established approach to distribution. In a turnaround every established practice must be questioned, including distribution.

Distribution must first be looked at from the point of view of cost-effectiveness. How much does it cost to do the job? The section on sales expenses described the example of Alloy Rods, which was able to reduce its sales force from sixty to twenty-five persons. They accomplished this by converting from selling directly to small distributors, to use of master distributors who, in turn, service the small distributors. The lesson is that sometimes less expensive means of distribution can be found.

Distribution methods must also be examined for strategic purposes. Baldor Electric, for example, adopted a policy of opening its own regional warehouses, in preference to other means of distribution, to be more responsive to customer needs. The goal was to substantially increase market share. Baldor now has 25 percent of its market segment.

A company must take into consideration that shifting sales responsibilities may change its market intelligence-gathering abilities. Your own salesmen are your prime source of market intelligence. This aspect cannot be ignored.

COMPETITIVE RESPONSES

The turnaround company must be able to respond to competitors' actions, in general, and to competitors' responses to its own actions.

Usually it takes a company a long time to become truly troubled. During this period it invariably has either ignored or not been aware of many of the actions of its competitors. It frequently doesn't know their strategy, cost structure, or ability to compete worldwide. In the turnaround it must become knowledgeable with regard to these aspects and devise responses to competitor actions, some of which may be of long standing.

The first priority, therefore, is not devising responses to anticipated competitor reactions to your own actions. Rather, it is your devising long-delayed reactions to many existing competitor actions.

The earlier section entitled "Assessing the Current Status and Competitive Situation" describes learning those things about competitors that have been long ignored. Benefiting from this information, you can test your proposed action against your competitors' capabilities. If your competitor has intrinsically lower costs than you do, for example, he can easily match a contemplated price decrease, which would then harm you more than it would him.

Once the turnaround is firmly under way the company's actions will begin to be felt in the marketplace. Competitors may feel compelled to respond. It is important to become aware of these responses as they occur. You cannot afford to just learn the current competitive situation and ignore this aspect afterward. This must be a continuing effort. It requires ongoing contacts at the customers, at all levels. A dialogue with mutual suppliers can provide information. Attention should be given to any information in newspapers, including the local newspapers where your competitors are located, and government filings.

This vigilance can lead to unanticipated beneficial actions. For example, specialty steel companies competing with foreign imports of stainless steel discovered that some of these producers are in countries that encourage trade with Cuba. This meant that Cuban nickel was going into their stainless steel. As the U.S. maintains an embargo on Cuban products, the embargo was then used to exclude the imports of this foreign stainless steel.

Because no two companies are identical, it may be difficult for competitors to match some of your actions. You would only know this by truly understanding your competitors.

An example is a company making specialty springs in a plant near Chicago, some of which are exported to Belgium and the rest of the Common Market. The firm also has a small spring operation in Brazil, primarily serving the Brazilian market. Its main competitor has all of its plants in the United States. By switching its production of springs for Belgian shipment to Brazil, it eliminated a 5.5 percent Belgian tariff, which the competitor could not do.

The turnaround company must also monitor the competitiveness of its product designs. It must decide where the responsibility for product ideas and product line design changes must reside. If the product lines are technology driven (e.g., capital goods), then the responsibility must reside in Engineering or in a research and development organization that coordinates closely with Marketing.

11

TECHNOLOGY

Every manufacturing company has a number of organizations concerned with developing or applying technology. Product engineering, engineering analysis, material engineering, test laboratories, and similar groups going by other names all deal with the specification and creation of the company's products. Manufacturing engineering, process engineering, and the like are concerned with how the product is to be cost-effectively manufactured while meeting product specifications. A separate research and development or new products group may exist whose concern is developing new products and sometimes new manufacturing processes. New product development is dealt with in a following chapter.

Each of these groups represents a considerable overhead expense and impacts present and future product cost. Arbitrarily reducing these overhead expenses can probably decrease, but not eliminate, the company's current losses. But the long-range result of this action may be the elimination of any prospect of future viability.

An optimum level of expenditures is needed that balances future gains against current costs, within the limits of what can currently be afforded. Troubled manufacturing companies generally must spend more, rather than less, on technology as part of their total effort to reduce product costs.

Technology organizations must be made receptive to change. This perspective is often lacking in troubled companies, particularly if little change has occurred in upper-level personnel for some time. The periodic infusion of new upper-level talent from either suppliers or customers can infuse new thinking into an organization relatively quickly.

PRODUCT ENGINEERING FOR CURRENT PRODUCTS

The Product Engineering group controls the configuration, dimensions, tolerances, materials of manufacture, and other physical elements of today's products. For manufacturers of highly engineered products, this is a major function within the business. At the opposite end of the industrial spectrum are build-to-print job shops, manufacturing products designed by others, having little product control. Product Engineering, in a sense, is where the cost of the product is intrinsically set. The greatest impact in reducing product cost can be achieved by this function. If a product design is improved to be inherently less expensive to manufacture, the benefit can far exceed that achieved by making many other types of economies.

The Product Engineering and Manufacturing functions of a company all too often don't talk with each other. For this reason it is often functionally better if Product Engineering and Manufacturing Engineering report to the same person.

Aggressive leadership is particularly needed in Product Engineering in a turnaround situation. Usually one finds just the opposite—an unwillingness to depart from tried and true designs. The mind-set is "It works, why change it?" The answer is that the company is going broke doing it this way.

New Product Development is another function and quite distinct from Product Engineering. It deals with products that are not part (or not a significant part) of current business. A major question must be the scale of resources devoted to this subject and the time frame of expected results. New product development is fully discussed in another chapter.

Product Engineering (in many companies simply called Engineering) must be organized to be effective. Poor organization is the most common, but least appreciated, reason for ineffectiveness. Small-sized Product Engineering groups can be organized functionally in the realization that aspects that cut across functional lines will be resolved by interpersonal relationships and the physical proximity of all members of the group. When the Product Engineering organization is large, however, a strictly functional form of organization inhibits the achievement of timely and "cost" optimum results. The different groups within Product Engineering, such as Mechanical Design or Electrical Design, and Engineering Analysis, all working on separate elements of the same project, will frequently not be effectively coordinated and have schedules that do not properly coincide. Two characteristics of this failure to coordinate or integrate related activities is (1) an almost routine lateness of completion of engineering efforts and (2) great difficulty by the Engineering organization in absorbing changes in product technology and engineering methods.

Figure 11–1 shows a typical Product Engineering activity, in this case for a heavy machinery manufacturer, organized on a strictly functional basis. Certain supporting technological functions, such as Stress Analysis, have been omitted for purposes of simplicity. As you can see, each functional group is self-contained. There is no way to properly integrate related efforts among the various groups or to allocate changes in manpower needs so as to achieve a common engineering completion schedule. Figure 11–2 shows a reorganization of this Product Engineering organization, made to overcome these problems. In an integrated type of Product Engineering organization, most of the human resources potentially applicable to more than one functional group now report to a resources manager. He tracks the progress on related efforts of the various groups and reassigns manpower to achieve on-time completion of the total effort.

There are many ways to organize Product Engineering. The example in Figure 11–2 illustrates that organizational approach is a key element that should be examined if current results are not satisfactory.

When a multiplicity of Product Engineering efforts are under way, a system is needed to track progress and identify needed corrective actions before a milestone or completion date is missed. Today much software is readily available that allows this to be done using a personal computer. It is the responsibility of the resources manager to do this. Tables 11–1 and 11–2 show a typical such tracking of engineering efforts, allowing management to know the current status: what is ahead of schedule; what is behind schedule; what is taking far more time than needed; and how much more time will be necessary to complete an effort. The resources manager assures that the engineering schedules dovetail into the program master schedule.

The overall program manager, described later in this chapter, will frequently track the customer order as a whole. Using similar software, he will track all major elements of purchased items, subcontracted activities, manufacturing, and engineering, to ensure meeting the customer's requirements and delivery schedule.

Being properly organized, well-managed, and sufficiently staffed are not all that is needed for the Product Engineering organization to succeed in significantly reducing the company's product costs. Two additional key ingredients are required. These are the possession of specialized staff skills and the use of advanced engineering methods. The specific specialized skills and advanced engineering methods will depend on the product and industry. Product Engineering must allow a company to trade brains for brawn. In other words, raising the sophistication of a company's engineering approach and increasing the intellectual content of the product by performing more extensive engineering analysis allows companies to achieve a significant reduction in manufacturing cost. For example, in designing something a half-inch thinner than before, through use of sophisticated engineering analysis, the resulting manufacturing savings are usually much greater than the cost of doing the needed engineering analysis.

Many large Product Engineering organizations are primarily staffed with generalists knowledgeable in the overall product. For the detail design of specific elements, internal design standards are usually consulted. Design standards freeze

Figure 11-1.
Product Engineering Organization

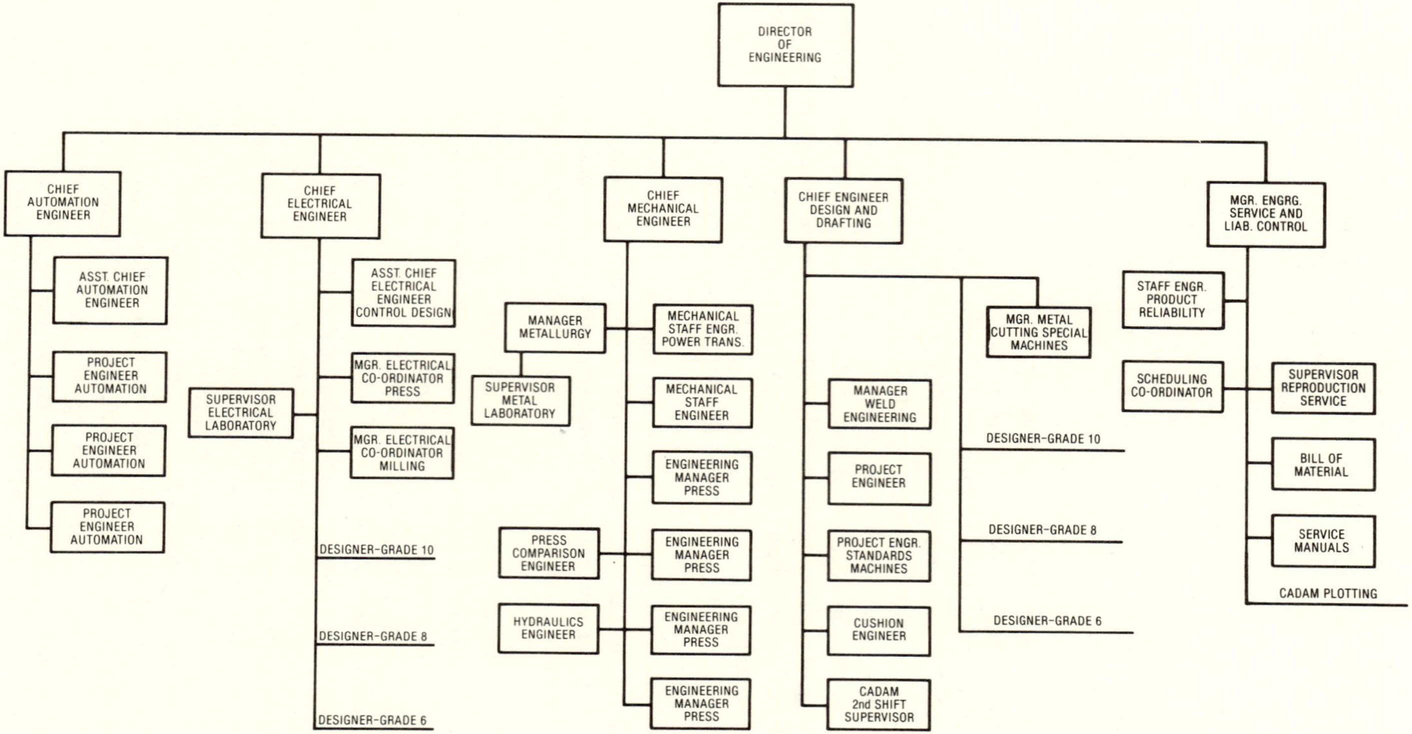

DIRECTOR OF ENGINEERING

CHIEF AUTOMATION ENGINEER
- ASST. CHIEF AUTOMATION ENGINEER
- PROJECT ENGINEER AUTOMATION
- PROJECT ENGINEER AUTOMATION
- PROJECT ENGINEER AUTOMATION

CHIEF ELECTRICAL ENGINEER
- ASST. CHIEF ELECTRICAL ENGINEER CONTROL DESIGN
- MGR. ELECTRICAL CO-ORDINATOR PRESS
- MGR. ELECTRICAL CO-ORDINATOR MILLING
- SUPERVISOR ELECTRICAL LABORATORY
- DESIGNER-GRADE 10
- DESIGNER-GRADE 8
- DESIGNER-GRADE 6

CHIEF MECHANICAL ENGINEER
- MANAGER METALLURGY
- SUPERVISOR METAL LABORATORY
- MECHANICAL STAFF ENGR. POWER TRANS.
- MECHANICAL STAFF ENGINEER
- ENGINEERING MANAGER PRESS
- PRESS COMPARISON ENGINEER
- ENGINEERING MANAGER PRESS
- ENGINEERING MANAGER PRESS
- HYDRAULICS ENGINEER
- ENGINEERING MANAGER PRESS

CHIEF ENGINEER DESIGN AND DRAFTING
- MGR. METAL CUTTING SPECIAL MACHINES
- MANAGER WELD ENGINEERING
- PROJECT ENGINEER
- PROJECT ENGR. STANDARDS MACHINES
- CUSHION ENGINEER
- CADAM 2nd SHIFT SUPERVISOR
- DESIGNER-GRADE 10
- DESIGNER-GRADE 8
- DESIGNER-GRADE 6

MGR. ENGRG. SERVICE AND LIAB. CONTROL
- STAFF ENGR. PRODUCT RELIABILITY
- SCHEDULING CO-ORDINATOR
- SUPERVISOR REPRODUCTION SERVICE
- BILL OF MATERIAL
- SERVICE MANUALS
- CADAM PLOTTING

144

Figure 11-2.
Reorganized Product Engineering Organization

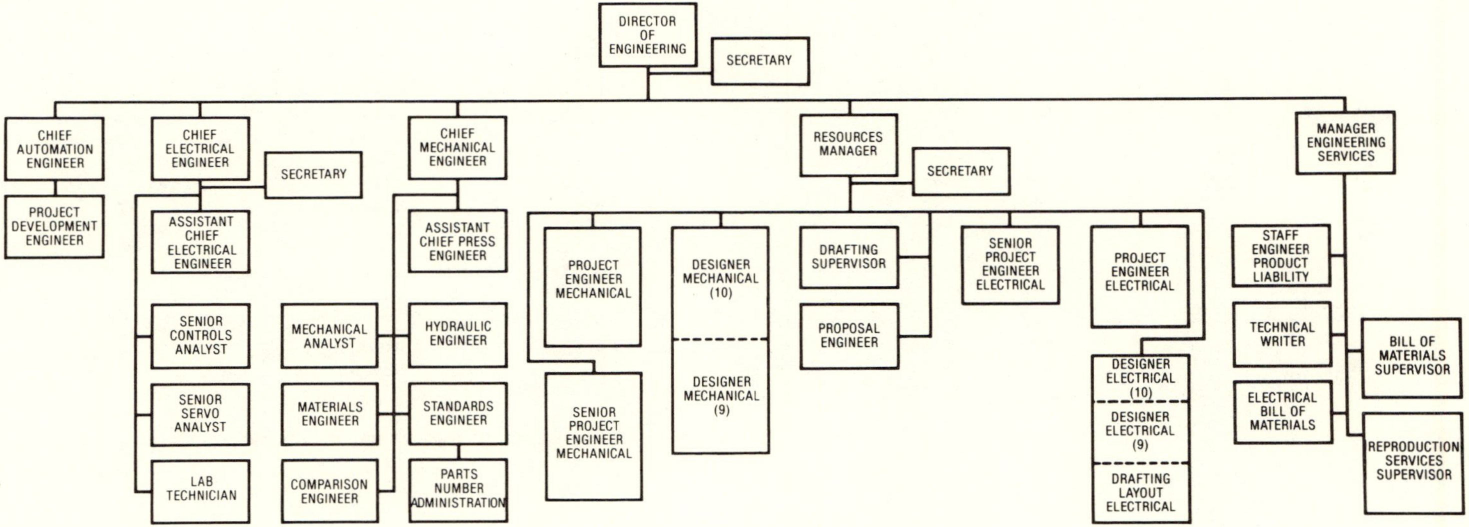

Table 11-1.
Engineering Department Performance—Mechanical

JOB NO.	DUE DATE	BUDGET HOURS	HOURS SCHEDULED TO DATE	HOURS USED TO DATE	% COMPLETION DATE ACTUAL	% COMPLETION DATE SCHEDULED	+AHEAD -BEHIND SCHEDULED	+AHEAD -BEHIND SCHEDULED	+OVER -UNDER BUDGET	% EFFICIENCY	BACKLOG AT 100% EFFICIENCY	BACKLOG AT ACTUAL EFFICIENCY
4156	HOLD	200	150	260	33	75	-42	-84	194	25	134	528
4164	1-12-85	3625	3625	6127	100	100	0	0	2502	53	0	0
4165	1-12-85	1600	1600	2938	100	100	0	0	1338	54	0	0
4166	3-29-85	400	328	142	32	82	-50	-200	14	90	272	302
4168	2-2-85	2500	2500	5066	95	100	-5	-125	2691	47	125	267
4170	2-16-85	4725	4725	6796	95	100	-5	-236	2307	66	236	258
4171	2-16-85	1600	1600	2280	97	100	-3	-48	728	68	48	71
4173	5-18-85	350	225	231	36	64	-28	-99	105	55	224	411
4182	11-10-84	1350	1350	1759	100	100	0	0	409	77	0	0
4184	2-22-85	350	350	145	41	100	-59	-207	2	99	207	209
4186	1-26-85	3015	3015	2512	90	100	-10	-302	-202	106	302	279
4188	4-27-85	4300	2795	1005	30	65	-35	-1505	-285	128	3010	2345
4189	8-17-85	4300	0	89	2	0	2	71	18	80	4229	5305
4190	11-24-85	2965	0	41	1	0	1	42	-1	101	2923	2888
4191	11-3-85	2850	0	65	2	0	2	66	-1	101	2784	2761
4193	2-16-85	3480	3480	2390	95	100	-5	-174	-916	138	174	126
4194	3-29-85	3480	2780	1154	65	80	-15	-518	-1108	196	1218	621
4195	1-26-85	1000	1000	3112	95	100	-5	-50	2162	31	50	164
4196	9-15-84	50	50	58	100	100	0	0	8	86	0	0
4264	5-3-85	2000	860	218	15	43	-28	-560	-82	138	1700	1235

Total Backlog 17636 17668

Table 11-2.
Engineering Department Performance—Electrical

JOB NO.	DUE DATE	BUDGET HOURS	HOURS SCHEDULED TO DATE	HOURS USED TO DATE	% COMPLETION DATE ACTUAL	% COMPLETION DATE SCHEDULED	+AHEAD -BEHIND SCHEDULED	+AHEAD -BEHIND SCHEDULED	+OVER -UNDER BUDGET	% EFFICIENCY	BACKLOG AT 100% EFFICIENCY	BACKLOG AT ACTUAL EFFICIENCY
95-4096	8-31-84	1300	1300	769	97	100	-3	-39	-492	164	39	24
4207	3-8-85	450	450	302	67	100	-33	-149	1	100	1	149
4208	5-10-85	100	0	29	90	0	90	90	-61	310	10	3
4209	4-19-85	200	50	85	90	25	65	130	-95	212	20	9
4211	5-10-85	250	25	49	20	10	10	25	-1	102	200	196
4212	5-17-85	450	105	9	2	23	-21	-96	0	100	441	441
4213	2-15-85	710	710	63	100	100	0	0	-647	1127	0	0
4214	2-22-85	200	200	80	100	100	0	0	-120	250	0	0
4215	5-24-85	100	0	7	7	0	7	7	0	100	93	93
4216	4-26-85	200	0	27	14	0	14	27	0	100	173	173
4217	6-7-85	250	0	38	15	0	15	38	1	99	213	215
4218	10-11-85	450	0	0	0	0	0	0	0	100	450	450
4219	4-6-85	455	250	36	20	55	-35	-159	-55	253	364	144
4223	4-26-85	40	5	0	0	13	-13	-5	0	100	40	40
4224	7-5-85	750	0	459	61	0	61	458	2	293	293	293
4225	7-19-85	125	0	1	1	0	1	1	0	100	124	124
4226	6-26-85	40	0	11	28	0	28	11	0	100	29	29
4227	8-2-85	500	0	156	31	0	31	155	1	99	345	347
4234	2-21-85	500	0	10	2	0	2	10	0	100	490	490
4239	12-7-84	350	350	521	100	100	0	0	171	67	0	0
4244	1-19-85	100	100	70	100	100	0	0	-30	143	0	0
4249	2-2-85	30	30	0	100	100	0	0	-30	100	0	0
4250	3-16-85	960	920	758	97	96	1	11	-173	123	29	23
4251	3-30-85	660	580	651	90	88	2	14	57	91	66	72
4253	12-7-84	100	100	256	100	100	0	0	156	39	0	0
4254	2-2-85	200	200	230	100	100	0	0	30	87	0	0
4255	2-2-85	200	200	159	100	100	0	0	-41	126	0	0
4256	3-30-85	270	230	40	15	85	-70	-190	-1	101	230	230
4257	2-16-85	150	150	10	7	100	-93	-140	-1	105	140	133
4259	2-15-85	25	25	26	100	100	0	0	1	96	0	0
4260	9-27-85	200	0	0	0	0	0	0	0	100	200	200
									Total Backlog		4138	3875

147

technology in time. If the company must reduce product costs, the way something was previously done can no longer be left unquestioned. The only way to depart from design standards is to have staff who have expertise in these areas, that is, who know more than the design standards. If the product has hydraulics aspects, the company needs a hydraulics engineer. If the company uses electronic controls, it needs controls specialists. If bearings are important to the company's designs, the company needs to obtain bearings expertise. Such specialized knowledge returns its expenditure fast through reduced product cost.

If a company's design standards do not lead to optimum cost designs, then an important task of the staff specialists is to supersede them with new design standards that reduce overall cost. If necessary, staff should be recruited for this specific purpose. They should also develop lists of preferred parts, sizes, and subassemblies that will create economies in purchasing and manufacturing and lower requirements for inventory.

Advanced engineering methods are the key to a "brains for brawn" strategy. Computer-aided design is an example. Here, designs are created on a cathode ray screen and stored in a computer, instead of having people bent over drafting tables. The economic savings do not result from the time saved in drafting, although this is a popular misconception. Rather, one obtains a significant expansion in engineering capability. Things that were never done before because it wasn't practical to do so now become everyday occurrences. A typical such consequence is the advent of user-friendly drawings. Previously used hand-drawn designs had to contain all dimensions, manufacturing notes, and the like, necessary for all the processes in the creation of the part. Hence, for a machined weldment, the welder and the machinist would use the same drawing. It was cluttered and difficult to read. Making interpretive mistakes was easy. Now, with the design stored in a computer memory, it is an easy matter to create specialized drawing variants tailored for each specific user. In these specialized drawings all extraneous information is removed; all dimensions are taken from where the user would like to take them; all special geometric allowances are already figured in—a user-friendly drawing.

Other applications of computer-aided design that provide significant productivity increases include the following:

- Proposal efforts—quick layout sketches of intended product
- Technical publications—repair manuals and parts books
- Kinematics—moving the machinery dynamically through its cycle to check for interferences, as well as for force, velocity, and acceleration analysis of linkages
- Sheet metal fabrication—flat patterns and nesting to minimize scrap
- Group technology—grouping of parts with similar characteristics in a data base, i.e., fasteners, springs, fittings, frames, bases, to achieve standardization or minimize redrawing, since the new design may require "the same except for" drawing task

- Packaging and crating
- Weight and volume calculations
- Schematics and wiring diagrams
- Numerical control—machining, welding, sheet metal fabrication, etc.
- Facilities layouts
- Bill of materials generation
- Tool design

The list goes on and on. Productivity increase ratios for these activities will range from 1:1 to 30:1 or higher. In the aggregate the total engineering effort will be improved by at least 3:1. What is perhaps even more important is that many tasks cannot be performed any other way and the *quality* of the engineering effort is significantly enhanced.

Great advances have been made in engineering analysis. For instance, sophisticated finite element engineering computer software is readily available whose use, however, requires a staff with a high level of engineering education. Now, old rules of thumb can be reexamined and one can know in detail how much safety and excessive conservatism exist in a design. Using these advanced approaches may necessitate bringing in new blood. The gains from adopting advanced methods occur with almost lightning speed. For example, a part designed with a hole used only for convenience in lifting could be found to have that hole in the worst possible location, negatively affecting the strength of the product. Moving the hole in accordance with the analysis would allow the part thickness to be reduced from 10 inches to 8 inches, with a savings of hundreds of dollars per part.

Another example is shown in Figure 11–3, a cast gear hub, used in making large, fabricated industrial gears, containing cast-in holes for the purpose of weight reduction. The upper figure shows the standard design, evolved over many years. The lower figure shows the new design, developed using finite element analysis, enlarging the "lightening" holes to leave only the material that is mandatory for safety and effectiveness. The new design weighs 1,047 pounds less. It cost $1,047 less.

As this process of analysis and change is repeated again and again throughout the product designs, intrinsic manufacturing costs dramatically decrease, while product integrity and quality increase.

Design engineers are often not sufficiently sensitive to the cost implications of their design choices. This is why a Value Engineering function is needed (usually placed within Manufacturing Engineering). A strong interaction and rapid feedback from Value Engineering to Product Engineering help to evolve lower-cost product designs. Creation of this process is frequently required in a troubled firm.

Figure 11–3.
Comparison of Old and New Cast Gear Hub Designs*

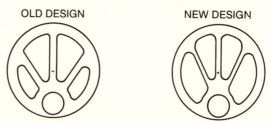

OLD DESIGN   NEW DESIGN

*The new design, developed using finite element engineering analysis, contains larger and repositioned lightening holes, resulting in a savings of $1,047 per hub.

MANUFACTURING ENGINEERING

Manufacturing Engineering comprises that group of functions that are related to production technology. Manufacturing Engineering is responsible for providing the know-how needed to manufacture products. It has the primary responsibility within the company for achieving meaningful product-cost reductions through changes in the methods, processes, and equipment used to manufacture the products. It must also provide guidance to Product Engineering on product design changes and simplifications needed to improve product producibility and lower manufacturing cost. In a troubled company, Manufacturing Engineering is normally understaffed. It is also usually missing key technical skills and may be weakly managed. As a result, it is probably not focusing attention on what is most deserving of high priority.

Manufacturing Engineering should be involved early in the design process, through program or design reviews. Their purpose should be to consider manufacturability of designs and design simplification and to suggest possible cost reductions.

In a properly functioning Manufacturing Engineering organization, the manufacturing cost reductions achieved each year range from four to six times the amoung expended on the effort. So why do companies spend so little on this activity? The answer lies in a general lack of perception of this multiplier effect in obtaining savings. Manufacturing Engineering is often considered just another necessary overhead function, whose cost is to be minimized as part of overhead containment. In this environment Manufacturing Engineering will often not be as productive as it should be and the multiplier effect will be absent.

The troubled company has usually not met its Manufacturing Engineering needs for many years. Therefore, if, as part of the turnaround, it is restaffed and revitalized, many fast payback opportunities will be identified and successfully implemented. The Manufacturing Engineering function should be expanded, even though staff reductions are under way in other functions.

Some of the key activities of the Manufacturing Engineering function in a turnaround must be:

- reduction or elimination of labor intensive operations;
- identification of parts or manufacturing steps that can be more economically obtained by outside subcontracting;
- proposal of design simplifications that significantly reduce manufacturing cost;
- product and process quality improvement;
- elimination of rework and scrap.

Specific Functions

The Manufacturing Engineering activity comprises a number of specific functions.

Machinery Evaluation. There is more than one way to make something and, for a given approach, a choice of different vendors' equipment to do so. If a machine or process has been used for some years, a more optimal approach may exist. It is the responsibility of those in Machinery Evaluation to identify these alternatives, propose a course of action, prepare a supporting return on investment and payback analysis, debug the new equipment when it arrives, and bring it into successful use.

An example was a production process of Danly Machine Corporation to routinely drill more than 100 identical, equally spaced holes, in a helical pattern, around the outside of a cylinder. A special machine had been developed about fifteen years before that did this job reliably and productively in about 4-1/2 minutes. During a two-year period many alternative approaches were examined, with the goal of finding a better process. Finally a little-known machine tool, made by Sakazaki, a small Japanese machine tool builder, was discovered. With minor modification this machine could perform the hole-drilling operation on four parts simultaneously, taking about 1.1 minutes per part. What had taken four employees, two men on two shifts, could now be done by one employee working a single shift—a significant cost savings.

Special Process Engineering. Depending on its industry, a company may have an area of process technology that is particularly important to its manufacturing. For a chemical company, this could be organic chemistry; for a powder metal parts producer, it would be powder metallurgy; and for a machinery company using welded structures, it would be weld engineering. In each case the logic is similar. The company needs to have well-educated, experienced engineers or applied scientists in this special process area who can keep the company's processes at the state of the art, which means lowest manufacturing cost.

An example of the benefit of having an effective special process engineering activity, in this case welding, is shown in Figure 11–4. The figure shows substituting current American Welding Society weld specifications for an older specification, in joining two thick steel plates, allowed the weld area to be reduced by forty-two percent. This reduced costs in welding labor, weld metal, and the

Figure 11–4.
More Recent American Welding Society Specifications Used in Weld Area
(Allowing Reduction of 42 Percent in Welded Area)

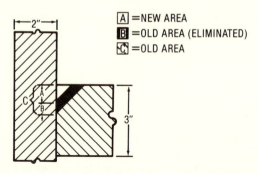

A = NEW AREA
B = OLD AREA (ELIMINATED)
C = OLD AREA

labor in chamfering preparation by $11.41 per foot of welded structure—a dramatic savings.

Value Engineering. Value Engineering advises Product Engineering on design changes, questions tolerance requirements and choices of materials, conducts standardization studies, and examines product reliability and quality assurance effects. It examines the need to improve product producibility and reduce product manufacturing cost. This function serves as a critic for new designs, helping to reduce their costs. An example illustrates this function in action. The design group of a molding machine manufacturer produced a design containing a small, relatively unimportant access cover with rounded corners that was located on the back of the machine. Value Engineering questioned the purpose of the rounded corners. The answer was the designer happened to draw it that way. Because the cover with rounded corners would cost 25 percent more to produce than a rectangular cover, the design was changed to a rectangular cover.

Tool Engineering. This activity designs and develops special tooling, fixtures, and feeders, selects standard tools, and, in a great many ways, optimizes the productivity of current manufacturing equipment. A turnaround demands that a company's existing fixed assets be used to best advantage and provide the lowest possible product costs.

Facilities Engineering. This function examines plant layout and work flow with the purpose of reducing materials handling requirements and, thereby, costs. It seeks to minimize the amount of manufacturing plant needed to meet manufacturing requirements. It is also responsible for plant engineering, that is, engineering aspects of maintaining existing facilities.

Assembly Engineering. This activity identifies better procedures and methods for assembling the company's products, reducing the amount of assembly labor required.

In many companies, Industrial Engineering functions, such as production routing preparation, labor standards preparation, and the like, are also part of

Manufacturing Engineering. These have been omitted from this discussion but may need improvement as well.

Manufacturing Engineering also frequently plays an important role in a company's make/buy decisions. This is due to its ability to judge the manufacturing capability of potential suppliers and its ability to estimate the company's internal costs of manufacture.

PROGRAM MANAGEMENT

Manufacturers of highly engineered custom products often find it difficult coordinating the various technological elements of a customer's order. They find difficulties in integrating the various activities that must act in concert, including engineering, manufacturing, purchasing, and field installation. Companies fail to meet their delivery dates and are organizationally unable to effectively respond to the demands presented by numerous customer-originated design changes.

For these technology-driven products, the solution to the problems above is the creation of a Program Management function. It must report to the president, executive vice-president—operations, or other officer capable of working across functional lines.

Program Management typically consists of a small staff of highly competent engineering specialists with excellent organizational and interpersonal skills. It may be organized by product line, customer, or project. Theirs is the ultimate product responsibility, ensuring that the product requirements of function, quality, cost, and delivery are met.

Once Marketing/Sales has identified an opportunity and secured a contract, it is assigned to the appropriate program manager, who has the responsibility for the product from concept through production and delivery to the customer, what may be termed "from lust to dust." He is the primary interface with the customer's Engineering and Operations Departments, as well as with the company's internal functional groups (i.e., Marketing, Engineering, Manufacturing, Quality, etc.). Marketing, meanwhile, continues to provide the interface with customer purchasing, conducts contract and price negotiations, and so on, and has ultimate account responsibility. However, once an order is received, all subsequent changes to the product, its "mission," and schedules are negotiated by and cleared with the program manager *only*.

Although the program manager has no administrative control over other functional groups, his ultimate product responsibility makes him one of the most powerful people in the organization, in that the other organizational groups *must* respond to his resource requirements to ensure that the program is completed satisfactorily.

He typically performs the following:

• Develops and maintains the program schedule
• Tracks time and cost performance

- Conducts customer, internal, and supplier meetings as required
- Conducts program and design reviews according to the schedule
- Provides the engineering, manufacturing, quality interface with the customer
- Ensures that human resources are adequate for successful program execution and completion by identifying tasks and responsibilities
- Reports progress and problems to the president and other functional heads on a timely basis

It becomes obvious that this individual must possess finely tuned interpersonal skills, be authoritative without being dictatorial, be sensitive to the needs of Marketing, customers, other internal functions, and be an effective communicator at all organizational levels. Through continual monitoring he must be able to anticipate problems that will affect program performance and respond accordingly.

For upper management and the customer, it identifies the key individual on whom the success of the program depends. Therefore, he is given the authority to do all that is necessary to ensure its success or to report impediments to success. With his ability to cut across organizational lines, the program manager is in the best position to ensure that the company's and customer's objectives are met. He also frees the other functional groups from the mundane tasks associated with program administration.

Generally, Program Management is not well received by Marketing and, sometimes, Engineering, at least initially, since it is perceived as a diminishing of their responsibilities and prerogatives. In actual fact Program Management frees them to do their jobs better (sell more products) and provides assurance that the program is adequately covered and nothing will "fall through the cracks." It also helps them in that any customer-requested change must be responded to immediately, both internally and externally, for its cost and schedule impact. Marketing is then obliged to immediately transmit this information to the customer and renegotiate the price and schedule change accordingly, with the program manager providing the backup data to support the negotiations. The two eventually become an effective team.

Engineering, on the other hand, is free to conduct its business of engineering and provides backup to the program manager on his customer interactions as required.

Although organizations such as this have functioned for years in the military/ aerospace and electronics industries, they are only now being generally adopted by the automotive and special machinery industries.

12

NEW PRODUCT DEVELOPMENT

Statistics show that successful product development and commercialization require a time span of nine to eighteen years. A troubled company usually cannot afford to devote resources to such a long-term payoff. Most new product development has a longer time horizon than is usually commensurate with a company turnaround. The common perspective in a turnaround is to identify new product development activities that can be eliminated. Occasionally, however, new products do become an important turnaround element. With this in mind, self-funded new product development efforts should be carefully scrutinized and, owing to such scrutiny, most will probably need to be eliminated. If a current market need truly exists for a product similar to that of an uncompleted product development, and such a product has been successfully developed abroad, then consider licensing it. Ceasing their own product development and licensing a European design, for example, helped in the turnaround of Fairbanks Morse, the diesel engine manufacturer.

Sometimes the long-term viability of a company requires a significant new product development effort. In these instances ways exist to have others pay for it. The advent of research and development (R & D) limited partnerships means that new products can now be developed with other people's money. A negative cash flow is no longer inherent. This will reduce the necessity of drastically curtailing this activity.

U.S. tax laws make R & D limited partnerships attractive to investors. Such a partnership, with a promise to commercialize the product if it is successfully developed, for a stated royalty percentage, should allow the development to proceed at little cost and no risk to the company. Joint technology ventures between companies in which the troubled firm contributes know-how and the other firm, cash are another emerging alternative.

WHAT IS A NEW PRODUCT?

A new product can be an item new to your company but previously commercialized by others, or it can be truly new to the world. But to be a new product, it must contain at least one of these tactical dimensions:

- Performs a new function
- Performs an old function, using a different technology (with a different cost structure)
- Different customers
- Different competitors

There are many other possible ways of listing these same dimensions that contain market and technology elements. By this test, much of what passes for new products can be seen to lack the basis for such an appellation. Many companies believe that any change in the products they are currently making constitutes a new product effort. This is false because product line extensions and alterations do not contain the basic management considerations intrinsic to new products. The common corporate public relations claim that fifty percent of their products didn't exist five years ago is seldom, if ever, true.

STAGES IN PRODUCT COMMERCIALIZATION

Product development and commercialization usually pass through the following steps (sometimes without the company being aware of the process):

- Conception
- Economic and technical feasibility
- Product and process development
- Pilot production and sales
- Full commercialization

The cost of conception is little, say, under $5,000. The cost of feasibility studies are often modest, say, under $50,000 (depending, of course, on the industry). The cost of product and process development may not be straining, say, typically twenty times the cost of establishing feasibility. The costs of pilot production and sales, including outlays for fixed assets, will probably be substantially greater than those of development, say, by a factor of twenty. This is an economic critical point in the process, for it requires financial commitments far beyond the scope of the typical product development organization. Full commercialization will raise the tab still higher.

The increase in cost associated with going from stage to stage in product development and commercialization is often unappreciated when the initiation of a product development effort is approved. This may be the single greatest reason why new product ideas do not eventually become successfully commercialized. Amazingly, this fact seems little known.

New product efforts usually fail, in my observation, in going from the developmental stage to the pilot production and sales stage because of lack of understanding of the increases required in funds, people, equipment, and time. Many managements expect this stage to be accomplished solely on good intentions.

In mature industries most family-owned firms or industrial firms with under $100 million in sales spend somewhere around one percent of sales, year after year, on new product development. These firms almost never have a new product success. The reason lies in the unwillingness to provide the required funds at the expenditure escalating points of the new product process for what are potentially viable new products.

It is important for the troubled firm to realize the scale of future monetary requirements. If the money will not be available to complete the project, it should be terminated.

TYPES OF NEW PRODUCT APPROACHES

Most new product development efforts follow and can be classified as belonging to one of two approaches. These are frequently referred to as technology push and market need/market pull/demand pull.

Technology Push

Technology push results when the driving force of the effort is the perceived potential of the technology itself. Marketing's role is secondary, becoming important only after the product or process has been developed. Most of the truly great inventions of the period 1830–1915 fell into this category (e.g., steam turbine, triode, telephone). For great inventions, it is truly impossible to estimate the ultimate size of the market. Who, at the outset, could have foreseen the market for computers or xerography? In fact, Sperry Univac is purported to have initially estimated that the size of the total computer market by the year 2000 would be 1,000 or 2,000 machines. This type of product, in effect, follows Says Law in economics: "Supply creates demand." It is this kind of success that inspires all technology push efforts, whether warranted or not.

Most new products, however, do not fall into the catgory of the 500 greatest inventions. The problem arises when minor innovations are treated as if they did. Most corporate and division R & D groups have one or more inspired new product idea generators. These people often become obsessed with the cleverness of an idea and will push its development with little market information, in the simple belief that a market will automatically develop later. This can be termed an answer looking for a question. The frequent result is a technical success and a commercial failure. In this category we can put some of the highly publicized technical innovations of the past twenty years—the heat pipe, rolamite, and laser (most firms developing lasers in the 1960s lost large sums of money without discovering a real market for the products).

One test of the appropriateness of the technology push approach for specific product efforts is its level of innovativeness. Does the product perform a new function and employ a substantially different technology? If not, are we actually faced with a substitution of new technology in existing products (e.g., changing from electromechanical to solid state electronic technology), a materials substitution, a size change, or the addition of new features? Technology push, as it involves great business risk, is an inappropriate management approach for a troubled company.

By and large, technology push is an unproductive corporate approach to new products. However, it usually proves difficult to kill such an effort in the typical industrial corporation when the project is of long standing because such efforts develop a constituency.

Market Need/Demand Pull

Most successful new products, say 80 percent, were developed as solutions to perceived market needs. This is the most reliable way to succeed in new products, for it means diminished business risk because there is less chance the fully developed product will fail to be successfully sold. This approach is much more difficult to manage than technology push because it requires a significant input and coordination with elements outside the new products organization. It also requires skillful handling of the temperamental egos of inventive engineers and technical managers, who must be prevented from doing what is personally technically interesting, but of little potential commercial merit.

IDENTIFICATION OF NEW PRODUCT OPPORTUNITIES

Some companies have a product planning group independent of R & D, frequently tied to the Marketing organization. In such companies this group identifies and specifies the characteristics of the product to be developed and its performance/cost requirements.

In most companies, however, particularly those in industrial products, new product identification is usually the province of the Product R & D organization. A company's Product R & D organization is poorly positioned to see market needs for new products, yet it is often almost exclusively relied on to perform this task. Those people in a company who deal directly with customers—salesmen, service people, and so on—are often the best potential sources of new product needs (although they don't know what is technologically possible). This potential source of new product ideas is seldom exploited. It takes a deliberate effort to do so.

One important but often neglected way to identify market needs is to sensitize your sales force to be on the lookout for them when meeting with customer purchasing agents or engineering personnel. This is particularly effective in small and medium-sized firms where the salesmen are headquartered at the same location as the product development organization. These customers often consider your development of a new product that meets their needs to be a favor and will, consequently, be unusually loyal customers.

A good example of this process occurred when the sales manager of a machined foundry products operation of Amsted Industries called on the purchasing agent of Detroit Diesel Allison Division of General Motors, a major diesel engine manufacturer, to obtain an order for rocker arms. The purchasing agent told the sales manager that he didn't need any. As the conversation progressed the purchasing agent mentioned that he needed a new source of valve guides, and if the price and quality were right, he might place an initial order of 10 million pieces. This information was carried back to the supplier's R & D organization. In time a new, more cost-effective manufacturing technology was developed, a sales agreement negotiated, a plant built, and a successful new product line introduced.

TESTING ECONOMIC FEASIBILITY

It is surprising how far new product programs can progress before someone asks the questions "What can happen if we succeed? Is the potential market large enough to warrant an effort?"

Two examples from my own experience will illustrate the importance of asking the latter question:

Example 1: A government aerospace facility said it needed a substitute for a special grease containing Japan wax. When I investigated how much was used per year, I learned that it was fifty pounds. End of interest.

Example 2: When I learned that it might be possible to manufacture small, single-cylinder engine crankshafts by new, proprietary, lower-cost methods, I wanted to know how many such crankshafts were used in the United States in a year. According to data obtained from the Outdoor Power Equipment Institute, it was about 11.5 million crankshafts. This was worth exploring further.

Another major aspect of economic feasibility is the likelihood of the intended customer to buy such a product. This subject is far too often neglected, particularly when firms wish to develop an industrial product for sale outside their usual product area. For example, many firms have developed automotive components for sale to major automobile companies only to learn the hard way that Detroit has a strong "not-invented-here" attitude. It is foolish to develop technology for automotive original equipment manufacturer use on speculation. This holds true for other industries that are disinclined to accept either outside or new suppliers.

An aspect that is sometimes overlooked is the willingness of a supplier to provide a proprietary component essential to the new product. For example, a chemical mixture may require a compound made only by Monsanto. Monsanto, however, may have other preferred uses for their output. Besides chemicals, this type of problem may also occur in electronics, materials, and a great many other areas. Availability of critical purchase items should be established as part of the economic feasibility examination.

For nonconsumer goods, another important consideration is whether or not the new product would perform the function of what it replaces, at a lower cost. If not, be wary. Most human needs are already met, in some way or another. The question is, at what cost? Even unique new products can be examined from this viewpoint. In the days before copying machines I observed that when a Japanese businessman wanted a copy of an article or a book chapter, a secretary was sent to the library with a portable typewriter to type the material. We now know that xerography is clearly a less expensive alternative.

TECHNICAL FEASIBILITY STUDY

Before embarking on full technical development, it is important to know how likely it is that the product can be developed to achieve its intended purpose. Spending $5,000 to $50,000 trying to show that it can be done, even crudely, by the people who will have to do the actual development will save many times that cost if an unexpected but fundamental problem is uncovered.

Most organizations that have a pattern of technical development failure can be found to have neglected the feasibility study phase in order to rush prematurely into full technical development. The establishment of technical feasibility before embarking on full-scale product development should be a requirement in all firms.

A good example of a fiasco resulting from lack of a technical feasibility study is the Cheyenne helicopter. Developed by Lockheed for the U.S. Army at a cost of many millions of dollars, the design of the Cheyenne helicopter uniquely combined the power and control systems. Several crashes and near crashes later, the U.S. Army insisted that Lockheed call in outside consultants to examine the feasibility of this technical approach. As part of the consulting team, I performed an analysis and found that the control system was inherently mechanically unstable—the basic concept was not feasible!

FINANCIAL EVALUATION

When should a complete financial and business evaluation take place? Obviously, at a decision point. Two such natural points exist. The first is whether or not to progress from product development to pilot production and sales; and the second is whether or not to proceed with full-scale production and commercialization. Of course, before entering product development, a preliminary financial evaluation is needed. At the decision point before entering pilot production, market potential can be reassessed using additional market research, direct product and overhead costs estimated, and capital investment requirements established for fixed assets and working capital. If the probable return on investment is attractive and other company criteria are met, going forward is permissible.

However, once started down a road, one need not feel compelled to go to its end. Pilot production and sales will be educationally important. They will allow for a much more accurate assessment of the probable level of sales that can ultimately be achieved and a better ability to estimate production and overhead costs. If costs creep up, as they often do, so that significant further investment is no longer attractive, a complete financial and business analysis before committing to full production should reveal this. If this is so, a decision should be made to either liquidate or sell off the specific new product effort.

An often neglected but critical question that needs to be addressed during the financial evaluation is whether or not the firm can afford to have the new product succeed. A successful new product makes significant demands on working capital; as sales mount, the resulting requirements for inventory and accounts receivable surge. Does the firm have the resources for this? A significant new product success may also present major demands for new plant and equipment to deal with the additional sales volume. Is this practical? If a firm doesn't have the resources needed for the new product if it succeeds, it should realize this as early as possible. A good example of a product whose requirements were too extensive for its innovators is the Weed-Eater lawn tool; they were forced to sell out while nearing insolvency.

MARKET SHARE CONSIDERATION

The results of most new product development efforts are without meaningful patent protection (except in a few high-technology industries). A firm usually has to rely on the know-how it acquired through the development process and the marketing advantage of being the first to offer the product in order to inhibit the entry of competitors.

When a new product falls within the scope of a firm's existing product lines and those of its present competitors, current market share becomes an important consideration in assessing the long-range prospects for the new product. If the product innovating company has a small market share relative to those of its competitors, these larger competitors can copy the product (i.e., reverse engineering) and, by dint of their greater marketing power, shoulder the innovator aside. This has happened countless times.

USE OF EXISTING BUSINESS RESOURCES

Every industrial enterprise has specialized expertise, based on its current products and markets, in engineering/R & D, marketing, manufacturing, purchasing, and technical service. New products have requirements in all of these areas that may or may not coincide with the existing company know-how or culture. The closer the match, generally the higher the probability of success because of the better understanding of what is at hand. Also, the use of existing corporate resources lessens the need for additional resources, thereby improving the economics of the proposition.

If a match in existing and required capabilities does not occur in at least two, and it is hoped three, of these critical areas, it is necessary to reconsider the likelihoods of gain and risk.

Most firms departing too far from businesses they understand underestimate their chances for failure. If hurdle rates are used as part of the new product decision-making process, then it is judicious to adjust the required hurdle rate to degree of resource match.

OUTSIDE RESOURCES

Most aspects of the new product effort include learning from the experience. It is important to keep the knowledge base in-house and instantly available. For this reason it is undesirable to use outside resources in a significant way, unless the product is being obtained under license. Few firms are inclined to make significant use of outside resources. Because of this lack of a market, there isn't a great breadth of suitable services available. It is not possible to farm out the bulk of the effort.

Market research firms (e.g., Technomic Consultants or Pierce–Suter Associates) can be useful in learning about the size, structure, and characteristics of existing markets. They can also help in assessing sales strategy alternatives.

Manufacturing job shops can make dies, parts, prototypes, test rigs, and sample batches. They often provide the fast turnaround so necessary in a product development program. The large contract R & D organizations are not well-suited to assisting in specific product development. Their staffs, by and large, do not have the ''business sense'' needed to make a product design cost-effective, and they lack insight into your company's current manufacturing capabilities.

Most well-known new product idea identification consulting firms and brokers are of no use. What they have to sell are either very specialized developments with no market to speak of or inferior products that have not previously succeeded. One notable exception to this is the New York City-based firm Rain Hill Group, Inc. In general, if you are missing some professional skills that you will need on an ongoing basis, it is best to obtain them by hiring people. This also provides continuity.

LICENSING

If you wish to make a product similar to that already being made by another company, particularly a foreign one, licensing may be highly desirable. Often, for a modest royalty, you obtain access to specific information that would otherwise cost your company many times that amount to duplicate. It can also save several years of effort. On the other hand, if the royalty is steep or a license not available, there is nothing wrong with reverse engineering. Little product technology is under meaningful patent protection; a few high-technology industries are an exception to this.

In order to negotiate a license agreement and determine a royalty, you must be able to analyze the worth of the license. Most firms find this difficult to do. I suggest that you first assess the likely return on investment from your making and selling the product. You can then assess how various royalty rates will affect return on investment, thereby come to some conclusion about the maximum royalty you can afford. If you can enter the business readily by reverse engineering, you can estimate the savings in development costs that would result from a license and use this as another criterion in your licensing strategy.

It is a temptation for a firm that has successfully recently developed a new product to license it to others, and thereby recoup some of its development costs. This is dangerous thinking. First, it creates a future competitor. U.S. antitrust laws are often interpreted so as to make it illegal to license a Japanese or other foreign firm on the provision that they cannot export to the U.S. market. There are also Third World country considerations. Many U.S. firms find that they are being undersold in Third World countries by their Japanese or European licensees.

Second, licensing creates multiple sources of supply, which inevitably reduces profit margins. Many firms license new products with the knowledge that multiple sources of supply increase market acceptance and market penetration for a product. They expect their royalties from these sales, which they would otherwise not have obtained, to materially benefit them. In reality, in case after case, their profits are less than they would have been if the total sales of the product were, say, only half or a third as great and the profit margin was significantly greater. The specialty metals industry is a particularly good example of this. Within the industry, over the years, Allegheny Ludlum Steel Corporation has licensed practically everything it has developed, whereas Carpenter Technology has licensed very little. Carpenter Technology has materially benefitted from its new product developments, whereas Allegheny Ludlum Steel has not. Apart from a few exceptions, it is not judicious to grant licenses. It seldom pays. First compare the contemplated benefits with the expected reduction in margin and lost sales, using a discounted cash flow approach.

ORGANIZATIONAL RELATIONSHIP OF MANUFACTURING PROCESS DEVELOPMENT AND NEW PRODUCT DEVELOPMENT

The organizational relationship of Manufacturing Process Development and Product Development in a company is a key element in the commercial success of new products. The importance of this structural relationship is never written about and is generally misunderstood.

Essentially, one of three possible organizational relationships may exist. Product Development may report to or be part of Engineering, while Manufacturing Process Development may be part of Manufacturing or Operations. In this scheme of organization, Manufacturing Process Development usually enters the scene when Engineering is nearing completion of the product's development. Another type of organization may exist in which elements of the Engineering and Manufacturing Process Development groups are brought together to form a project team for a particular product, while simultaneously continuing their normal functions. A third, and rather unusual, organizational arrangement has both Product Development and Manufacturing Process Development as parts of the same technology organization, with a single functional head. Schematically, this is shown in Figure 12–1.

Of the three organizational approaches, the first is the most common and least effective. It requires a great deal of additional time in the total product development cycle because the actions occur in series rather than in parallel. In most instances the resulting final product dissatisfies the product developers, owing to manufacturing-induced changes, and an increased likelihood exists that the final product cannot be made at a competitive cost.

The adoption by companies of CAD/CAM (Computer Aided Design/Computer Aided Manufacturing) systems forces better coordination of Product and Manufacturing Process Development activities. This is an important, but frequently misunderstood, benefit of using such systems.

A significant percentage of failed new product efforts arise from this poorly understood organizational problem. Product Development and Manufacturing Process Development function best when integrated. Optimum product development that is optimum in respect to development time, development cost, product utility, and product manufacturing cost can only arise when combining Product Development and Product Manufacturing Development functions. The same people must be concerned about what the product is intended to do and how to accomplish this cheaply.

The third organizational approach, combining New Product Development and Manufacturing Process Development, has been found to be the best of the three approaches by those few corporations that have tried it. It has the additional advantage of allowing management to easily shift resources between the two

Figure 12–1.
Three Organizational Approaches to New Product/Process Development

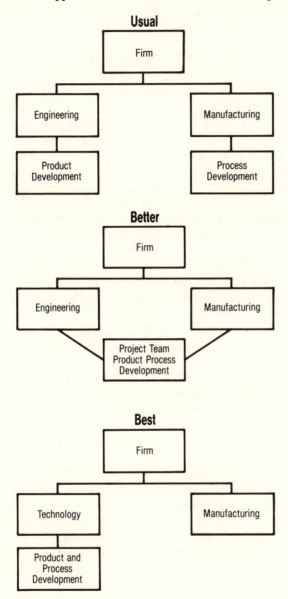

activities to better fit transitory changes in program needs, as the engineers and technicians involved are members of the same organization.

PHYSICAL LOCATION AND ISOLATION

New product efforts are often placed in a central R & D center, physically separated from the rest of the company (often in an attractive building whose picture may appear in an annual report). The common result is few, if any, commercial successes. Why?

In most companies, particularly those in industrial products, new product identification is the province of the R & D organization. It is often almost exclusively relied on to perform this task. A company's R & D organization, however, is poorly positioned to see market needs for new products.

New product R & D organizations have an inherent tendency to be too removed from the marketplace and the input from the company marketing and sales functions. It normally takes considerable perceptiveness and effort to overcome this. Geographically removing the organization compounds the problem. The physical isolation degrades the ''business sense'' of the organization.

Usually the new product will ultimately have to be made by the company's present Manufacturing organization, possibly in an existing plant. Technology transfer is largely a matter of human relations. The Operating people will have to want the new product to succeed and will need assistance with a myriad of minor, but critical, details that will continue to arise over a considerable period of time. Being there helps. It cements personal relationships and allows the Operating organization to receive answers informally and instantly from the R & D organization. All this is inhibited, if not frustrated, by a geographical separation of R & D and Operations.

Geographical separation also lessens New Products staffers' direct knowledge of the manufacturing capabilities in existing plants that can be used in commercializing new products. Seeing the machinery every day creates an awareness that would otherwise be lacking.

Putting the New Products organization in the same location as the manufacturing plant intended to receive its creative output has a strong logic. Yet example after example can be found that show this, too, doesn't work. Why?

In such instances there usually is insufficient organizational isolation. An Operating organization always has immediate and important problems hindering it from accomplishing its mission of ''getting the stuff out the door.'' An attached R & D organization, possessing manufacturing technology know-how, will be called on for immediate help with these problems. In time, the natural consequence is for this ''fire fighting'' to overwhelm the resources of the new product effort, which cannot be continually interrupted by short-range tasks if it is to effectively execute long-range programs.

The best solution seems to be locating the New Product R & D organization at the manufacturing site intended to use the bulk of its creative output, while keeping it organizationally separate. It should not be placed under the Operating organization at this site. It should have its own budget and resources. A firm understanding must exist about the level of technical support it will provide to the plant with its problems. Having the New Product R & D organization provide some support, say, up to 20 percent of its total effort, will teach the New Products organizational staff realism about what can be accomplished on the manufacturing floor, as well as the actual capabilities of machines and processes.

A schematic of these approaches is shown in Figure 12–2.

POSITIONING OF NEW PRODUCTS IN THE COMPANY STRUCTURE

New products either have some fit with the firm's existing resources, including manufacturing, selling, engineering, technical service, and purchasing, or no fit at all. If there is no fit, the new product is really a new business investment. Logic dictates that it be run as a separate business, as a division, subsidiary, or venture. Management problems often arise with regard to a product that does actually fit, which is the usual case. The best way to kill a new product, particularly in its early commercialization stage, is to put it under normal functional control. Let's examine why.

Manufacturing likes the longest possible runs and hates to stop for set-up changes, particularly when it has not had the benefit of significant prior experience in making the same item. A new product violates all the established norms. As a result, the Manufacturing organization inevitably creates a production schedule with excessive lead times for the new product—lead times that make selling the new product impractical.

Salespeople would much rather visit an old customer and exchange a few pleasantries, knowing that they will most likely walk away with a good-sized order, than visit a new customer and have to battle to possibly, just possibly, receive a small order. In fact, among themselves, salespeople refer to this as a "missionary" sales activity. Consequently, salespeople for ongoing products are usually a poor resource to use to sell new products. The exception is when the new product is a natural adjunct to an existing product and would be sold to the same purchasing agents.

Engineers frequently don't know when enough is enough. They will forever propose and test modifications of the product and process. A point of diminishing returns is frequently passed by a substantial margin. Consequently, the decision of when to proceed from development to commercialization must often be made by someone other than those directly doing the development.

For a new product to be successfully commercialized, manufacturing must not be controlled by normal manufacturing management, and sales responsibility cannot be entrusted to the usual sales organization. A new product in the pilot production and early commercialization stage requires full control to be vested in a single project team. In time this project management team will be either disbanded or made the nucleus of a new division. The key responsibilities of

Figure 12–2.
Alternative Physical Locations for New Product Development

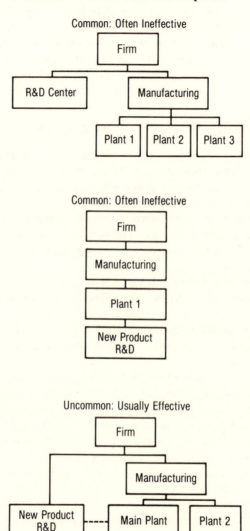

this team are development, manufacturing, and sales. In order for the product to be made in a timely manner, the team will often have technicians doing some of the manufacturing, assembly, and testing. They will argue with and push conventional manufacturing to get what they need made in an acceptable time frame. They will overcome bottlenecks by going to outside vendors and job shops. As a result, the product will be available as needed. Similarly, they will visit key potential customers, often accompanied by regular salespeople, for introduction purposes, and carry out the "missionary" sales activity themselves.

The commercialization of the new product, its sales and manufacture, must be a specific responsibility. Divided authority here often leads to a premature end to the project. The question of sponsorship—who's in charge—must not be left unresolved.

TIME CONSIDERATIONS

It is a common belief of general management that a new product R & D effort that is succeeding will provide meaningful additional profits in another two or three years. This is usually a false notion. When you consider the difficulty of getting customers to accept a new product—any new product—and the need to pass from the development stage, to a pilot production stage, to full commercialization, it is no wonder that the time needed to achieve meaningful profits is extensive. This period is usually in the range of six to seventeen years, with seven to eleven years being typical. Edwin Mansfield, a technology historian, has made similar findings. This time consideration is never stated at the outset of product development efforts because it would cause most product R & D to be terminated. Nevertheless, this is a fact of life.

An implication of the long time frame required for new industrial products to capture significant market share is that business for present products will seldom decline precipitously because of the commercialization of competitive new products. An automobile piston engine parts company, for example, concerned about the Wankel engine at the time General Motors announced its adoption, concluded that it would be years, if ever, before they would be seriously affected. History proved them right.

The long time it takes to commercial viability means that troubled firms, in general, have no business in pursuing new product development. The payback is simply too far off.

13

STRATEGIC PLANNING

The management team organizing and implementing the turnaround of a troubled company needs strategic planning. But the perspectives of this planning will differ greatly from what one normally associates with the words "strategic planning." Instead of a three- to five-year time frame, the planning will deal with issues of today and coming months. Strategic planning in a turnaround must be accomplished quickly, whereas normally, planning is carried out at a leisurely pace. Normal strategic planning is often observed to have the problem of a lack of urgency and follow through. In a turnaround, action is imperative and the purpose of strategic planning is to provide understanding necessary to choose the right actions. Hence strategic planning in a turnaround differs considerably from normal strategic planning.

The primary reason for devoting the substantial time and effort required for strategic planning is that it enables the chief executive to make rational decisions. A planning process brings to the fore alternatives to choose from and data needed in making these choices. making these choices. This reduces the use of intuition, guesswork, and emotion. However, it will not eliminate them because of lack of sufficient data, time, and resources.

For the chief executive officer to make realistic and appropriate choices and have the means to implement them, he must be able to relate causes and effects based on the best available information. This information must include definition of the business environment, competitor advantages/disadvantages, and operational aspects. Assumptions must be confronted by fact and, where they contradict one another, changes in perspective must occur.

A troubled company often maintains inappropriate perspectives, and its executives frequently cannot come to grips with problems dependent on these perspectives. For example, executives may believe that the company is the product leader and preferred supplier, when this is no longer true. In this example, a common occurrence is the company charging a price premium for its products when the market will not permit it, resulting in a precipitous decline in market share. Sunbeam Corporation, in its small consumer appliances division, seems to have been an example of such a situation.

Strategic planning is needed to impose discipline in the setting of business objectives and establishing methods of implementation. Without a corporate strategy the company may be likened to a ship without a rudder. There will be much motion, but the ship will not arrive at its destination. In the absence of a company strategic concept, the various functional elements of the company, each believing that it is doing the right thing, will act at cross purposes. Failure will be only a matter of time.

Another common result of the absence of a strategic concept is that Operating and Marketing people will spend a great deal of their time and resources trying to improve a product or business segment that should be either abandoned or, at best, allowed to decay. Only if understanding exists about the course of the company can a company's scarce resources be directed away from what are ultimately unprofitable uses.

Strategic planning in a turnaround is usually a sequential process. First, the informal hypothesizing of a strategic concept. Then the evolution of a preliminary analysis that goes beyond an initial gut feel but is far less than a segmented, formalized strategic plan. This preliminary analysis marshals data and prepares an exposition of the company's actual strategies and tactics compared with the requirements for business success. By looking at the company's strengths and weaknesses with a view toward what is needed for business viability, let alone true competitive success, judgments can be made about the ability of the company's businesses to survive. Some time later a more comprehensive strategic plan emerges, although not always. The development of the more comprehensive plan, although beneficial, is usually not an essential ingredient for company survival.

The corporate strategy, or strategic concept, is a rather permanent statement usually articulated by the chief executive officer. The distinguished academics Arnoldo C. Hax and Nicolas S. Majluf have pointed out that strategic planning usually addresses three issues:

• An expression of the mission of the firm in terms of product, market, and geographical scope

- The identification of the company's strategic business units (SBUs) and their interactions in terms of shared resources and concerns
- An articulation of corporate philosophy in terms of policies and cultural values

The definition of mission should be a clear enunciation of the scope of the present and future business that broadly describes the products, markets, and geographical coverage of the business today and in the near future. The mission should define the basis on which the company will maintain or regain competitiveness.

Communicating the corporate strategy to management and employees gives them a unified sense of direction to which they can all relate. This aspect is often overlooked. Without broad internal communication of the corporate strategy, a company will not have everyone pulling in the same direction. A myriad of decisions have to be made on a day-to-day basis by a great many people. If they all know the direction the company is taking, its mission and objectives, they can make decisions consistent with the company's best interests, and they can do so with confidence. Otherwise, vacillation and inconsistent decisions will exacerbate the company's numerous problems.

Most troubled firms of any size are in several businesses, which may be related, but have not defined their SBUs and differing degrees of viability. Hax and Majluf have pointed out that the cornerstone of strategic planning is segmenting the firm's activities in terms of business units. One of the first questions to be addressed is deceptively simple, yet often a challenge: What business are we in?

A business can be defined as an operating unit or a planning focus to sell a distinct set of products or services to an identifiable set of customers, in competition with a well-defined set of competitors. The resulting entity is normally referred to as an SBU. Most strategic planning is centered at this level.

A true SBU, as an entity, must have the following characteristics (as pointed out in a recent article by William Rothschild):

- It must serve an external, rather than an internal, market; it must have a set of external customers and not merely serve as an internal supplier or opportunistic external supplier.
- It should have a clear set of external competitors with which it is vying.
- It should have control over its own destiny; it must be able to decide, by itself, what products to offer, how and when to go to market, and where to obtain its suppliers, components, or even products. This does not mean that it cannot use pooled resources, such as a common manufacturing plant, or a combined sales force, or even corporate R & D. The key is choice. It must have options from which it may select the alternative that best achieves its business objectives.

The chief strategic planner in a turnaround is the turnaround leader. In a freestanding company this is usually the chief executive officer. He will rapidly and informally develop an initial strategic concept for the company based on his assessment of the situation, his past experience, and the knowledge at hand. This viability analysis is usually largely intuitive. The next stage is to acquire supporting information needed to test the assumptions intrinsic to the strategic concept and render better definition of vague areas. These tasks normally must be performed on a part-time basis by those executives who are at hand in Finance and Marketing, and whatever planning staff exists. Outside market research firms and other consultants can be used on a short-term basis to gather specific information that is not readily available to the company. The chapter on Marketing describes the information needed in making a good market and competitive assessment. Much of the same information is needed here. The planning itself, being a reflection of the turnaround leader's vision, cannot be performed by an outside group.

The fundamental element of the chief executive officer's strategic concept is postulating what viable business is to be created or salvaged from the existing configuration of the company. If no sizable business segment can be identified, a turnaround is not possible. A turnaround leader is usually selected, however, with a belief that he will be able to identify a viable business and make it prosper. If the company can be turned around, he will be able to accomplish it. This is a reasonable expectation if a person of the right skill and experience is put in charge of the turnaround.

Every business has one or two elements that are most essential to its success. In the construction machinery business this is believed to be replacement parts availability—24 hours to obtain a part. In the steel industry it is lowest price. In some segments of the computer industry it is compatibility with existing software. In automobiles it includes a dealer network of sufficient size and strength. For the turnaround leader to be able to decide whether or not a company's various businesses are potentially viable, he must first identify these vital one or two business requirements. Then he must relate the company's position to these requirements. If the company cannot currently meet the requirements imposed by these essential elements, the turnaround leader must judge the practicability of actions needed to meet them. Anything that would take considerable capital is usually out of the realm of possibility in a turnaround situation. The essential elements for the success of a business are usually dictated by a market. If these elements are not obvious, then a comparison of succeeding and failing competitors will often reveal them.

The strategic planning process in a turnaround evolves from being highly informal to being reasonably thorough and documented. During this evolution a clear definition develops of such aspects as the following:

- The major business assumptions concerning the external environment
- The intended scope of the business, including such matters as products, markets, manufacturing strategy, and geographical coverage—the company mission
- The resources and organizational arrangements needed to support the company mission
- The key indicators to signal whether or not the strategy is succeeding

- The elucidation of specific company objectives—the ambitions toward which the management will work
- The specification of company goals—milestones along the path of achieving the company objectives

In clarifying the company mission, certain fundamental questions need to be addressed:

- What is our business? To some extent this question can be answered by stating what is not the company's business. This must be done for each SBU.
- Who are our customers?
- What do our customers want? This may not be what the company has been trying to sell.
- How much will the customer buy and in what relation to price?
- Does the company have to be a product leader? If so, in what way? If not, what makes a good follower?
- What market share is needed to be successful? A 5 percent market share would be high for a custom gear maker but not for a specialty steel company.
- Does the company have any advantages in meeting customer's needs? If so, how can this be utilized further?
- What is the role of existing and potential competition?

When management's thinking has progressed to the point that it is able to prepare and properly use a comprehensive strategic plan, even more issues will have to be considered. These normally include the following:

Economic Characteristics of the Business

- Where is value added? By you? By competition?
- What have been historical margins, asset turnover, cash flow? How will these change in the future?
- Why do margins and return on investment vary across products/markets?
- What is the asset composition of the business? (net fixed assets, inventories, receivables, payables, etc.) For you? For competition?
- Is relative cost a function of market share?
- How can you or competition achieve and sustain a cost advantage?
- What competitive barriers exist? How secure are they?

Appropriate Strategic Business Definition

The appropriate SBUs may differ from current definitions or reporting groups. The definition is probably correct if (a) you can achieve and sustain a cost advantage relative to competition and (b) you can make decisions in one business without significant impact on others.

- Where are the significant differences in economics between businesses or products?
  —Within manufacturing
  —Distribution/geography
  —Customer segments and buying behavior
  —R & D
  —Marketing service
  —International/domestic
- Do these differences allow you to manage these businesses reasonably independently of one another?
- Is domestic share or worldwide share critical in achieving cost advantage?
- Do you have different competitors in different products or markets? Why?

The External Environment

- What is the business growth potential?
  —Total market, customer segment, product lines
  —Is demand primary or substitution based? What is the saturation level?
- What is the impact of changing technology on the product? On the nature of competition?
- What is the impact of international market development and competition?
- How will changes in production factors, particularly material supply, affect you? Your competitors?
- What will be the impact of government regulation or macroeconomic factors such as inflation, balance of payments, currency trends?
- Are critical cultural factors developing that will impact marketing?

The Competitive Environment

- What is your relative market share and competitive situation?
  —Historical trends
  —Future projections if strategy is unchanged
- What are your key competitors' apparent strategies?
- What are your key competitors' resources, capacity, and limitations?
- What are your resources, capacity, and limitations?

Strategic Options and Feasibility

- Should you remain in or withdraw from the business?
- What are the required actions in broad terms (price, capacity, focus, timing)?
- What are the investment and profit implications of the strategy selected (cash flow projections)?

Strategy Statement

- What is the business mission?

- What are the market share, profit, growth, and cash flow objectives?
- What actions are required for implementation?
    - —Capacity additions/new facilities
    - —Price and nonprice decisions
    - —Product line/market focus (pruning or expanding)
    - —New market/product offerings
    - —International expansion
    - —Cost reduction investments
    - —Accounting, reporting, organizational changes

Some of the important analyses that may be the basis for strategy formulation include the following:

Value-Added Analysis by Product Line or Business

- Manufacturing/processing steps and costs (yours and competitors')
- Postmanufacturing costs (yours and competitors')
- Competitive barriers resulting from different levels of value added

Product Line or Customer Group Profitability and Return on Investment

- Revenues by business
- Material, labor, and realistic allocation of indirect labor and overhead costs
- Realistic allocation and understanding of variances
- Allocations of marketing, service/repair, R & D to products/customers, etc.
- Allocation of net fixed assets and net working capital

Differences in Profitability or Competitive Position as a Function of Product Mix

- Standard versus custom product
- Long versus short run length
- Large versus small customer orders
- Heavy versus light service requirement
- Product size
- Fixed asset intensiveness of business or products
- Inventory investment required

Estimate of Relative Competitive Cost Positions

- Capacity, equipment, facility assessment
- Material purchasing power
- Labor rates
- Scale economy differences

- Geographical locations
- Tariff barriers and governmental policy

Sensitivity of Profitability or Return on Investment as a Result of Changes in Key Variables

- Product mix changes
- Scale
- Location
- Value added
- Purchasing
- Asset management

Size and Magnitude of Competitive Barriers

- Scale and investment
- Patent
- Technical know-how
- Marketing/service

Market Segment Analysis

- Differences in customer buying behavior
  —Volume
  —Service requirements
  —Price sensitivity versus nonprice needs
- Demand forecasting and historical trends
- Impact on differential growth rates among segments of product mix and competition
- Estimation of saturation level for products with substitution-based growth

Impact on Changing Technology

- Changes in value added by suppliers
- Potential dramatic cost discontinuities
- Implication of shorter product life cycle for pricing and capacity decisions
- Attraction of new competitors as a result of their capabilities in substituting technology

Evaluation of International Market Potential and Threats

- Effect of new demand growth on the length of the product life
- Additional volume improvements in competitive costs
- New international competitors moving down their experience curves

Figure 13–1.
Factors to Analyze in Identifying Industry Characteristics

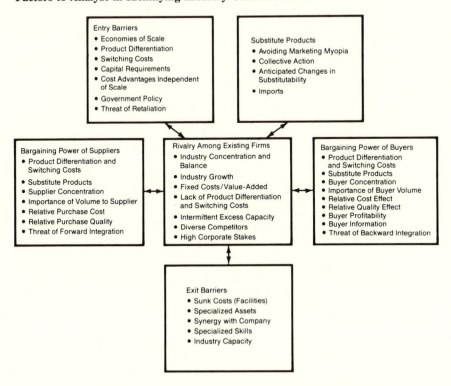

Figure 13–1, developed by Roland Roehrich (*Journal of Business Strategy*, Fall 1984, pp. 60–73), is a good graphical depiction of the many issues addressable in analyzing a business.

Strategic planning and business planning are distinctly different activities, which are sometimes confused. Strategic planning deals with the questions of what business is the company in and what does this business need for success? Business planning deals with company financial performance, actual against projection, and the results of specific operating activities, such as sales and cost reduction plans. Many of the same people are involved with the formulation of both types of plans, but the two types shouldn't be confused or commingled. Strategic planning tells you where you want to go. Business planning tells you how things will go along the way. The earlier chapter on Finance discusses formulation of the business plan in some detail.

14

FOREIGN OPERATIONS

A troubled manufacturing company often has small foreign subsidiaries. If the parent is mismanaged, the subsidiaries are usually in worse shape. They may have all the problems of their parent company magnified and added to by lower-quality management, an absence of staff resources, an inattention to problems that remain unknown to the parent's chief executive officer owing to great distance, foreign government regulations, and cultural differences. In a turnaround a company is fighting for its very survival. It cannot allow small, badly performing foreign operations to absorb cash or make significant demands on the time of key managers.

A new trend, globalization, is replacing multinationalization in many industrial and consumer products. In the globalization concept, products are manufactured in a single location for worldwide use, instead of for a regional or national market. The specific location is chosen because of cost advantages compared with regional manufacture. The cost advantage may arise purely from the scale of manufacture. This philosophy, which has only recently become the predominant management concept, is significant in viewing the necessity of continuing foreign manufacture. In important industrialized countries a company can usually continue to sell into a market once it has ceased manufacturing there, particularly if name recognition has been established. It would, thereby, retain market share and other consequential advantages. In less developed countries this is not so, as significant barriers to product importation frequently exist. These include quotas, product exclusion regulations, foreign currency allocations, and license requirements. However, this limitation is usually not important, since the typical troubled U.S.-based manufacturing company has minor sales in less developed countries.

Foreign operations need to be put into historical perspective. In the thirty-year period from 1945 to 1975, many U.S. companies/divisions became multinational, opening small plants or acquiring small companies in Canada, the United Kingdom, Western Europe, Latin America, and elsewhere. This was popular. These foreign operations, for the most part, were really miniatures of their parents, making the same products for smaller national or regional markets.

Small foreign manufacturing subsidiaries may be a legacy of the multinational era. Careful study is needed to discern if this is so. A comparison of the product costs at these plants and the home plants may find little cost advantage, or even a cost disadvantage at the foreign plants.

The smaller size of a foreign subsidiary means that it intrinsically has a much lower availability of skilled internal staff resources in such areas as manufacturing management, manufacturing/process engineering, product application engineering, purchasing, marketing, and financial management. The troubled nature of the parent usually implies that the foreign subsidiaries have not been receiving much help for a long period. In addition, there is likely an absence of effective management control of their activities. A potentially damaging drift in parent company attention commonly occurs as the parent company's troubles increase.

The managers of foreign subsidiaries are usually local nationals, possessing skills and abilities commensurate with the size of the operations. These skills and abilities may not be adequate for a turnaround situation and are frequently far below those found in the parent company. To properly convey the perspectives and sense of urgency permeating the parent company, executives may need to be transferred from the parent to the subsidiary.

The foreign subsidiaries cannot be ignored in the turnaround of their parent company. However, the turnaround of the parent company must take priority over the management problems of small foreign subsidiaries. The foreign subsidiaries' product offerings, pricing policies, and other activities must be in concert with those of their parent. As a first step, someone at the parent company who has the confidence of the turnaround's top management must be put in charge of foreign operations. This person will be responsible for the changes to be effected in the foreign subsidiaries that parallel and support those in the parent firm. He will also have to do this with fewer resources, reflecting the usual relative size of the two sets of activities.

The same strategic concept governing the U.S. firm's turnaround must be tailored to the circumstances of the foreign subsidiaries. If a foreign operation has unrelated products or businesses, extraneous to the major thrust of the parent company, these should be considered by the chief executive officer as immediate candidates for divestiture.

Every firm needs a manufacturing strategy—what to manufacture, at what location. It needs this strategy for the firm as a whole, not for the parent company and each subsidiary separately. One must look at present costs and future probable currency movements. The outcome of such an analysis may be to close some foreign plants in favor of existing U.S. plants; to close U.S. plants in favor of foreign plants; to close both types of plants and purchase the products instead; or to open new plants in low-wage countries to meet global needs.

If the foreign subsidiaries are engaged in what are really national or regional businesses, their ownership or non-ownership cannot fundamentally affect the parent company's market position. In this case divestiture is certainly called for. As an example, Chemetron Corporation owned regional industrial gas businesses in various parts of the United States, Colombia, and Venezuela. The foreign operations could not benefit Chemetron's industrial gas businesses in the United States. Their sale would end a diversion of management time from more important business concerns. Once Chemetron Corporation was acquired by Allegheny International, the decision was made to sell the South American businesses, although this took longer than expected to accomplish.

If worldwide market participation is an important part of the company's strategic concept, then the retention of foreign subsidiaries needs to be viewed in this light. To an ever-growing extent, worldwide market participation is important, almost indepedent of matters related to market share. If a significant competitor has a home market without foreign competition, it tends to charge higher prices and earn higher margins in this market, which will subsidize the assault of foreign markets. By entering a company's previously protected home market, you destroy these unusually high margins, thereby making it financially more difficult for the company to compete in other markets. As an example of this, the entry by Komatsu, Ltd., into the U.S. market for earth-moving equipment, and its obtaining only a 3 to 5 percent U.S. market share, so depressed prices that Caterpillar Tractor Company was permanently injured.

The foreign operations need detailed, well-thought-out business plans no less than the parent company. The head of foreign operations must monitor these plans against performance and just as strenuously control cash flow.

Marketing responsibilities between the various subsidiaries and the parent, particularly concerning third countries, must be carefully administered. A wise customer may attempt to play one against the others by sending each the same sales inquiry and placing the order with the one with the lowest effective price (including tariff and transportation). Some companies encourage this competition among their subsidiaries without realizing how much overhead it will absorb.

The final pricing of goods moving from the parent to the subsidiary or among subsidiaries cannot ignore currency changes. Maintaining a given price in Belgian francs, say, when this currency devalues in terms of the U.S. dollar, means a significant erosion in margin. If raising the price is inhibited by Belgian price levels, this calls into question the firm's manufacturing strategy. If nothing else can be changed, low foreign margins necessitate an examination of the desirability of continuing to participate in this foreign market, save an overriding strategic consideration.

Foreign manufacturing operations may be experiencing higher manufacturing costs than need be because of the absence of the transfer of improved manufacturing technology from U.S. plants. This improved technology provides cost reductions. Technology transfer occurs by people going, seeing, and doing. To accomplish this transfer of improved technology, appropriate employees from the U.S. operation must be sent abroad, and vice versa, for what could be an extended period. The costs of doing this are usually trivial compared with the benefits obtained.

The various cost reduction approaches, described elsewhere in this book, such as improved purchasing techniques and the reduction of staff overhead, apply equally as well to foreign operations. They must be implemented there, with a sense of urgency and great determination.

The poor performance of the foreign subsidiaries may be the result of differences in cultural values and unspoken differences in business objectives. This is often unrealized by executives of the parent company. Several such examples will now be used to illustrate this.

Chemetron U.K., Ltd., maintained two manufacturing operations in the United Kingdom, a weld flange plant in Wales and a forged pipe fitting plant in Scotland. These two plants made the same products that their parent, Tube Turns, Inc., manufactured in the United States. In both plants the native workers, Welshmen and Scots, respectively, resented the English management, more or less on general principle. In addition, the management understood neither the desirability nor the means to measure and control manufacturing productivity; this was part of the national culture. The consequence of poor management and ethnic antagonism was one-half the labor productivity of the American plants. The subsidiaries' hourly labor costs were also about one-half of those of the U.S. plants. As a consequence, the product costs were about the same. The products were sold worldwide, as were those made in the American plants. Therefore, what was the purpose of maintaining two sets of plants? No one had thought to ask. Another culturally based problem of this foreign subsidiary was its penchant to export to Australia and other British Commonwealth countries, while virtually ignoring sales opportunities in the Common Market.

Electrodos de Monterrey was the Mexican subsidiary of Alloy Rods, the U.S. welding products firm, manufacturing welding rods for the Mexican and Latin American markets. Its ability to make certain high-quality welding products that were needed but difficult to obtain in Mexico implied that the firm should have been profitable. It was not. In examining their facilities, one observed many idle employees. The firm had sold another, labor-intensive business and had kept many of its employees, although it had no work for them. An unspoken business objective was to provide employment. The identification of this problem and consequent elimination of the excess employees gave a significant boost to profitability.

These two examples illustrate the need for on-site inspection of foreign operations and firsthand knowledge of their business practices. They also emphasize the need to be flexible and not locked into narrow cultural or national interests.

The costs of a company extricating itself from a foreign operation, or improving the operating performance of a foreign operation by eliminating unnecessary employees, can be extreme owing to local statutory requirements. For example, Belgium, France, Italy, the Netherlands, and the United Kingdom require employee severance payments, which are excessive from a U.S. point of view. Many less developed countries have similar laws. There may also be requirements to immediately fund enormous pension fund obligations. Other limitations may be imposed as well. Mexico, for example, requires capital gains distributions to employees of 8 percent of the gain when property such as a plant or business is sold. In some countries—France, I believe, is one—you need government permission before you can close down a plant. If the subsidiary has received loans from the foreign government, these may have to be automatically repaid in the event of a close down. These aspects need to be considered when analyzing strategic changes.

If an undesirable foreign subsidiary cannot be either sold or closed out without using cash, then consideration should be given to bankrupting it. This may hurt the parent company's reputation in this local area. This harm, however, must be weighed against the need of the parent company to take steps in the short run that ensure its survival.

It is difficult enough to manage the turnaround of the parent firm let alone that of the foreign subsidiaries, simultaneously. If the subsidiaries are *small*, the best advice might be this:

If profitable	Leave more or less alone (unless significant cash could be realized from their sale)
If unprofitable	Close down or sell (unless a compelling strategic need exists)

Closing down or selling the foreign manufacturing subsidiaries may offer a number of benefits:

1. Freeing up capital (although close-down costs will often absorb much of the cash generated)

2. Elimination of the diversion of management time to less important areas

3. Increased production level of parent plants, by means of increased exports, which can often be used to increase productivity

4. Decreased company overhead, since staff positions tied to managing the foreign operations can be eliminated

   A troubled company with foreign operations cannot ignore those foreign operations while achieving its turnaround.

15

OPERATING DURING STRIKES

The troubled company may have fundamental operating cost problems arising from the bargaining agreement with its labor union. These costs may stem from complex and debilitating work rules and excessive wages and benefits. Management may conclude that long-term company survival will not be possible without corrections in one or both of these categories.

Local union leaders do not view the world as management does. Many are not reasonable men. Opening the company's books and presenting a cogent case that work rules changes and wage reductions are needed to help the company survive, and thereby preserve the workers' jobs, should be attempted in the hope that a strike can be averted. However, the likely result will be no, or at best token, concessions. This is particularly true when dealing with heavy "smokestack-type" industrial unions. Many union leaders are ideologically motivated and will see a company fail before agreeing to a concession.

This chapter assumes that a strike will occur over operating cost-related issues, and the company will continue to operate during the strike. That is, raw materials will continue to arrive. Production will continue. Finished goods will continue to be shipped. In a strike the plant will initially be manned by office personnel; and new hires will soon take the jobs of the strikers.

If the company shuts down for the duration of the strike, or achieves only limited production using office personnel, it is playing the game on the union's terms. The basic purpose of a strike is to prevent production, thereby putting a crushing burden of unmet overhead costs onto the company. Limiting production allows the union to meet its objective. International Harvester virtually committed suicide by choosing not to operate during its long strike by the United Auto Workers.

By operating during a strike, a company is in a much more favorable position. Sales are occurring and resultant cash is coming in to meet the bills.

More and more, companies are realizing that operating during a strike is the preferred method of managing a strike. It also allows a company to implement vitally needed changes in work rules and pay practices.

In studying turnarounds that have failed, you find case after case where a company realized it had to change the work rules and pay practices, asked for these concessions in labor negotiations, and backed down when the union negotiators refused to budge. Soon thereafter these firms went bankrupt. If they had shown the courage of their convictions, a viable turnaround may have been possible.

The company has to analyze the costs and benefits of a possible strike and decide if taking a strike is sufficiently attractive to bear the risk. If the alternative to the strike is a marginal existence at best, taking a strike looks much more attractive. The economics of taking a strike are frequently quite favorable; this is little known. A payback of twelve to eighteen months, from the start of the strike, is possible.

Can the company afford to take a strike? This is an important question whose consideration must be coordinated with the firm's financial sources. Strike costs are considerable.

A strike pits the continued existence of the company against the continued existence of the union local (or its existence at this particular company). A company decision to continue operating during the strike, and all that implies, means total war. There is no sensible way for a company to approach a possible strike except on this basis.

A company that has properly planned for operating during a strike, and hires new workers, should expect to achieve full production and prestrike productivity by month six to eight of the strike. Certain strike expenses, say, additional plant security and legal costs, will continue for twelve months or more. After that it is possible that the new employees will request a decertification election from the National Labor Relations Board, and the old union will be thrown out.

Organizing the company for a strike needs to start six to eight months before the event. It must be a specific person's responsibility. This person, the strike captain, must be intelligent and energetic. The individual chosen for this responsibility may be the number two or number three man in Employee Relations. It is his job to coordinate the preparation of the strike plan, all supporting aspects, and to supervise its implementation.

The strike plan should consist of the following seven elements (based on the discussion of Charles R. Perry, Andrew M. Kramer, and Thomas J. Schneider, *Operating During Strikes*, Philadelphia: University of Pennsylvania, 1983):

1. Security

2. Communications

3. Production

4. Supply, shipping and receiving

5. Maintenance

6. Personnel

7. Legal representation

These topics will now be examined separately, based largely on my own experience.

SECURITY

The company's security effort has to be more comprehensive than many people realize. Its activities are among the most important in neutralizing the possible negative effects of a strike. These efforts must start many months in advance, with the first task being building bridges of friendship and understanding with the local police department.

Meetings with the police department heads should take place to review what will be required of them. It should be made clear that they will be expected to uphold the law. Plant security officers will be unarmed and undeputized, so as not to interfere with the police department's ability to do their job properly. Police attendance at all plant shift changes will be expected.

Many police officers hold second or third jobs. This is part of police culture. The company, therefore, should hire local police officers, including high-ranking ones, as part-time security officers. These actions will serve two purposes. It will familiarize the police with the plant layout. It will also make them less hesitant to enforce the law in the event of a strike.

The ability to protect the plant should be improved. All external fences should be examined and repaired as needed. Unused entrances should be locked. The perimeter should be cleaned up, and "No Trespassing" and "No Parking" signs installed as needed. All employees should be required to wear photo identification badges, with a color code for classification. These badges must be shown to enter the property.

Security lighting should be improved where needed. Plans need to be made for improved patrols, including patrol routes, times, and manning. Arrangements should be made to obtain additional guard service as needed.

The overt placement of video cameras (some with night vision capability) will have a chilling effect on violence. It will let it be known that all incidents will be recorded and that these recordings will be available as hard evidence in legal proceedings.

The security group should encourage employees to enter and leave in cars, so as to minimize interactions with pickets. This will help prevent incidents.

Windows should be boarded up a few days before the strike. This will prevent needless damage and communicate the steadfastness of the company.

Alternate telephone communications and radio systems should be in place, just in case the telephone system is temporarily disrupted. Set up a C.B. monitor.

Incidents are bound to occur, so establish a procedure for quickly obtaining affidavits.

Be prepared for fires. Be certain all fire equipment is in good working order and the sprinkler system is fully functional.

The security group should be expected to develop informants who will advise them of criminal actions being planned. Countermeasures can be taken, usually publicly, so as to discourage the planned activity.

COMMUNICATIONS

Strikes are political events. They get newspaper and television coverage. They sometimes turn into a battle of public relations firms. Choose and work with a public relations firm some months before the strike starts. Have them ready to produce a press release and use their influence with the press and television stations at a moment's notice, particularly to counteract unfair and untrue reports.

A media spokesman needs to be appointed; often this is the head of Employee Relations. He should be coached by the public relations firm, who will provide simulated television minicam and newspaper interviews. As little as one day of such training will turn an ineffective, confused presentation of the company's position into a forceful, convincing statement. All media questions should be referred to the spokesman.

An effective communications program addressed to all employees for the four to six months before a strike will not prevent a strike. However, it will most likely change its outcome. It can lessen the resolve of the union members. They may still go along with their union leadership, but not, by and large, enthusiastically. The consequence will be fewer pickets and far less strike violence. A large number of salaried employees will come to approve of the company's position and enthusiastically welcome the opportunity to pitch in by leaving their offices and manning the factory (this psychological high lasts for about a month). Effective prestrike communications are, therefore, essential to be able to continue operating during a strike.

The communications program must continue during the strike. Letters sent to homes should tell how well the company is managing. A hot line, available to employees and strikers who telephone in to the company, can carry important news items.

Customers have to be informed that, although a strike is under way, the company is continuing to operate. Concerned customers should be invited to visit the plant to prove to themselves that their goods are actually being made.

Suppliers should be told that the company is operating, and on-time shipments are expected. They should be urged to use nonunion truck lines.

PRODUCTION

Assume that, initially, all members of the union bargaining unit will participate in the strike. What can the company continue to make? The shop supervision (foremen, general foremen, and so on) are all skilled operators. In addition, many salaried employees have shop skills, owing to having once worked in this or other plants. Other salaried employees can be taught to do unskilled and semiskilled shop tasks, such as assembly, loading and unloading of machine tools, driving forklifts, and plant/office cleaning. An inventory of available skills and people who can be temporarily drafted for production invariably shows many more people than anyone would have expected. A specific job assignment plan should be prepared. Engineers, by actually making the things they have designed, will often come to be more sympathetic to the complaints they have heard over the years, and better, simpler designs will be one favorable outcome. Employees should be informed of their job assignments just before the strike begins.

Similarly, a list of production priorities must be prepared, based on market needs. The two sets of information should be put together to form a strike production plan. This plan must include three other important elements. First, an inventory build-up plan is necessary. For the six months before a strike, significant inventories will have to be built, particularly of those items that will be most difficult to produce during the strike. Second, a subcontracting plan is necessary. It will take at least six months to identify and qualify subcontractors who can do the job at reasonable prices. Trial orders will need to be placed to assure that they are capable of producing quality products, on schedule. It may be some time into the strike before subcontracting efforts begin to produce meaningful results. Third, an employee recruitment plan is necessary. Hiring strikebreakers is illegal, and no company should even consider it. But hiring employees to be permanent economic replacements is well sanctioned in law. The distinction is that the former are hired to intimidate strikers into returning to work, whereas the latter have no interaction with the strikers and are hired just to do the job. The plan must estimate how many economic replacements will be on the payroll and the time frame involved.

Just before the strike, locate materials for convenient use by a reduced labor force. Also, have the foremen train themselves on important manufacturing tasks. This will be resented by much of the labor force, which will have no recourse except to file grievances.

In the first few months of the strike, people will be unavailable to prepare much of the normal paperwork (e.g., shop routings, time standards), since these same people will be in the factory manning machines. There will also be less need for paperwork, as salaried employees will be doing the work and tracking time will be of lessened importance. Therefore, prepare to run on a system of abbreviated paperwork that still captures the most vital data. As hourly workers are recruited, it will be necessary to phase the normal systems back in and return people to their office roles. The first such step is for foremen to begin directing activities in lieu of actually doing them.

SUPPLY, SHIPPING AND RECEIVING

Successfully operating will require being able to regularly bring goods into and out of the struck plant. With trucking deregulation, this has become relatively easy to do. The traffic manager should check in advance with the truck lines normally servicing the plant as to whether or not passing through the picket line would present a problem. If it will, a change in vendors should be considered.

Sometimes, in the initial phase of a strike, an individual driver is willing to drive within a few blocks of the plant but not across the picket line. In such cases a company employee may meet the truck and drive it through for the driver.

If the company runs any of its own trucks, they should continue to go in and out in a normal fashion. If their movements are impeded, the police should be expected to intercede. A company truck may be required to deliver goods to the terminals of truck lines whose employees will not drive across the picket line.

Arrangements should be made for use of a public warehouse to stage inbound or outbound shipments, if this should become necessary.

Rail service cannot be interrupted by a strike. Railroads will provide supervisory personnel to man their locomotives and give normal rail service.

If people and goods move freely in and out of the struck plant, the strike is half won.

Sufficient supplies will need to be on hand to allow office workers to take on production functions. These include safety shoes, safety goggles, hard hats, overalls, and the like.

Purchasing arrangements for strike-related items should be made. This includes food, contract services (perhaps janitorial), and extra vehicles.

The overall perspective should be that nearly normal shipping conditions will exist. Whatever steps are needed to accomplish this will be taken.

MAINTENANCE

Well before the strike a review should be made of maintenance needs. All major projects must be completed long before the contract expiration. All outside contract work should be scheduled for completion before the strike as well, unless the contractor understands that a strike is likely and can be expected to have his employees cross the picket line.

Routine maintenance needs will exist during the strike. These should be identified and the strike plan should allow sufficient manpower for this task. The plant has to be kept running. When new employees are hired, this is usually one of the first areas to staff.

Your Engineering organization should be the primary source of assistance when a machinery breakdown occurs and skilled repair personnel are unavailable.

Plans should be made to use specific outside contractors for major breakdowns or maintenance work beyond the scope of existing in-plant personnel.

PERSONNEL

A strike gives the Personnel function a new importance, which their managers usually relish. They have to be able to show good judgment and much tact. If the strike is mismanaged, the problem will emanate from Personnel.

Negotiations with the union have to be carried out in good faith on what sometimes seems an interminable basis. Nothing has to be conceded, however. Bargaining in good faith doesn't imply making compromises contrary to the best interests of the enterprise.

Consultations with the labor attorneys will be needed every step of the way. This area is a minefield of precedents, many of them murky. But they are equally difficult for the union.

Strikers who wish to abandon the strike should be welcomed back. Your goal is cost-effective production—not retribution.

After a suitably brief period the company should hire economic replacements, that is, recruit a new work force. Only experienced people should be sought, as the company does not have the resources or the time for training programs. All new employees, including skilled ones, will still need to go through a learning curve in operating your equipment to manufacture your products. Usually well-chosen employees can accomplish this quickly and, in about two weeks, be reasonably productive.

Interviewing and qualifying large numbers of potential employees are major tasks. They require assigning sufficient people to do the job, having adequate company literature and employment forms available, and being able to test large numbers of people at once (in, say, blueprint and gauge reading). Screened employees can then be passed on to foremen for final evaluation. Although thousands of persons may respond to your large newspaper advertisements, only 10 to 13 percent of applicants will meet all your requirements.

Once on the job, scrutiny must be given to the new employees' performance, and those that don't come along fast enough should be fired. If your hiring procedures are correct, this will not be a large percentage of the new hires.

As a practical matter, it is necessary to promise new employees job protection. That is, you will not fire them in order to replace them with returning strikers once the strike is settled (assuming that a negotiated settlement is reached). Unless you take this step, skilled workers will not quit their jobs at other companies (even though lower paying) in order to join your company. Taking this step makes a negotiated settlement with your labor union almost impossible, as a union is normally willing to strike almost indefinitely over the issue of whether its members or your new workers have employment preference once the strike is over.

You must produce continual reassurance that new workers will not be fired to make way for returning strikers. If striking workers try to return to work, and their jobs are filled, you must explain this to them. Their names should be put on a preferential recall list, to be notified when a suitable position opens.

During the strike you are legally obligated to operate under the work rules and compensation rates set forth in your last offer to the union. Be certain the offer contains what you really want. Of course, at any time the union may be presented with an amendment to the last offer, and this change is then immediately implemented in the plant.

In the conduct of the strike, Personnel will have a larger than usual number of administrative tasks. It must make certain that it has an up-to-date list of all employees' names, addresses, telephone numbers, and automobile license plate numbers. It must establish and issue policies on pay, method of keeping track of hours worked, and charges (if any) for food service. It must establish procedures for notifying employees of the times for starting work, which may undergo several changes. It must instruct people on how to prevent incidents with pickets.

Personnel is responsible for special help, supplies, and the like. It has to plan for the unlikely event that employees are temporarily barricaded into the plant, and provide for rented cots and recreation activities.

Because questions will be directed to Personnel, they must be capable of answering them clearly and with authority. This is most important.

LEGAL REPRESENTATION

The company needs the services of a firm of experienced, competent labor lawyers. It is foolish to take on a strike without this support.

An accurate log of strike-related activities should be maintained. Evidence such as videotapes, photographs, and sworn affidavits should be collected of all union-related criminal behavior. Victims or witnesses of picket line violence, vandalism and malicious mischief, assault, arson, and threats should be urged to press charges.

Pressing charges has three favorable consequences:

1. It ties up union attorneys in defending the criminals and costs money, including bail money for the individual.

2. It's prima facie evidence of conduct for which the striker may be formally fired.

3. It shows a pattern of union-sponsored conduct, which will allow the company to obtain a restraining order from a court.

The company should use every legal avenue available against the union and its strike. It should try to convert a restraining order into a permanent injunction. Continual arrests by local police of strikers for minor illegal acts will both inhibit further illicit activities and generally demoralize the pickets.

Unemployment compensation and welfare claims should be fought by the company. They will only subsidize the strikers.

The union may file frivolous lawsuits against the company. Every one must be hard fought.

The legal area is but another theater of what is a total war.

16

SUMMARY

An advanced market economy, such as the United States, will at any given time have a large number of industrial firms in trouble. These are companies whose survival is open to question. How these companies arrived at their precarious situation is not important. What is important is whether or not they will survive— can they be turned around?

The key to resolving the question of business survival is the company's management. Successful turnarounds usually require the installation of a new management, of unusual competence, experienced and skilled in turnaround management. The continuation of the old management and its inappropriate attitudes and perspectives is a prescription for failure.

A troubled company must make radical changes. These changes may include the abandonment of historically important products, the closure of plants, the firing of many longtime employees, changes in internal organization, and the adoption of substantially different policies and procedures. All of these changes are psychologically stressful to an organization. The people responsible in the past cannot usually bring themselves to make these types of changes, nor would these changes have the acceptance of the organization if they would try to make them.

Although many of the most important aspects of managing a successful turnaround have been examined in this book, each of these subjects has nuances not covered here, which only become important in specific circumstances. Understanding and control of these nuances will favorably affect the outcome of your turnaround effort. No two turnaround situations are ever exactly alike. Therefore, no single approach is satisfactorily applicable to every case.

Time and resources do not exist to improve everything at once. Those factors that have the greatest impact on cash flow and profitability must be the center of attention.

Because the troubled company's management is often misinformed and isolated from the day-to-day business, details must be investigated. Common sense is the key to a company turnaround. For each troubled business, you must ascertain what is most urgent and then focus your attention on those elements.

The leader of the turnaround, while soliciting ideas from all, must usually be more authoritative than otherwise. He must make the hard decisions. It is a matter of company survival. In a turnaround this is usually the only technique that will work.

PEOPLE ASPECTS

People are at the heart of a successful turnaround. The employees must be motivated and feel personally involved in achieving the company's survival. A sense of urgency must pervade the environment. All employees—management, salaried staff, and hourly workers—must feel involved. What the company achieves will be through the actions of all its employees, not just its top management.

Employees have to know the company's objectives and how they are expected to help accomplish them. Manufacturing supervision and lower-level staff management often welcome and need training to perform their jobs more effectively.

The turnaround management must take whatever steps are necessary to ensure that it has the proper mix of critical skills. Those key skills that are missing will have to be obtained by hiring new employees, at competitive market rates.

Executives and other employees who are found wanting will have to be terminated. The company cannot afford the luxury of carrying dead wood. Not acting decisively in this area will prevent the development of the sense of urgency and self-sacrifice that needs to exist. But there must be no rush to terminate employees without good cause. It is foolish and needlessly expensive to replace an entire management. Some continuity is required to serve as a bridge between the new management, and its new perspectives, and the majority of the staff who worked for a long time under the old regime.

COMMUNICATIONS

The establishment of new values and priorities, and motivation of employees, depends on communications. People are at the heart of the majority of the company's problems. They are also at the heart of the solution to these problems. People are influenced through good communications. With the help of outside specialists, the company must explain to its employees why change is needed.

They must be given the facts. When people are treated as if they are part of the team, they become part of the team.

Employee demoralization must end and their confidence must be restored. It is essential that employees become confident in the competence of the new management and in their own ability to succeed in turning the company around. Fearful, demoralized employees are ineffective employees. The employee communications program must be thorough (e.g., speeches, bulletins, letters to homes, supervisor chats) and continuing. It is a mistake for a company to communicate with its hourly employees through a union, whose messages tend to be one-sided and adversarial.

The turnaround management faces a number of powerful constituencies to whom communications is important as well. These include the board of directors (or parent company in the case of a subsidiary), lenders, government (as customer, regulator, or protector of the public weal), perhaps a powerful labor union, customers, and suppliers. These constituencies also must be made to feel confident in the ability of the new management to achieve a successful turnaround. They must be motivated to support the turnaround program. Obtaining their support will require an ongoing, information-laden, convincing communications effort.

STRATEGIC PLANNING

Early on, the turnaround leader must hypothesize a strategic concept of the business. He must analytically segment the company into its separate businesses—its strategic business units. He must develop an understanding of the one or two key elements vital for the success of each business and measure the current state of the business against these criteria. Then he must decide which of the businesses can be made viable and which must be disposed of. For the potentially viable product segments or businesses, he must decide what changes will be needed to make them viable. Understanding must lead to action. Survival depends on implementing change.

Strategic planning is needed to impose discipline in the setting of business objectives and establishing methods of implementation. In the absence of a company strategic concept, the various functional elements of a company, each believing it is following the correct course, will act at cross purposes. In these circumstances, failure will only be a matter of time. Only if general understanding exists about the course of the company can a company's scarce resources be directed away from what are ultimately unprofitable uses.

Strategic planning in a turnaround is usually a sequential process. First is the informal hypothesizing of a strategic concept by the turnaround leader, usually the chief executive officer. Then there is the evaluation of a preliminary analysis, which goes beyond an initial gut feel but is far less than a formalized strategic plan. This preliminary analysis marshals data and prepares an exposition of the company's actual strategies and tactics compared with the requirements for business success. The fundamental element of the chief executive officer's strategic concept is postulating what viable business is to be created or salvaged from the existing configuration of the company.

Strategic planning and business planning are distinctly different activities, which are sometimes confused. Strategic planning deals with defining what business the company is in and questions concerning what this business needs for success. Business planning deals with the company's financial performance, actual against projection, and the results of specific operating activities, such as sales and cost reduction plans. Strategic planning tells you where you want to go. Business planning tells you how things will go along the way.

FINANCE

A business plan is a necessary tool in accomplishing a turnaround. To manage the situation you have to know what to expect in terms of losses and cash flow, on a month-by-month basis, for the foreseeable future. You have to know if the company is likely to become illiquid and, if so, when. You have to know how much additional cash the turnaround will require.

The consistent achievement of operating results that follow the business plan will help create confidence in the company's management by lenders and other constituencies. The confidence is needed to obtain their support at various critical moments.

The monthly financial statements will tell how well events follow projection. When a serious miss occurs, it will compel corrective action. The product and sales/administrative cost reduction plans are important in their own right and should be tracked monthly as well. It is from these specific activities that much of the company's improvement in financial health will derive.

Cash is the lifeblood of a company. In a troubled company, becoming illiquid is a real threat and requires special attention. Troubled companies must examine methods for reducing their operating cash needs. They must find ways of providing additional cash, by freeing up cash currently used nonproductively, and obtaining it by other means.

As the thrust is to decrease cash needs and make more cash available, often by one-time actions, great caution must be shown in pursuing any course that will increase the need for cash. If the strategy dictates actions that look as if they would absorb cash, then alternatives that do not require as much cash but allow the objectives to still be met, albeit less efficiently, must be examined.

The accounting system has to be a key tool providing vital data needed in cutting costs, pruning product lines, making pricing decisions, and the like. A company in trouble usually doesn't know its costs. Frequently it has an accounting system that obscures rather than reveals true costs.

It is important to know costs, by individual product, in great detail. The data should allow identification of those items for which selling price does not cover cost and that, therefore, should be considered for abandonment or repricing.

In a turnaround you usually have neither the staff nor the time to fully overhaul the accounting system. However, steps must be immediately taken to properly reflect the true costs of important items and generate this information on a timely basis. Actual sample measurements should be taken of the amounts of materials used in making various products and of the outputs/productivities of the various manufacturing steps/operations. The information gained from these efforts will frequently be quite different from what had been generally believed. Probably some products that had been thought to be profitable, and thereby emphasized, will be discovered to be unprofitable. The reverse situation is sometimes found as well.

Commonly, a small portion of sales may be responsible for a disproportionate share of costs. Elimination of these sales can bring a significant operating profit improvement.

OVERHEAD

An important type of cost that you must come to fully understand, justify, and control is staff overhead. Some staff overhead is vital; control and cost management would be jeopardized without it. Other staff overhead does not return its costs by decreasing other costs or by increasing profits elsewhere. These unnecessary costs must be identified and eliminated. A sense of urgency must pervade this task.

To achieve the lowest overall costs, companies should not minimize staff overhead. This is a common mistake. They should attempt to optimize the level of overhead, making trade-offs in which increased overhead leads to significantly decreased total costs. Adding the overhead of a make/buy function, for example, can lead to substantially decreased total costs. Common sense must be the guide.

The location of staff functions within the organization of the company is an important element in overhead efficiency. The examination of organizational location is a route to overhead containment.

For a reduction of staff to accomplish its aims, the functions performed by the displaced employees have to be either eliminated or accomplished with improved procedures and systems. Simply eliminating jobs and expecting the remaining employees to carry the increased work load will seldom work.

One useful way to approach reduction of staff overhead is to look into the possibility of subcontracting the activity to another firm. Essentially this means applying the logic of a make/buy decision to services instead of goods. By buying the service from specialized firms who achieve greater productivity because they are doing this function as a business, you can eliminate the relevant internal manning and achieve lower costs.

When looking at fixed costs and administrative nonstaff costs, there is no such thing as a stupid question. Every item should be examined, even those that seem above question. Real estate taxes, utility rates, and office space requirements are examples of these. The fact that an expense or practice is of long standing is not an acceptable reason for it to continue.

INVENTORY

Inventory ties up much of the capital and is the origin of many of the costs of any manufacturing business. The cash needs of the company will be highly dependent on how well it is managed. Inventory mismanagement is a common characteristic of a troubled company.

Obsolete inventory has to be recognized as such. Products or raw materials in storage, unlike wine, do not improve with age. If the obsolete inventory contains purchase items, still in good condition, there may be a good opportunity to return them. Although the entire purchase price may not be refunded, a significant portion of the original cost may be recaptured.

Usage over time needs to be examined in determining whether or not goods are obsolete and in establishing proper inventory levels. Raw materials inventories are often excessive because of extreme conservatism in their estimation. Operations must be forced to work with lower lead times, relying on the supplier of the material to make it quickly available. In almost any industry there are suppliers who will place material on consignment, or at least store it for immediate customer requirements.

It is often better to experience some loss of business than to pay the economic price of overstocking, giving up your potential profit through incursion of inventory costs of approximately 24 to 28 percent per annum.

Firms use a variety of criteria for selecting order quantities for goods that go into inventory. The most rational way is to use the Economic Order Quantity, which is the quantity that provides minimum cost from both manufacturing/purchasing and carrying cost points of view.

PROCUREMENT

Purchasing is a key factor, and sometimes "the" key factor, in the profitability of a company. Improved purchasing should be looked on as a potential source of important savings and must be managed to ensure that savings will be achieved. Many troubled companies do not understand the importance of purchasing and focus relatively little management attention on this area. A small reduction in purchase costs can often have a greater effect than large reductions in labor costs.

Purchasing controls an important portion of the cost of your manufactured product. It represents an alternative to a company's own manufacturing cost. By sourcing abroad, it may be able to counter a present cost advantage of foreign-made products. Purchasing may be able to obtain needed technology quickly, through product purchases, with little investment. These are far broader considerations than the common purchasing perspective of merely ensuring that production doesn't run out of raw materials or parts.

Poor purchasing frequently results from improper organization, unsatisfactory operating procedures, and lack of integration into business plans. People with the proper skills and experience are needed to head and staff the Purchasing function. It is penny-wise and pound-foolish to have anything but a first-rate Purchasing function. Remember, this small group of people may control between one-quarter and one-half of the company's product costs.

Many troubled manufacturing companies subcontract infrequently and have limited experience in make/buy decisions. Considerable savings are often realized if make/buy decisions are systematically pursued. However, to be successful, the company must be organized to make them, think through the various business implications, and provide the effort with sufficient staff resources.

MANUFACTURING

A troubled manufacturing company invariably requires significant improvements in the management of this activity. Good manufacturing plant supervision and skilled hourly manpower, no matter how well intentioned, cannot produce good manufacturing results if a capable manufacturing staff organization is absent. Manufacturing has grown too complex for that. The manufacturing staff organization must be properly staffed in terms of manning level and appropriate skills.

Manufacturing must be conducted in a manner consistent with the company's overall strategic concept. It must be responsive to the company's strategy and cannot exist in a world of its own, making decisions contrary to this strategy.

How do you go about assessing the current status of manufacturing? There is no substitute for walking a plant—every aisle. Observing housekeeping, scrap, the work pace, the amount and distribution of work in process, which machines are in use, and the like often tells a skilled observer more about the current status of an operation than a myriad of reports. It will also reveal problems not committed to paper.

No manufacturing is without problems. Materials arrive late or are defective. Customers change their specifications. Engineering makes design errors, which are discovered only in the midst of production. Machinery breaks down. However, if shipments are always late, quality problems are endemic, and production costs go up rather than down over time, there is a problem in Manufacturing management.

Companies need a manufacturing strategy—what is to be made and where. If the company has a number of manufacturing plants, the question often is which one to use. This is as important to established products as it is to new ones.

The key to obtaining greater efficiency in using direct labor is detailed monitoring of how labor is actually used. This means putting in a labor analysis system that categorizes all uses as percentages of productive use. This gives management a means to identify and focus attention on productivity problems.

Fossilized or restrictive work rules governing the use of production employees in manufacturing plants can be a severe economic burden on a company. In achieving a company turnaround, management must squarely face the work rules issue. In general, the fewer the work rules, the better—the better with regard to working environment and manufacturing productivity.

Plant consolidation is a painful process that has to be considered when a company has permanent significant excess capacity. Combining, besides reducing, costs may force you to look at which products to move and which to eliminate. It forces you to face the psychologically difficult task of pruning the product line.

MARKETING

Company and division managements usually believe that they are fully aware of the structure of their markets and how their market position compares with that of competitors. In the troubled company this is usually simply not so. To learn the actual current competitive situation, market research has to be done on a continuous basis. This often requires using a market research firm initially.

To properly assess the current marketing and competitive situation, the turnaround management needs reliable in-depth knowledge about:

* market structure, dynamics, and size;
* key competitors;
* product requirements;
* pricing;
* sales requirements/issues;
* distribution;
* product positioning.

The test of the appropriateness of the organization of a Marketing and Sales function is its effectiveness. Usually it must be made more effective in a company requiring a turnaround.

What level of sales expense should be maintained in a turnaround? To answer this question you must look at the specific business and determine whether or not salesmen and other sales expenses are truly the basis of obtaining sales. Norms for travel and entertainment have to be developed and enforced; otherwise, significant costs will be needlessly incurred.

Pricing decisions must reflect the competitive situation, uniqueness of the product, and alternatives available to the customer. Decisions in troubled firms are often based on limited and faulty information.

An understanding of the costs and, more important, of the probable costs of competitors must exist before price leadership is attempted. In general, a troubled company should avoid leading the market to lower price levels.

Once the price level has been lowered, it is a difficult task to restore it. If a troubled company lowers prices and is not the lowest-cost producer, it will be in worse shape than before, with even greater losses, as competitors quickly match their lower prices.

Many companies and their Marketing Departments like to boast that they are a full-line supplier or to say that they have the broadest product line in the industry. Such a situation can be the basis of excessive cost. Virtually no troubled company should feel that remaining a full-line supplier is an important consideration.

TECHNOLOGY

Every manufacturing company has a number of organizations concerned with developing or applying technology. Arbitrarily decreasing these overhead expenses can probably decrease, but not eliminate, the company's current losses. But the long-range result of this action may be the elimination of any prospect of future viability. Troubled manufacturing companies generally must spend more, rather than less, on technology as part of their total effort to reduce product costs.

For Product Engineering to succeed in significantly reducing the company's product costs, it must:

• have a form of organization that permits good communication and an efficient use of its resources;
• be well managed;
• not consist entirely of generalists, but have specialists with key skills and knowledge;
• use advanced engineering methods (e.g., computer-aided design, finite element analysis).

A properly functioning Manufacturing Engineering organization can achieve manufacturing cost reductions each year in the range of four to six times the amount expended on this effort. Why do troubled manufacturing companies spend so little on this function? The answer is a lack of perception of this multiplier effect in obtaining cost savings.

NEW PRODUCT DEVELOPMENT

Most new product development has a longer time horizon than is usually commensurate with a company turnaround. The common perspective in a turnaround is to identify new product development activities that can be eliminated. Occasionally, however, new products do become an important turnaround element.

Licensing a successfully developed foreign product is frequently less expensive and less risky than completing a half-finished product development effort.

The use of R & D limited partnerships may provide a means of developing products with other people's money. It also lessens the company's product development risk.

FOREIGN OPERATIONS

A troubled company with small foreign subsidiaries usually follows the rule that if the parent is mismanaged, the foreign subsidiaries are in worse shape. The foreign subsidiaries cannot be ignored in the turnaround of the parent company. Their activities must be in concert with those of their parent.

The same strategic concept governing the U.S. firm's turnaround must be interpreted for the circumstances of the foreign activities. If a foreign operation has unrelated products or businesses extraneous to the major thrust of the parent company, these should be considered immediate candidates for divestiture.

OPERATING DURING STRIKES

The troubled company may have fundamental operating cost problems arising from the bargaining agreement with its labor union. These costs may stem from complex and debilitating work rules and excessive wages and benefits. Management may conclude that long-term company survival will not be possible without corrections in one or both of these categories. If taking a strike is necessary for the company to obtain these corrections, the issue should be faced squarely.

The company should expect to continue operating in the event of a strike. Raw materials will arrive, production will continue, and finished goods will continue to be shipped. Office personnel will initially be required to man production. In time, new hires will replace the striking workers, permitting the return of salaried employees to their normal staff functions.

The economics of taking a strike are frequently quite favorable; this is little known. Removal of debilitating work rules and reductions in wages and benefits, when balanced against strike costs, can provide a relatively fast payback.

INDEX

About the Author

Eugene F. Finkin, Ph.D., is one of America's leading turnaround executives. He was formerly Executive Vice President (Chief Operating Officer) of Blaw Knox Corporation: an independent, seven division, $250 million in sales, industrial conglomerate. He took Blaw Knox Corporation from a $12 million a year loss to break-even in ten months.

Dr. Finkin was previously Executive Vice President of Danly Machine Corp., a large machinery and industrial products manufacturer, headquartered near Chicago. He attracted media attention with the successful turnaround of Danly. In less than two years he increased sales from $65 million to above $150 million. This restored competitiveness was the result of a comprehensive cost reduction and technology improvement program. Danly was able to win back market share from the Japanese—something few American firms have accomplished.

Prior to Danly, Dr. Finkin gained extensive first hand experience as a turnaround executive at Allegheny International, Inc., and Westinghouse Electric Corporation. He has published articles, given invited speeches, and advised companies on the management of turnaround efforts.

Dr. Finkin received a B.S. in Mechanical Engineering from M.I.T. in 1962. He received an M.S. and Ph.D. in Mechanics from Rensselaer Polytechnic Institute in 1964 and 1966, respectively. He now resides in Upper St. Clair, Pennsylvania, a suburb of Pittsburgh.